STATE AND SOCIETY
IN AFRICA

State and Society in Africa

Perspectives on Continuity and Change

Edited by
Feraidoon Shams

University Press of America, Inc.
Lanham • New York • London

Library of Congress Cataloging-in-Publication Data

State and society in Africa : perspectives on continuity and change /
edited by Feraidoon Shams.
p. cm.
Includes index.
1. Africa--Economic conditions--1960- 2. Africa--Politics and
government--1960- 3. Africa--Social conditions--1960- I. Title.
HC800.S715   1995   330.96--dc20   95- 12677 CIP

ISBN 0-8191-9977-X   (cloth: alk: paper)
ISBN 0-8191-9978-8   (ppr: alk:paper)

CONTENTS

Tables and Figures

Contributors

Dr. Wilfred L. David (Ph.D., University of Oxford), is an economist and currently a senior Professor of Development Policy and Planning in the Department of African Studies at Howeard University. Before joining the Howard Faculty in 1978, Dr. David held senior academic appointments in a number of institutions, including Fisk Universtiy where he was Chairman of the Department of Economics and Management, Vanderbilt University, the University of Delaware, and Brooklyn College of the city University of New York. Dr. David has served as a consultant to the World Bank, the U.S. Agency for International Development, and the United Nations. His many publications include: *Conflicting Paradigms in the Economics of Developing Nations, The IMF Policy Paradigm, Political Economy of Economic Policy, and the Washington Consensus: From Structural Adjustment to Authentic Development.*

Dr. Peggy A. David (Ph.D., Howard University), is a sociologist and currently an international consultant on organizational reform and the sociology of development. She has held appointments with Fisk University, the World Bank, and the Joint Center for Educational Studies in New York.

Dr. Charles Jarmon is Professor of Sociology and Associate Dean of the College of Arts and Sciences at Howard University, where he has taught in the area of urbanization and Development. He has served in an editorial capacity for several journals relating to Asian and African Affairs. Professor Jarmon's major research in urbanization and development has focused on Nigeria, and is currently conducting research on public policy and poverty in the United States.

Dr. David Kowalewski is Professor of Comparative and International Politics at Alfred University. His works have appeared in the *Journal of Conflict Resolution, American Journal of Sociology* and elsewhere.. He is the author of *Global Establishment* (Macmillan, 1995).

Dr. Sulayman S. Nyang is Professor of Political Science in the Department of African Studies at Howard University, Washington, D.C. Dr. Nyang has written extensively on Africa, the Middle East and Islamic Affairs. Dr. Nyang holds a Ph.D. ,from the University of Virginia and is the author of numerous scholarly works, noteably, *Islam, Christianity and African Identity,* (1984).

Dr. Feraidoon Shams is Associate Professor of Political Science, and International Affairs, Division of Social Sciences of the College of Art and Sciences at Howard University, Washington, D.C. Within the past twenty six years at Howard University, Dr. Shams has taught undergraduate and graduate courses in Comparative Politics, International Relations, African Political Systems, the Middle East and survey of Social Sciences. He is the author of numerous scholary works on Africa and the developing world and currently is the Editor-in-Chief of the *Journal of the Third World Spectrum.*

Dr. Timothy M. Shaw is Professor of Political Science and International Development Studies at Dalhousie University in Nova Scotia, Canada. Dr. Shaw Holds a Ph.D., from Princeton University and has taguht at universities in Nigeria, South Africa, Uganda, Zambia and Zimbabwe. He is General Editor of the Macmillan/St. Martin's Press Series in *International Political Economy* and serves on the Editorial Boards of *Journal of the Third World Spectrum,* and *Third World Quarterly.*

Dr. Larry A. Swatuk is SSHRCC Post-Doctoral Fellow at the Center for International and Strategic Studies, York University, Toronto, Canada. He was Rrecently a Visiting Research Fellow At Rhodes Universty. He is the author of *Between Choice in Hard Place:* Contend*ing Theories of Internnational Relations* and co-editor with Timothy Shaw *of the South at the End of Twenieth Century*

Dr. F. Ogboaja Ohaegbulam is Professor of Government and International Affairs at the University of South Florida, In Tampa. Dr. Ohaegbulam holds a Ph.D., in International Studies and Politics from the University of Denver, Colorado and is the author of numerous scholarly publications.

Dr. John C. Weidman is Professor of Education and Sociology and Senior Associate in the Institute for International Studies in Education at the University of Pittsburgh. He is the author of numerous works on educatational development.

Design and Typesetting Production by Lina Vanessa Jaramillo.

Introduction

The state and society in the African continent, more than any other in recent decades have undergone profound metamorphosis. These changes, both positive and negative were highlighted by the end of European colonial rule in the late 1950s, 1960's, and 1970s. From intense and prolonged East-West rivalry of the post independent era, to its demise in the early 1990s Africa has experienced repeated economic, political and social crisis. The Balkanization of Africa across tribal and ethnic divide, together with apparent lack of success on the part of many emerging African states to forge long term reconstruction of societies in terms of both economic mobility and political egalitarianism have adversely affected the human prospect for an equitable and descent existence.

This volume examines divergent themes on African polity and society. It is a collective effort by a host of scholars from the United States and abroad who analyze the prevailing political, economic and social conditions in Africa. Essentially, the book in its organization is designed to assess major challenges that confront Africa societies. These include forces and factors that impose constraints and pose dilemmas to African societies', national, regional and international viability. In its approach, however, the book is eclectic, representing alternative paradigms to the continent's economic, political and social malaise.

Thus, the first article: "Resolving the African Developmental Cathexia: Empowerment of the People" is written jointly by Professor Wilfred David and Peggy David. It addresses the "African Developmental crisis and how it can be resolved." The authors in their treatise expound on human struggle and human prospect in Africa and maintain that "In essence, the development struggle represents a human quest for access to the ordinary opportunities of life, land, water, work, living space and basic social services." Further, they hold that "Inherent in this is struggle for political, social and economic power, or the basic human motivation of people to meaningfully participate in the decisions governing their lives." Conversely, however, they continue that many African societies have failed to achieve the desired end of national and state reconstruction. In reality, "perceptible structural contradictions or inconsistency has apparently become a chronically reproduced property of societies in Africa and parts of the less developed sector of the world." these factors, according to authors may be explained by the"historical perpetuation of antithetical relationship between traditional or indigenous and the national" context within which developmental processes take place.

The second article: "Cities and Development in Sub-Saharan Africa" is offered by Professor Charles Jarmon who views "urbanization in Africa" to be marked by the "small proportion of the continent's urban population, its rapid growth and its uneven distribution." In turn, according to the author, "these conditions are significantly related to an accelerated increase of large African cities," which in essence create, " a spectra of economic and political dilemmas and issues closely identified with the problems of development in African nations."

The third article: "The African Periphery in the World System: Kondratieff Longwaves of Exports and Indebtedness" is written by Professor David Kowalewski. The author relies on cyclical upswings and downswings in world capitalism of the past several centuries, sets forth empirical evidence and rational on "core-periphery" spectrum of world economy and their relations to Africa. He raises pertinent questions on the application of the "global paradigms" in economics and the appropriateness of the "world system theory, using historical African data on exports and indebtedness in the last two centuries" to economic realities in Africa. The writer also maintains that " as core nations made their inroads into underdeveloped or 'periphery' areas the structure of their respective economies were correspondingly established." Furthermore, the processes of modernization, industrialization and post-industrialization in core countries to some extent were achieved "on the basis of wealth extracted from periphery. Periphery areas, in contrast became locked into various dependencies(technology, finance, investment, trade) on Core countries. Consequently, they have continued to lag behind the latte

The fourth essay: "Third World Political Economy and Foreign Policy in the Post-Cold War Era: Lessons from Africa" is written by professor Timothy M. Shaw and Dr. Larry A. Swatuk, who provide an illuminating study on the impact of the Post-Cold War international character on African foreign policies. They address traditional and contemporary assumptions in the Post-Cold War Third World arena in general and their relevance to Africa in particular. The authors contend that profound shifts and realignment in East-West relations, including the "transition to harsh economic, rather than diplomatic or strategic realpolitik in the 1990s, expose African unity and power both as hollow and obfuscatory." In essence, and as a result of these developments, Africa as whole is now "more marginal and vulnerable, but also, perhaps more flexible and fluid."

The fifth article: "Prospects for Regional Integration in post Apartheid Southern Africa," by Dr. Larry A. Swatuk examines varying scenarios and hypothesis regarding the region's economic integration. The author contends that despite post Apartheid "South Africa's emergence as the regional hegemon" the country "faces innumerable problems of its own. Debt not strategic minerals will mark South Africa's major link to North in the Post-Cold War and *Apartheid* era." Moreover, South Africa's position within greater Southern Africa must be viewed within the context of "Southern African Development Coordination Conference, which may be viewed "as a proposed counterweight to the economic and political power of South Africa." Moreover, the author notes that "Given the ubiquity of debt and state-by-state negotiated structural adjustment programmes in the region, the prospects for state initiated, *de jure* regional integration remain limited.

The sixth article: "Colonialism and the Integration of the Gambian Ethnic Groups by professor Sulayman Nyang is offered as a synthesis of the Gambian society, including factors of religion, institution of marriage and inter-ethnic social processes of rivalry conflict, cooperation, assimilation and accommodation. In professor Nyang's view the "inter-ethnic struggles for resources and living spaces and foreign encroachment in Gambia" have together shaped the nature of relationship between different groups. perhaps the ethnic scene in Gambia, is not dissimilar to inter-ethnic relationship in the rest of Africa, where social integration of various groups within a national settings becomes an important factor in "nationally representative of social integration."

The seventh article: "Africa and the Demise of soviet Block," by Professor Ugboaja Ohaeghbulam is an exploration of many faceted implications and challenges posed by the end of the Soviet Union's presence in Africa. As a whole, according to the author, "the demise of Soviet block has had additional salutary impact on Africa. It has reduced the opportunity for the politicizing of Western aid to Africa as a cold war weapon-a prophylactic against the spread o communism to Africa."

The eighth article: "Prospect for the Development of Higher Education in Kenya" is offered by Dr. John c. Weidman. He considers the Kenyan higher education within both regional and continental contexts. And Analyzes various themes and their significance in the growth of African and Kenyan higher education.

The ninth article: "The Dynamics of the State Boundaries in Post-Colonial Africa: The Prospects for the Future" is presented by Professor Ugboaja Ohaegbulam. In his view, "The post-colonial experience in African states, especially the current genuine crisis of the nation-state in Sub-Saharan Africa, has demonstrated that European-carved boundaries have proven to be more of liability than an asset to the emergent African State."

In conclusion, this volume represents a modest contribution to the vast body of knowledge on Africa. Each contributor, of course, is responsible for the analyses, views, data and conclusions presented. The work by no means has pretensions to being considered a definitive treatise on contemporary State and Society in Africa; nevertheless it brings to the fore the painstaking efforts of a number dedicated scholars, who contribute significantly to a greater understanding of African states, economies and societies. Undoubtedly, the volume will open up greater possibilities for research by those interested in Africa's economic viability, political development and social progress.

I wish to thank my colleagues for their gracious permissions to include thier scholarly works in this volume. Also I am grateful to Ms. Michelle R. Harris, the Acquisitions Editor and Ms. Helen Hudson, the production Editor of the University Press of America and to Ms. Lina Vanessa Jaramillo for the typesetting production of the present book.

Feraidoon Shams, Ph.D.
Associate Professor
Howard University
Washington, D.C., U.S.A.

Chapter I

Resolving the African Development Cathexia: Empowerment of the People

Dr. Wilfred L. David and Dr. Peggy A. David

Despite global megatrends favoring liberal market economies, multi-party democracies, and decentralization of the development process, the masses of people in Africa and elsewhere in the less developed sector of the world still have very little control, if any, over their lives. What is now an entrenched development crisis is exemplified by the disempowerment of rural dwellers, ethnic minorities, women, children, the aged, and disabled. These and similar cadres have very little power to change the increasingly miserable conditions under which they live. There is now a plethora of literature interpreting the African development crisis and how it can be solved. Needless to say, the climate of opinion has changed over the years. Contrary to the conventional wisdom, the problem stems not so much from burgeoning balance of payments deficits, macroeconomic imbalances, and uncontrollable budget deficits. Rather, it is more a reflection of the failure of the state elite to create and nurture the conditions necessary for sustainable human development. The persistent reality of human misery is evidentced by dilapidated social and infrastructural systems, schools without teachers, textbooks, or chalk, medical clinics without pharmaceutical drugs, hungry and undernourished children, and premature death. In essence, the development struggle represents a human quest for access to the ordinary opportunities of life--land, water, work, living space, and basic social services. Inherent in this is a struggle for political, social, and economic power, or the basic human motivation of people to meaningfully participate in decisions governing their lives. As explored in this chapter, the failure to achieve this end is part and parcel of a perceptible structural contradiction or inconsistency that has apparently become a chronically reproduced property of societies in Africa and parts of the less developed sector of the world. This is reflected by the historical perpetuation of an antithetical relationship between what we term the "national" vis-a-vis the "traditional" or "indigenous" environment.

The national environment refers to the state or urban-based systems of governance that have been created and shaped by the political and technocratic elite in their articulation of state power. The traditional environment is defined by rural hinterlands or tradition-bound communities in which the majority of people live. They have historically reflected the value systems and motivations of farmers and small-scale producers whose economic activities now support about 500-600 million people, and continue to shoulder the primary burden of generating the lion's share of the socio-economic surplus in the form of foodstuffs for domestic consumption and cash crops for export.

This chapter focuses on the developmental consequences underlying the interaction between the two environments. The guiding premise is that the nature and direction of this interactive process hold the key not only for attaining viable forms of agricultural and rural development, but more importantly, for long-term structural transformation at the societal level. The latter is a *sine qua non* of authentic and sustainable development. The argument is marshalled in three stages. First, an account is provided of main factors governing the socio-economic dynamics of the traditional environment. Second, the deleterious effects of national policies on its potential for survival and growth are highlighted. Third, this is followed by a discussion of the relative merits of three alternative policy paradigms and their implications for effecting legitimate and balanced forms of national development in which all Africans participate.

The Traditional Environment as a "Moral Economy of Affection"

Through the lens of the orthodox development paradigm, the traditional environment is often portrayed as a "backward", aberration that stands in the way of meaningful change. From the African cultural perspective, however, it represents a vibrant socio-cultural system with its own internal logic governing patterns of production, consumption, distribution, and exchange. The structure and functioning of this system can be interpreted from the perspective of the so-called "peasant economies" in which the majority of people in the developing world live. In general, the value orientations of such economies have been identified with a "moral economy" or "economy of affection" in which the behavior of rural dwellers is linked to certain principles of collective action. According to James C. Scott (1976: vii), "the study of the moral economy of the peasant, while it begins in the domain of economics, must end in the study of peasant culture and religion."

The underlying premise is that such communities are primarily interested in their survival in the face of uncertainty about food and other basic necessities. This leads to a "subsistence ethic," which is reflected in values and social relations that help to mitigate hardship in the worst of times. Rural dwellers typically accept a significant level of mutual dependence and obligation, and tend to assert these through various rules of allocation and communal obligation as a means of providing a basic level of subsistence to all members of the community. Such practices are believed to represent a "moral economy" because the rules of village life tend to produce moral outcomes. Such rules impose an obligation to protect the subsistence needs of the less fortunate and the larger community from the costs of inequality through a process of consensual decision-making, and by allocating burdens according to means.

Contextually, rural communities cannot be viewed merely as associations of profit-seeking farmers or producers but more as "cultural units" that typically betray a strong sense of identity through subscription to an all-inclusive moral code. The pervasive and unifying force is provided by the entrenched or extended family system, which functions as a corporate body whose goals are rooted in the "economy of affection" than in the objective of profit maximization. Being born into a family and having to subscribe to its basic cultural rules provides something roughly equivalent to the Western concept of "insurance". The family not only functions as a source of economic support in any type of circumstance, but also as a business unit in which individual and collective resources are utilized to meet consumption and investment needs of members.

In the case of Africa, economic arrangements in the traditional environment are typically guided by more embracing indigenous cultural orientations or an organic value system based on principles of communality, social cooperation, and participation (Ake 1990). Traditional values emphasize communication, people's concern for others, the oneness of being, and group solidarity. The latter is reflected in the fact that, compared to Western cultures, a high value is placed on interpersonal relations and the timely execution of certain social obligations than on individual achievements. The strength of group commitments and obligations inherent in the social contract are usually the result of group pressure associated with ritualistic forms of behavior. The circumstances and forms of ritualistic behavior usually govern economic transactions and are therefore accorded greater significance than the principles of pure economic exchange.

The value of economic transactions is measured in terms of their capacity to reinforce group commitments. The overall objective is to maximize group welfare or social well-being rather than individual welfare based on the ruthless pursuit of the profit motive. Since individual economic motivations are secondary to those of the group, society, or collectivity, the pursuit of private productive gains tends to be constrained by the requirements of general social welfare. Within this framework, expansion of the system occurs infrequently, and only as a result of increased social need, e.g., as a result of population growth.

Land and other physical resources on which the traditional environment depends for its survival and growth are construed as "social capital," in the sense that the system of allocation is community-based (tribal, ethnic, etc.). This bears a sharp contrast to the resource allocation process encountered in classical and neoclassical economic theory where a distinction is commonly drawn between discrete earnings accruing to different sets of owners - rent to landowners, profits and interest to capitalists, and wages and salaries to workers. The emphasis is on maximum resource use and exploitation as a means of generating a private surplus. In the traditional African environment, heavy reliance is placed on the need to maintain an optimal balance between production and the natural resource system by pursuing a "satisfactory" path of resource exploitation and sustainable development based on "satisficing" and human-ecology dialectics no distinct class of landowners has existed because the community rather than individual landowners has historically controlled the land. As indicated above, land and other natural resources, as elements of aggregate social capital, have always been communally-owned and allocated by village leaders. The historical evidence suggests that when the social capital (including land) has been expropriated for "external" production, e.g., cash crop production during the colonial and post-colonial era, the system became destabilized, disarticulated, and impoverished (see David 1988).

The overall argument, therefore, is that the values and motivations associated with communality, participation, and sharing have traditionally played a pivotal role in helping African peoples to devise sensible and pragmatic strategies to take care of their basic needs and to survive in the face of the most wrenching forms of crisis. They are reflected in a system of income and wealth distribution based on the over-arching and inter-generational presence of the extended family and the imperative of community sharing of wealth. The guiding principles undergirding the socio-economic-cultural order have traditionally reflected cooperative relations of production and open access to kinfolk. In this context, the rural household or community remains the institution that continues to provide some sense of social security and acts as employer at last resort for those who might have failed in the open employment market that purportedly characterized modernization and urbanization.

National Policies, Government Failure, and Retreat of the Countryside

For the past three decades, development policy in Africa has been influenced by the Western model of modernization and has produced not only an antithetical relationship between the national and traditional environments, but also a visible wedge between producers and the economy. The underlying philosophy is that successful national development can be best achieved by policies based on rapid industrialization, an urban-bias in the development process, and discrimination against the countryside. The modernization ethic views rural dwellers in the traditional environment as being predominantly poor, lacking in organization, wedded to inappropriate values, and isolated from the market economy and modern world. These attributes, combined with the presumed inefficiency of small-scale production, have been interpreted as barriers to economic success and fuller participation in the development activities advocated by the state.

The historical evidence suggests that most governments became too bogged down in policies and strategies that were unworkable, resulting in colossal government failures and disasters of intervention. In many cases, what went wrong was not so much the overall objectives advocated, but rather the specifics underlying the day-to-day process of implementation. In general, this process was marked by bureaucratic centralization, authoritarianism, a lack of incentives to new producers, and a failure to sufficiently redistribute economic and political power. These outcomes reflected, among other things, what has been dubbed "policy induced, and thus far from inevitable, distortions created by irrational dirigisme" (Lal 1985: 1).

Though it may be subject to different kinds of interpretation, the early experience of Ghana under the leadership of Kwame Nkrumah is usually cited as one of the most prominent examples of the *dirigiste* approach. His policies, it is believed, chipped away at the very sectors, notably agriculture, which provided the best prospects for sustainable economic growth. In general, the goal of interventionism was the rapid redirection of predominantly agrarian modes of production toward heavy industrialization. Nkrumah followed a policy reminiscent of "primitive socialist accumulation" under Stalinism, whereby the state apparatus systematically siphoned off the surplus from the agricultural sector and redirected it to industry. Such policies eventually led to an annihilation of property rights at work in the rural sector and a destruction of farm income. Meanwhile, for all the vast resources being pumped into the industrial sector, the industrialization drive failed to get off the ground, and was a classic story of throwing good money after bad.

A spiralling effect was set in motion: as the state sector continued to fail, further ad hoc measures were imposed to support it, and the circumvention of private property rights became increasingly severe. However, the failure to establish a self-sustaining industrial sector was certainly not due to any laxity in the policy implementation process. Among the factors commonly cited is the role of the "petit bourgeois" class interests in sabotaging the early efforts at socialist-based development. The reference to class interests is sometimes taken as a special case of a more general explanation based on corruption as the underlying factor contributing to the collapse of Nkrumah's, development efforts. To the extent that corruption was a factor, it remains true that political elites of the day found their roles quite lucrative.

The experience of the Nkrumah era clearly demonstrated the distorted environment that can be created when political objectives clash with the requirements of economic rationality. The primacy given to the political reform and state power were reflected in Nkrumah's now famous dictum: "Seek ye first the political Kingdom, and all else will be added unto it." The politicization of the development process was to become a pervasive feature of African political economy. Many governments deliberately concentrated more on policies that promised to build and stabilize their political base at the expense of others designed to increase productive activity. Military budgets were upgraded and policies and projects were often geared toward distributing benefits to regions or ethnic groups on which politicians relied for the consolidation of their power.

As a result, the available resources were misallocated and the foundations for an efficient and balanced process of economic development could not be established. The overall environment has been depicted as one in which many governments, in the face of conflicting objectives, have had to deal with a variety of constraints to development, including rapid population growth, underdeveloped human resources, a lopsided economic structure, mal-developed institutions, and a generalized scarcity of financial resources in relation to objective needs. Under the circumstances, political actions have always played a predominant role in the struggle to control available resources. In Africa, as in other parts of both the less developed and more developed world, political behavior is primarily motivated by self-interest, i.e., the use of state power to accumulate wealth and other forms of private gain. The resultant centralization of the decision-making process dealt an inevitable and severe blow to the dispersed knowledge at work in the system of communal ownership and property rights, and systematically circumvented the discovery process at work in the "moral economy of affection."

This inflammatory process was fuelled by the perceived need of politicians to appease or otherwise coopt urban-based cadres such as civil servants, teachers, soldiers, and unionized workers. Under the circumstances, small farmers and rural producers in the countryside were deliberately paid lower prices for their wares as a means of guaranteeing higher living standards and economic privileges for the more favored urban interest groups. Accordingly, the market was manipulated in order to control increases in the cost of living, and especially the cost of food, for urban consumers. The surplus produced in rural areas was appropriated and frittered away in "steel -and-glass" urban-based industrial projects, and only a relatively small proportion of the revenues generated from commodity exports originating from the rural sector was reinvested for its own survival and development.

It comes as no surprise, therefore, that African political economy has often been described as one in which leaders are wont to build palaces, cathedrals, airports, international conference arenas, and then declare that the people are happy. As alluded to earlier, this reflects a widespread subscription to a modernization ethic, which has produced a number of dysfunctional development consequences for the majority of people living in the traditional environment. Robert Bates (1981: 6, 119) has aptly interpreted the relevant trends in the following terms:

> The collective optimism of the nationalist era has given way to a sullen and embittered recognition that the sacrifices of the many have created disproportionate opportunities for the few. How do policy choices, ostensibly made for the public good, become the basis for private aggrandizement? By what process does a vision of public order erode?

Agricultural policies in Africa are characterized by attempts to set prices in markets in a way that is harmful to the interests of most farmers. The economies of Africa are overwhelmingly rural in nature, but the government elites in Africa seek to industrialize. It is hardly surprising, therefore, that these elites should attempt to extract resources from agriculture and channel them into manufacturing and industry. All nations seeking to industrialize have done this. The African policies are thus notable not as exceptions but as examples of a large class.

It may be added that such policies have been reinforced by other government actions designed to control the political power of the rural majority. In order to build and consolidate their political base, governments have tried to create a privileged class of large-scale producers or "progressive farmers" as a buffer between the national and traditional environments. In many cases, political alliances were forged with influential traditional leaders who made large fortunes from agriculture. The process of political manipulation was further buttressed by a "bi-modal" strategy of agricultural development in which resources are contracted in a small subsector with large, capital-intensive production units existing alongside a large subsector or subsistence agriculture.

The denouément of this process has witnessed the creation of large landholdings, irrigation white elephants, and the adoption of farming technologies that have fundamentally altered the economic and social organization of the countryside. A new form of competition was orchestrated between the elite group of farmers and traditional producers for the available productive resources and services. The result has been continuous political conflict and a heightened distrust of the state by traditional farmers. More often than not, the situation has been exacerbated by a widespread proclivity of the state to place heavy reliance on force, with the ubiquitous presence of coercive power tending to inspire fear, retreat, and even resistance rather than cooperation.

In the overall scheme of things, small farmers and other traditional producers have always viewed the state as lacking any legitimate authority. The devolution of any such authority is construed as emanating from the historical forces of foreign domination and the establishment of amoral and acultural institutions, e.g., forms of governance, that are at odds with the traditional authority structure which remains very paternalistic and hierarchical. As Dia (1991: 11) describes the latter:

> Little prone to individualism, it tends to be egalitarian within the same age group, but hierarchical in group-to-group relations, with marked subordination of the younger members. Within each group, individuals possess equal legal status and the capacity to perform specific acts, but a person wishing to go beyond his or her own circle, can do so only with the permission of the father or some other authority (i.e., a tribal chief).

In the eyes of the rural masses, the primordial authorial system is not only synergistic with their needs and beliefs, but also displays the moral and cultural legitimacy required for the efficient exercise of power. As emphasized in this chapter, people who are in the main outside the modern or urbanized sector of the economy tend to place greater store on age-old customary practices rather than on "national" policies that have little meaning to them. When such policies are perceived to clash with their own interests, the response is minimal cooperation or a retreat to their traditional modes of life based on the subsistence ethic, self-sufficiency, and self-reliance. This is explained by the fact that rural producers can reproduce without any reliance on the state. Their relative independence, access to communal land, and ability to provide for their own means of subsistence enable them to make their own decisions about the nature and degree of participation in government-mandated activities.

The overall consequence, therefore, is that an antithetical structural relationship seems to define the interaction between national and traditional environments. On the one hand, the state esconced atop the national environment continues to dictate policies and constantly struggles to obtain compliance with them. On the other hand, various forms of resistance emanate from the traditional environment in which indigenous systems of authority and cultural sentiments rule the roost. The burning question is whether policies and strategies can be designed to effect a mutually supportive pattern of interaction between the two sectoral interests, or at least to minimize the fallout from antagonistic confrontation or potentially destructive conflict. The three alternative policy scenarios presented below should be assessed in this light.

Policy Scenario I: Market-Based Reform of the Traditional Environment

What has emerged as a Washington consensus, or universal convergence of ideas about development policy, is that successful patterns of rural and national development can be fostered by providing the requisite material incentives to small-scale farmers and producers in the countryside, and in general by building more conciliatory and cooperative bridges between national and traditional environments. Such a strategy is predicated on the belief that the impasse could be broken if governments were in some way able to persuade rural producers to accept the logic of reform and increasingly adopt modern technocratic methods to produce more for the commercial market. It is also believed that the state, through its interventionist and discriminatory agricultural policies, should bear the lion's share of the blame for the isolation and generalized condition of underdevelopment pervading in the traditional environment.

Accordingly, the reformist strategy is guided by three related principles: (i) "getting prices right" through greater reliance on the market mechanism; (ii) recognition of the primacy of economic responses to individual incentives, and in particular, the quick and rational responses of small farmers to incentives and disincentives; and (iii) minimal government intervention in the market process. The overriding philosophy is that the "peasant" or rural farmer is a "rational problem-solver, with a sense both of his own interests and the need to bargain with others to achieve mutually acceptable outcomes" (Popkin 1979: 30-31).

This rationalist perspective runs counter to the idea that the traditional methods of peasant farming tend to be driven more by "non-rational" factors associated with cooperative values and social obligations than by individual self-interest and the rational pursuit of profit. In other words, it poses a challenge to the conventional wisdom that peasants and small farmers are bound by tradition and therefore cannot be induced through market incentives to increase agricultural output, adopt new technologies, or change their ways. In this context, Nobel Laureate Theodore Schultz has championed the view that peasant farming is efficient, the implication being that there is no necessity to appeal to traditional cultural values to explain behavioral patterns encountered in traditional agriculture.

In his book *Transforming Traditional Agriculture* (1964) as well as in subsequent studies, Schultz advanced the thesis that responses to price and profit incentives tend to be universal and to not differ across countries or regions of a country. The assumption is that the farmer, whose behavior is substantively rational, tends to allocate resources in both modern and traditional organizational settings in order to maximize output gains and profits. This conceptualization of the behavior of the rural producer as *homo oeconomicus rusticus* ("rural economic man") strips him of all cultural traits that may have a bearing on the decision-making process. The Schultzian philosophy has had a significant influence in shaping the "Washington consensus" about development (see David 1994). In two influential reports- *Accelerated Development in Sub-Saharan Africa* (1981) [the Berg Report] ad *Sub-Saharan Africa: From Crisis to Sustainable Growth* (1989), the World Bank was to identify government policies as the major obstacle to agricultural and rural development. In consonance with the philosophy engendered in the Berg Report, most structural and sectoral adjustment programs contain a "reform package" that is designed to modernize agriculture through a policy mix that emphasizes market-based incentives, introduction of improved agricultural technologies, and the privatization of agricultural marketing through parastatal divestiture and/or restructuring.

Policy Scenario II: "Capturing the Peasantry"

Under a second policy scenario, the premises underlying the World Bank's reformist option are thought to be false, and therefore, unacceptable. It explains the fracture between national and traditional environments in terms of the inability of governments to "capture the peasantry" or sufficiently subjugate the rural sector by enforcing authority. Under the circumstances, palliatives based on more economic incentives to traditional farmers and efforts to integrate them more fully into the national decision-making process are likely to prove unproductive, and might even exacerbate the problems facing the traditional environment. According to this perspective, therefore, the answer lies in the "stick" and not in the "carrot."

In this context, one line of argument is a derivative of the classical Marxian thesis that exploitation and subjugation of the peasantry should be considered an inherent and inevitable part of the development process. The primary reason is that the history of development has always constituted a struggle among various interest groups with differential forms of access to power. In this process, it is argued, the weak and the powerless tend to lose their autonomy and are therefore exploited and subjugated. In the struggle for power, the state always imposes its will on various social classes. Hence, a reasonable expectation is that rural and national development in Africa and elsewhere will not be pursued for the benefit of the countryside, but more to promote the interests of the nation state and the privileged few.

The burning question remains whether this historical inevitability cannot be escaped. Here, protagonists rely on the radical heterodox theses that the process of developmental transformation is fraught with tensions, ambiguities, and antagonistic relationships. As a consequence, it can be expected that the process will be uniquely painful for the peasant class or traditional agriculturalists because of their dogged resistance to the forces of modernization. As Hyden (1980: 4) writes:

> In their case, development is not only a matter of improvement of material conditions. It is also a question of losses in respect for other values and, above all, it is a matter of trading social autonomy for increased dependency on other social classes. Modern society with its inorganic substance - or development as it has been historically defined - is not necessarily an attraction. Development in that context is not a temptation to people to sacrifice.

The meeting point between policy scenarios 1 and 11 lies in their implicit subscription to a philosophy of development based on the Western model of modernization. They also recognize that the nature of the polity essentially determines the environment in which people live, i.e., what sectoral or class interests shall prevail, the nature of participation by economic agents, patterns of equality and inequality, how rules are enforced, and the extent to which policies are legitimized on the basis of local values and institutions. They diverge, however, in their interpretations of the differential roles of the state *vis-a-vis* the market as alternative catalysts of authentic development.

The reformist or technocratic option is based on the premise that market-based inducements and "moral suasion" can be effectively used by a minimalist, "nightwatchman," or "benevolent" state to foster cooperative relations with the traditional environment. However, its conceptual focus is devoid of any critical interpretive analysis of the potential influence on farmer behavior of factors such as personality, motivation, and the socio-cultural and economic characteristics of rural households and families. Along Schultzian lines, peasant or small farmer behavior is explained by using the standard assumptions or orthodox microeconomic analysis, e.g., perfect foresight, certainty, and stable relationships between prices, production inputs, and outputs.

On the contrary, what is known from actual observations of rural households in Africa and elsewhere tends to suggest that such decisions are typically based on uncertainty and lack of information. In particular, rural producers continue to face uncertainty about the behavior of input relative to output prices, and are usually at a disadvantage when attempting to acquire information about the future behavior of such prices. Not only do they constantly face uncertainty about the behavior of the weather, rainfall patterns, the incidence of crop disease, pests, and so on, but they are often skeptical about the advice received from central government authorities. As indicated earlier, they live in a world that is usually antagonistic to the government machinery.

The latter forms the basis of the neo-Marxian option, which interprets the interactive process as one of open conflict between national and traditional environments. As Hyden remarks, the antithesis has its roots in the fundamental contradiction between "the modern development logic and the social logic of the peasant mode (1980: 231). The contradiction is thought to be irreconcilable because the state cannot introduce political, technological, and other forms of modernization without disrupting the traditional ethos of rural life. The only alternative, therefore, is for the modernizing state to utilize any means at its disposal to enforce compliance. It remains highly debatable, however, whether a reluctant citizenry can be effectively coerced to accept any form of modernization that they do not perceive to be in their own interests.

This is borne out by the failure of economic reforms in Ghana under the Nkrumah regime, the villagization schemes in Tanzania under Nyerere, and Mengitsu's efforts to relocate large segments of the Ethiopian peasantry. In particular, the Tanzanian and Ethiopian experiences provided ample evidence to show how attempts to wrench human populations out of their organic socio-cultural contexts can prove inimical to the requirements of authentic development. The Tanzanian Ujamaa experiment proved to be a virtual paradox of development because it disrupted the cultural cohesion of the rural community. On the one hand, it placed heavy reliance on the principles of cohesiveness underlying the traditional socio-cultural milieu. On the other hand, the organic process of rural socio-economic organization was violated by uprooting rural village communities, tearing them away from age-old and tested methods of production, and relocating them in comparatively modernized settings with access to upgraded social amenities and centralized organs of development. In the Ethiopian case, the relocation policy proved to be even more traumatic. It was designed to ameliorate the rigors of life facing drought-stricken nomads in the rural hinterland. The model failed because it was patterned on ill-conceived and dysfunctional notions, borrowed from the Soviet Union, about the possibilities of "scientific" economic development.

Nevertheless, one should be reminded that after the Second World War a few African leaders were able to mobilize small farmers successfully by incorporating them into the political base of the ruling party. The *Harambee* movement in Kenya and *investissement humain* in Guinea are cases in point. It is now known that while such mobilization campaigns were perceived as local complements to external assistance and as a means of boosting local productive efforts, they came to grief largely because expectations about the redistributive role of the state were not fulfilled and they lacked sufficient incentives for the most diligent and hardworking members of population.

Policy Scenario III: Endogenous Development and People Empowerment

A third alternative takes as a point of departure the conglomeration of values, ideas, institutions, and artifacts that have historically guided the behavior of African peoples in regional, country, or group contexts. It posits that an authentic process of socio-economic transformation must by necessity be rooted in the cultural dynamics of African society. As indicated earlier, this represents an evolving framework that establishes the bases on which diverse collectivities act and react in society. This cultural milieu has been undergoing constant change in response to the internal dynamics of group behavior, exocentric influences, and the continuous interplay between exogenous and endogenous factors.

In the articulation of the inherent features of the "moral economy of affection," the impression was probably conveyed of an eternally fixed, static, and never-changing value system and *modus operandi*. This is not the case. African societies have continuously displayed a dynamic "moral pluralism" (Martin 1991), based on the ability to accommodate unique balances or configurations of behavior of what would appear to the naked eye as totally contradictory forms of behavioral expectations. Forms of individualism and communalism, paternalism, competition and solidarity tend to coexist. On the surface, this poses a basic dilemma for a development quest based on values of social and cultural cohesiveness. On the one hand, people are wont to extol the trappings of material advancement as exemplified by the visible success of well-known business people and their entrepreneurship. On the other hand, they are often repelled by the individualistic and competitive forms of behavior engendered in the capitalist system. The moral imperative of solidarity and social cooperation has enabled people to surmount the opportunism in which collective interests are unrealized because each individual or group, acting in splendid isolation, has no incentive to abide by the collective will.

Based on the assumption that there is a set of consensual norms and values, the central task becomes one of building a civil community or societal ordering guided by four socio-cultural imperatives: civil engagement; political equality; solidarity, trust, and tolerance; and social structures of cooperation (Putnam 1992). Civil engagement refers to the participation of the citizenry in all facets of the life of the community. It involves the inculcation of "civil virtue," or the pursuit of individual self-interest within the context of the broader social good. Political equality connotes equal rights and obligations for all, or communities bound together by horizontal relations of reciprocity and cooperation. The relations of solidarity, trust, and tolerance imply that even in a conflict-ridden society there should be some minimal amount of mutual respect and tolerance for the views of others. In other words, disputes should not be settled by resort to violence and internecine warfare. The structures of cooperation refer to the associations and local institutions that are the conduits for effective self-government and participation.

The principles underlying the civil community are more or less supported by all cultures, and are synergistic with the true spirit of indigenous format of African society. The philosophical thrust has found a forceful expression in the writings and public statements of African scholars and leaders. Notable examples are Kwame Nkrumah's consciencism, Julius Nyerere's African socialism, and the Christian Socialism of both Kenneth Kaunda and Robert Mugabe. As emphasized earlier, however, there has been a wide divergence between the "record" ad the "rhetoric." The actual experience of the fragile nation states established in contemporary Africa generally demonstrates that either the pillars of civic society have not been successfully built, or they have been constantly eroded away by the self-serving and ruthless behavior of the ruling elite.

Yet, a civic community based on an ensemble of values holds the key to the creation of highly viable and coherent economic structures as well as an autonomous institutional capacity. In this context, the success or failure of African countries in achieving authentic development is intimately bound up with their ability to skillfully intermesh strategies for economic growth, income redistribution, employment creation, basis needs fulfillment, and others designed to remove the various structural and institutional bottlenecks to the development process. This involves an endogenous, organic, and multidimensional process of transformation encompassing output and capacity expansion, the building of competence levels, and corresponding organizational and institutional changes across society. The elements of such a unified and integrated approach must necessarily vary from country to country. Nevertheless, some general requirements with regard to the structure of governance, decentralization, and the role of local institutions may be briefly mentioned.

The structure of governance is usually defined by the amount of power vested in the central government and the structural arrangements linking the bureaucratic apparatus to groups, classes, and individuals in society at large. A distinction is sometimes drawn between "closed", "open", and "intermediate" systems (Cleaves 1980). As we have shown, the system typically encountered in Africa is relatively "closed", i.e. one in which the state apparatus has effectively monopolized economic and social power. As an integral part of this process, the state (national environment) has retained full discretion over policy initiatives, which generally respond to the personal and institutional interests of the individuals and/or groups dominating the government machinery. Accordingly, national elites in Africa concluded that their development goals for African society were effectively prejudiced by a nuisance - factor, i.e., the socio-cultural beliefs and patterns of economic organizations characterizing the traditional environment.

Whether or not this is true, this paper suggests that a first step in the authentic development path involves the establishment of "open" political systems. The latter are characterized by a relatively large number of autonomous interests associations (political, economic, social) based on competing, and sometimes mutually supportive, ideas about the paths governments should follow in the search for solutions to critical problems, as well as the scope and direction of change to be sought in society. This endogenous and participatory model essentially advocates that the decision-making process should be guided by the "word" or "voice" and not by the "sword" or "stick", as the case may be. It suggests an internalization of the tenets of what is now known as "good governance". The characteristics of good governance about which there is widespread international agreement include: accountability; the rule of law; equitable and sustainable economic development; and meeting people's basic needs.

Underlying accountability is the need to ensure the legitimacy of government through open processes of public choice such as free and fair elections. It also involves a process whereby the state elite and public bureaucratics are made accountable for their decisions and actions through transparent rules and mechanisms of implementation. The principle of accountability must be buttressed by the role of law. This requires the creation and maintenance of an objective, efficient, and reliable judicial system to guarantee the safety and security of citizens, as well as the fair enforcement of contracts. The prerequisite of equitable ad sustainable economic development is predicated on the imperative of ensuring that forms of economic and social development are not only responsive to people's needs, but also for the benefit of present and future generations. Good governance also means that the life-sustenance, intelligence, and other needs of the population should be met. This requires the ready availability of information to ensure that accountability is practiced, laws correctly applied, markets function adequately, and to encourage the creativity and innovativeness of people.

In the final analysis, bureaucratic and planning systems cannot be exclusively based on the abstract principle of efficiency, but must be compatible with local values in which a local institutional spirit is nurtured. The Japanese and East Asian success story is a case in point. It is through local organizations that the needs of the people could be best expressed and understood. They are the focal points for initiating and continuing the participation and involvement of people in the development process. The most successful organizational and institutional structures have typically represented indigenous, participatory initiatives in relatively cohesive local communities.

REFERENCES

Ake, Claude, 1990. "Sustaining Development of the Indigenous." In *Long-Term Perspective Study on Sub-Saharan Africa*. Washington, D.C.: The World Bank.

Bates, Robert. 1981. *Markets and States in Tropical Africa*. Berkeley, CA: University of California Press

Cleaves, Peter. 1980. "Implementation Amidst Searching and Apathy: Political Power and Policy Design. "In *Politics and Policy Implementation in the Third World,* edited by Merilee S. Grindle. Princeton, N. J., Princeton University Press

David, Wilfred L. 1988. "The Food Crisis in Sub-Saharan Africa. "*New Directions,* 15(3).

------------ 1994. *The Washington Consensus: Between Structural Adjustment and Authentic Development.* Washington, D.C. Howard University Press (forthcoming).

Dia, Mamadou. 1991. "Development and Cultural Values in Sub-Saharan Africa "*Finance and Development,* (December), 10-13

Hyden, Goran. 1980. *Beyond Ujamaa: Underdevelopment and the Uncaptured Peasantry.* London: Heinemann.

------- 1983. *No Shortcuts to Progress: African Development Management in Perspective.* London: Heinemann.

Lal, Deepak. 1985. *The Poverty of "Development Economics"* London: Institute of Economic Affairs.

Martin, Denis-Constant. 1991. "The Cultural Dimensions of Governance." In *Proceedings of the World Bank Annual Conference on Development Economics.* Washington, D.C.: The World Bank.

Popkin, Samuel L. 1979. *The Rational Peasant: The Political Economy of Rural Society in Viet Nam.* Berkeley, CA: University of California Press.

Putman, Robert D. 1992. "Democracy, Development, and the Civic Community: Evidence from an Italian Experience. "In *Culture and Development in Africa,* edited by Ismail Serageldin and June Tabaroff. Washington, D.C.: The World Bank.

Schultz, Theodore. 1964. *Transforming Traditional Agriculture.* New Haven, CT: Yale University Press.

Scott, James C. 1976. *The Moral Economy od the Peasant: Rebellion and Subsistence in South Asia.* New Haven CT: Yale University Press.

World Bank. 1981. *Accelerated Development in Africa: Agenda for Action.* Washington, D.C.: The World Bank.

--------- 1989. *Sub-Saharan Africa: From Crisis to Sustainable Growth. A Long-Term Perspective Study.* Washington, D.C.

Chapter II

Cities and Development in Sub-Saharan Africa

Dr. Charles Jarmon

Introduction

U rbanization in Africa, as in most developing regions of the world, is marked by several distinctive features: the small proportion of the continent's urban population, its rapid growth, and its uneven distribution. These conditions are significantly related to an accelerated increase of large African cities. This accelerating increase of cities is creating a spectra of economic and political dilemmas and issues closely identified with the problems of development in African nations.

Cities have existed for more than five thousand years, (Mumford, 1961), but those among the great wave of cities that helped to foster the industrial revolution in western countries contained the prime forces which have had the greatest consequences for transforming nations; in the present era of the evolution of African nations, cities contain the same potential for change, if the new demands brought about by the immense increase in the urban population can be met by the nation states of Africa through continuing the expansion of the political bureaucracy, the enlargement of industrial establishments, the indigenizing of commercial enterprises, the universal accessibility to large educational institutions, and the political and social integration of the great mass of highly differentiated populations. The phenomenal growth of cities, therefore, must be understood as having serious consequences for the social and economic development of African countries. Many scholars are reconfirming this reality (e.g., Gugler and Flanagan 1978; Jarmon, 1988; and Dogan and Kasarda, 1988). The aim of the present study, which is primarily limited to Sub-Saharan Africa, is twofold: to examine the growth of urbanization as a condition which necessitates the concomitant development of a number of economic variables in the modern economic sector and to examine industrial development as a basis for addressing some of the pressing problems of African countries that are identified with the emergence of big and giant cities.

In comparisons across nations, studies reveal the importance of urbanization and industry in national development (Gugler and Flanagan, 1978; United Nations, 1985; and Glickman 1988). To emphasize both urbanization and industry in this discussion, does not dismiss the multifarious nature of development, especially of the importance of concerns as political stability, nationalism, education, housing, transportation, and the like (Glickman, 1988; Jarmon, 1988).

Another reason to examine economic conditions in the modern sector is that agricultural production continues to be precarious and marginal in most African countries. Many of the management schemes for development in the agricultural sector have been disastrous (Pellow and Chazan, 1986, 163-164; Manning, 1988, 115; and James, 1991, 80-86). In this context, the significant question is whether industrial development in the modern sector is occurring sufficiently enough to meet the needs of countries which are increasingly becoming urban.

A discussion of these two focal concerns—urbanization and industry—will be required to make their implications for development clear. First, however, it will be helpful to establish a context for understanding the pattern of urbanization in Sub-Saharan Africa. This will be achieved by giving attention to the three distinctive features of urbanization which we referred to above. The first, the small proportion of the continents population living in cities, is particularly characteristic of most countries below the Sahara, with Nigeria being the most notable exception.

Urbanization and Cities

To gain a perspective of Africa's level of urbanization, let us consider levels of urbanization in the various major areas of the world. First, a brief comment should be made concerning what is meant by urbanization as we refer to it here. In recognizing that the definition of urban places varies with the country, the definition of urban in this work is the same as that recommended by the United Nations. Thus, it includes all localities with populations above 20,000 (United Nations 1969).

Table I provides data extracted from United Nations' estimations for major regions of the world. At all five dates between the period 1950 and 2000, Sub-Saharan Africa, excluding Southern Africa, is less urbanized than other major world regions save Southern

Asia. However, Eastern and Western Africa, with the smallest proportion of their population living in urban areas, are experiencing more rapid increases in urban growth rates. By 2000, the former will have increased nearly sixfold; the latter, nearly fourfold, ranging from 5.2 to 29.0 percent and from 10.2 to 39.8 percent respectively. At the other extreme, in Northern and Western Europe and Northern America, the most urbanized

Table 1: Percentage of Total Population Estimated and Projected Living in Urban Areas in World Regions, 1950-2000

Region	Percentage Urban					
	1950	1960	1970	1980	1990	2000
World total	29.2	34.2	36.6	39.5	45.2	55.1
Africa	14.5	18.3	22.9	27.8	33.9	40.7
Eastern Africa	5.2	7.3	10.3	15.0	21.8	29.0
Middle Africa	14.2	17.9	24.7	30.8	37.8	45.6
Northern Africa	24.5	30.0	36.0	39.9	44.6	51.2
Southern Africa	38.0	41.7	43.5	48.3	54.9	61.3
Western Africa	10.2	14.5	19.7	25.8	32.2	39.8
Latin America	41.5	49.3	57.3	65.3	71.5	76.4
Caribbean	33.8	38.3	45.6	53.0	59.5	64.8
Central America	39.8	46.7	54.0	60.4	66.0	63.5
South America	43.2	51.7	60.0	68.0	75.1	80.0
Northern America	63.9	69.9	73.8	74.2	75.2	77.3
Canada	60.8	68.9	75.7	76.0	77.1	79.3
United States	64.2	70.0	73.6	74.1	75.0	77.0
Asia	16.4	21.5	22.9	27.1	34.4	42.7
Eastern Asia	16.8	25.0	24.7	28.7	39.4	51.4
South East Asia	14.8	17.6	20.2	24.8	29.9	36.9
Southern Asia	16.0	17.3	19.5	23.1	27.3	32.8
Western Asia	23.9	32.9	43.2	51.5	62.7	70.3
Europe	56.5	61.1	66.7	70.4	73.4	76.7
Eastern Europe	41.9	47.9	53.5	60.1	64.7	69.4
Northern Europe	75.1	77.6	82.4	83.8	84.4	85.7
Southern Europe	44.6	49.4	56.1	61.0	65.7	70.4
Western Europe	66.6	71.4	76.4	79.1	80.8	83.0
Oceania	61.3	66.3	70.7	71.2	70.6	71.3
USSR	39.3	48.3	56.7	63.0	65.8	67.5

Source: Adapted from United Nations, *World Urbanization Prospects, 1990*. New York: Department of International Economic and Social Affairs, 1991.

regions of the world, the rate of urban growth is likely to continue to decline. Northern and Southern Africa, possess moderate levels of urbanization that have continued to be lower than that for the more developed regions of the world and higher than that for the less developed regions.

The dynamic character of urbanization in this part of Africa becomes more apparent if rates of urban growth since 1960 are compared with the three decades prior to this date. From 1920 to 1950, Sub-Saharan Africa had less than one percent increase in its urban population over each of the three decades; it was not only the least urbanized major world region but had the lowest level of increase in its urban population over the thirty year period. Since 1960, this region has experienced an enormous surge in its urban growth rates, greater than for most of the developed nations and similar to other developing countries.

The third feature, the uneven distribution of the urban population, is as evident within particular countries as between regions of the continent, with the former of greater interest from the standpoint of development than that of the latter. However, because of obvious limitations, the present discussion is on the latter. Tables 2 and 3 provide these data. In the first of these two tables, countries are arranged according to their level of urbanization in terms of the estimated averages for the continent of Africa in 1960 and 1989. Examining the two averages, thirteen and twenty eight percent respectively for the two dates, provides a clear picture of important differences within and between each of the two periods. For 1960, it is evident that the pattern of unevenness in urbanization follows along regional lines. For example, in Group I, are Egypt and South Africa, the countries with the highest level of urbanization. Each, with 36 percent of its population living in urban areas, had urban populations at least twice the average for the continent. They are located at opposite ends of the continent, northern and southern Africa respectively.

Countries which fall into Group II, comprised of those with more than the continent's average level of urbanization, but less than its double, display similar regional patterning. Three of the seven countries—Algeria, Morocco, and Tunisia— are part of northern Africa; three are part of southern Africa, Zimbabwe, Zambia, and Angola. Senegal, the single exception, is in the western region.

Group III and IV, composed of those countries with less than the continent's average level of urbanization, include the greatest number of countries, with most coming from western, central, and eastern Africa. Among this group, Nigeria and Ghana possessed the greatest number of inhabitants living in urban areas.

Group V discloses the uniqueness of the small African nations, those with populations below two million inhabitants. One of the salient characteristics associated with this group of countries is that most of the urban population tend to live in the primate city of these countries (United Nations, 1973) which is often the capital city. Moreover, they are unlikely to possess big cities. Libya and the Congo, possessing big cities, are the two

Table 2:   **Estimates of the Level of Urbanization for African Countries, 1960 and 1989**

Level of Urbanization	Percent Urban	
	1960 a	1989 b
Group I (more than twice the continent's average)	South Africa (36) Egypt (36)	South Africa (59)
Group II (more than the continent's average, but less than double)	Algeria (25) Morocco (24) Tunisia (23) Senegal (22) Zimbawe (16) Zambia (16) Angola (13)	Tunisia (54) Algeria (51) Zambia (49) Morocco (47) Egypt (46) Ivory Coast(40) Cameroon (40) Zaire (39) Senegal (38) Benin (37) Somalia (36) Nigeria (35) Ghana (33) Sierra Leone (32) Tanzania (31) Chad (29) Angola (28)
Group III (less than the continent's average, but more than one half)	Nigeria (12) Ghana (12) Zaire (9) Benin (8) Madagascar (8) Ivory Coast (8) Sierra Leone (8)	Zimbawi (27) Guinea (25) Madagascar (24) Kenya (23) Sudan (22) Niger (19) Mali (19)
Group IV (less than one half the continent's average)	Cameroon (6) Kenya (6) Chad (5) Ginea (5) Somalia (5) Niger (5) Ethiopia (4) Mali (4) Sudan (4) Uganda (4) Tanzania (3) Burkina Faso (3) Malawi (2)	Ethiopia (13) Malawi (12) Uganda (10) Burkina Faso (9)

Continued Next Page

Table 2 (Continued)

Level of Urbanization	Percent Urban 1960	1989
Group V (countries with less than two million inhabitants)	Libya (29)	(69)
	Congo (22)	(40)
	Central African (13) Republic	(46)
	Gabon (11)	(45)
	Gambia (9)	(22)
	Liberia (8)	(45)
	Togo (6)	(25)
	Mauritania (3)	(45)

a Continental average = 13; b continental average = 28.

Source: *World Development Report 1991: Challenge of Development*, The International Bank for Reconstruction and Development, New York: Oxford University Press, 1991; *Demographic Yearbook 1988*, New York: United Nations, 1990; and *Growth of the World's Population 1920-2000*, *op. cit.*

exceptions. Libya, with twenty nine percent of its population urban, actually surpassed the continent's average. The figures which are shown for the period of the most recent estimates, 1989, reflect the growth of the urban population which occurred over nearly three decades, a period during which Africa's population growth rate (3.2 percent between 1980 and 1990 compared with the world's average of 1.8) was higher than other regions of the world (see World Development Report, 1991, 181). Much of this growth occurred in urban areas. In examining for comparisons between the two periods, important changes are evident in the distribution of urbanization on the continent.

First, enormous change has taken place in the magnitude of the urban scale. Table 2 reveals a definite shift towards greater urbanization among the Sub-Saharan countries. While South Africa remained the only country whose urban population doubled the continent's average, more than twice as many countries had rates which exceeded the average. The Ivory Coast, Cameroon, Zaire, Benin, Somalia, Nigeria, Ghana, Sierra, Tanzania, and Chad moved into this category. This means that the urban boom is occurring most rapidly among the less urbanized regions, particularly among countries of West Africa.

Second, in 1989, no country in Africa was at the embryonic stage of urban growth which was observed by the very low levels of urbanization existing for many of the countries in 1960. Malawi (12 percent), Uganda (10 percent) and Burkina Faso (9 percent) are the only countries with urban populations below the average of that period.

Big and Giant African Cities

There has been a phenomenal increase of people living in African cities as well as a sharp increase in the number of big and giant cities. The previous discussion confirmed the increase in Africa's urban population. This section focuses on the regional distribution of big and giant African cities; that is, again using United Nations' definitions, cities which have 500,000 or more inhabitants and ones which have multi-millions respectively. Table 3 reveals that in 1960 Africa possessed only one giant city, Cairo. Alexandria, in Egypt, and Johannesburg, in South Africa, were the largest of the eight big cities.

For 1990, Table 3 shows a greater number, a wider distribution, and a higher scale for both big and giant cities. For example, by this date, the number of giant cities had increased from one to eight; the number of big cities of at least one million had increased from two to twenty four. In addition to the largest of the big cities that are included in the table, there were at least 25 cities which had reached 500,000 or more inhabitants. Although Northern Africa continued to have a greater number of big cities, Sub-Saharan Africa experienced a significant increase in such cities, including the cities of Kano, Yaounde, Freetown, Canakry, and Kampala which are not included in the table.

With respect to heightened scale of cities, Cairo grew to over six million inhabitants and twenty three of the cities with one million inhabitants or more in 1990 had not obtained a population of 500,000 inhabitants as late as 1960. Given this build up of cities in Africa, brief attention will be given to the demographic conditions which led to their rapid rise. In demographic terms, it has been customary to explain Africa's recent surge of urbanization by reference to natural increase and migration. The former is generally explained with respect to Africa's progress toward the demographic transition. This approach assumes that the demographic make-up of African countries, caused by social, political, and economic circumstances in the modern era, is determined by sharp decreases in the continent's death rates and a continuation of high birth rates. For example, data extracted from the World Tables, 1991 (World Bank, 1991b) demonstrate the relationship between infant birth and death rates. In 1969, the infant mortality rate per thousand live births in Nigeria (162), Ghana (112), Senegal (118), and Uganda (117) had, by 1989, declined to 102 for Nigeria; 87 Ghana, 76 Senegal, and 99 Uganda. The birth rate, on the other hand, continued at nearly the same level for these same countries. The average fertility rate for these four Sub-Saharan countries was 6.8 and 6.4, respectively for 1969 and 1989. This situation sharply contrasts with that occurring in Northern America and Japan. Their much lower infant mortality rates, averaging 8.4 for Mexico, the United States, and Canada, with the latter having the lowest at 6.9, and for Japan, 4.8, exemplify the advance stage of mortality in the demographic transition for these countries. Their average fertility rate was 1.8 for Northern America and 1.5 for Japan, which is an indication of the similar position of birth rates in these area in the demographic

Table 3: Regional Distribution of Big and Giant African Cities, 1960, 1990

Population of Cities (Thousands)[a]		
Region	1960	1990[b]
Northern Africa		
Egypt:		
Cairo	3,320	6,053
Alexandria	1,502	2,893
Gizza	...	1,858
Morocco:		
Casablanca	965	2,904
Marrakech	...	1,425
Rabat	...	1,287
Algeria:		
Algiers	722	3,250
Tunisia:		
Tunis	...	1,395
Libya:		
Tripoli	...	1,000
Sudan:		
Khartoun	...	3,000
Western Africa		
Cameroon:		
Douala	...	1,030
Ghana:		
Accra	...	1,400
Ivory Coast:		
Abidjan	...	1,423
Nigeria:		
Ibadan	575	1,296
Lagos	500	1,739
Ado-Ekiti	...	1.000
Ilorin	...	1,084
Ogbomosho	...	1,000
Senegal:		
Dakar	...	1,105

Continued Next Page.

Table 3. (continued).

Population of Cities (Thousands)a Region	1960	1990b
Central Africa Zaire: Kinshasa	...	2,654
Africa Ethiopia: Addis Ababa	...	1,686
Kenya: Nairobi	...	1,162
Tanzania: Dar es Salaam	...	1,096
Uganda: Kampala	...	1,000
Zambia: Lusaka	...	1,000
Southern Africa Angola: Luanda	...	1,300
Mozambique: Lourenco Marques	...	1,000
South Africa: Johannesburg	1,140	2,000
Cape Town	800	2,000
Durban	675	1,000
Port Elizabeth	...	1,116
Pretoria	...	1,000

a Big cities refer to cities with 500,000 inhabitants or more;
  giant cities refer to with multi-million inhabitants.
b Population figures represent both most recent estimates and projections.
Sources: *Europa 1991: Africa South of the Sahara*. London:
Europa Publications Limited; Europa.
transition.

Migration, the second dramatic contribution to the phenomenal growth of cities, refthe

move of migrants from rural villages to cities. As it results from a mix of "push" and "pull" factors, migration is a response to different motivations. Most migrants, whose stay in cities vary in length, are seeking work in the urban centers. They see in the city prospects for fulfilling a variety of interests which would be difficult to satisfy in the village. As evidence of the city's attraction, migrants leaving the village may constitute, in some cases, close to 70 percent of a village's male labor force, and all may be away from home at the same time (see discussion, Jarmon, 1988, 130-132). The failure of sustained development in the agricultural sector has been one of the primary factors pushing migrants to the city.

Industry as a Dimension of Development

Background to Industrial Development. It would be desirable to examine the structure of industrial development in several countries, but that is not feasible under the constraints of the present discussion. It appears appropriate to highlight significantly common features of industrial development in Sub-Saharan Africa, while giving descriptive details of industry for a country in which the range of obstacles can be shown. In Nigeria, because of its movement between periods of success and failure in this sector, these obstacles can be amply shown with respect to the history of foreign rule, independence, and subsequent dependent relations.

For Nigeria, as with other Sub-Saharan countries, industrial development cannot be separated from the history of the colonial imperative in Africa. The colonial empires of core European countries, successful in incorporating the region into a larger political and economic capitalist-world system (Rodney, 1972; Shaw and Aluko, 1984; Jarmon, 1988; and Boswell, 1989), tempered the scale of industrial evolution in these countries to the benefit of the empires. This history of subjugation and dependency among African countries makes it necessary to examine industrial development from a different perspective than would be used to examine it in industrially advanced countries of the core.

In essence, the Western experience with industrialism has little in common with what is occurring in the now independent countries of Sub-Saharan Africa. When the industrial revolution began in the West, it was industry that demanded a conformable labor force of urban workers. Urbanization increased with rural peasants being rapidly converted into an urban proletariat at the same time in which industrial production and markets for manufactured goods expanded. However, in Sub-Saharan Africa, the primary drive for industry emanates from the demand of the teeming populations in big and giant cities. Rural migrants who are in transition from rural farm workers to urban wage workers are swelling the ranks of the unemployed. Pressured by the great numbers of job-seekers, industrial development has become one of the primary objectives of national policy among most countries of the region, particularly for Nigeria whose oil exports were an important source of government revenue (Wickins, 280).

In the first decade of independence (1960-1970), industry in Sub-Saharan African countries heavily depended upon capital coming from the direct investment of foreign private sources and government related agencies. Thus, one of the first great obstacles derived from the lack of ownership and control over industry by African themselves. However, beginning with the early 1970s, the nationalistic movements that occurred in many of these countries were responsible for transferring much of the ownership and control over foreign-owned enterprises from foreign capitalists to national governments and indigenous entrepreneurs (Wickens, 1986, 299-302). In Nigeria, for example, the government promulgated the 1972 Nigerian Enterprise Promotion Decree which excluded foreigners from all but the largest wholesale enterprises (Jarmon, 1988, 85-86). Where the movement occurred, the question arose of the extent to which the transfer of ownership had benefited workers by additional wealth "trickling down" to wage workers.

Indicators of Industrial Development. Given the demands which have been induced by urbanization, the question that is critically considered here is: How has the industrial sector contributed to the economy of these countries within the last two decades? The evidence suggests that the performance has not been encouraging. In most Sub-Saharan countries, this appears to be related to insufficient capital, infrastructure, skills, and markets which have retarded industrial growth. This pessimism issues from continued declines in such indicators as contribution of industry to the gross domestic product, growth of the industrial sector, and increase in the export of commodities from manufacturing.

Contribution to Gross Domestic Product. In African countries where a substantial modern economy has developed, the underdeveloped and capital-intensive nature of the industrial sector has retarded its contribution to the gross domestic product (GDP) of these countries. Table 4 reveals World Bank estimates for industrial development from 1965 to 1989. The table discloses that Sub-Saharan African countries are still very much more dependent upon the agricultural sector for economic productivity than other world regions, with its percentage contribution to GDP in 1987 being six times greater than that for world regions. It is also evident that growth has occurred in the industrial sector, but the problem appears to be one of sustaining it. In 1980, the contribution of industry actually surpassed that of agriculture; however, by the end of the decade it had dropped to the levels of the early seventies.

World Bank (1991a) estimates suggest that from 1970 to 1990, in Sub-Saharan Africa, excluding Nigeria, the industrial sector contributed an average of less than one percent to the growth of the GDP. Further, the 2.1 percent rate of increase for the GDP in 1989 was a 50 percent decrease from the 4.2 rate of 1980. This decline in GDP constitutes one of the most important indicators of breakdowns in the development process. Nigeria's exclusion in the estimates for Sub-Saharan Countries was warranted because its vast revenue from the production of its petroleum in the first half of this period would have a confounding effect on the aggregate average for industrial contribution to the development of countries in Sub-Saharan Africa. However, beginning with 1980, the market for Nigeria's oil suffered a severe decline, and the industrial picture began to resemble that of other Sub-Saharan countries. For example, between 1970 and 1979, the industrial sector contributed nearly 6 percent to the growth of the GDP. In contrast, it contributed only 0.6 percent between 1980 and 1990.

Industrial Growth. The expected gains in the industrial sector have not occurred as measured by the gains in the number of new jobs created for an increasingly urban labor force. In 1980, for example, in Nigeria, 17 percent of those employed were in manufacturing and processing, but this was only 0.2 percent increase over the 16.8 percent in 1975 (Fourth National Development Plan, 1980-1985). Other declining indicators for industry would suggests that even this marginal growth has not been sustained. In this respect, in Nigeria, since 1983, factories have been working at only 50 percent of their capacities (Nyang'oro, 1989, 23-24).

Much of what is mentioned here regarding employment can only be inferred from inadequate and limited data. For example, the report of the International Labor Organization (ILO) on employment in industry and manufacturing since 1980 included uneven data for less than half of the African countries (ILO, 1990). But for the countries for which data were included, few countries showed significant gains in employment in manufacturing. It appears reasonable for us to conclude that employment in industry is related to the changes occurring in the industrial sector, which is integrally connected to the capacity of these countries to export manufacturing commodities.

The World Bank (1991) provides data for the average growth rate for the modern

Table 4: Agricultural and Industrial Production in Sub-Saharan Africa, 1965-1989

Percentage of GDP

Sector	1965	1973	1980	1989	
Sub-Saharan Africa					
Agriculture	41	31	28	30	32
Industry	20	25	32	25	27
World Regions					
Agriculture	10	8	7	5	..
Industry	40	37	37	32	..

Source: *World Development Report, 1991: Challenge of Development, op. cit.*

sector in Sub-Saharan countries. The most telling statistic is that for the decline in the annual rate of growth for expansion in industry. For example, between 1965 and 1980, the average annual rate of change was 7.5 percent; however, for the period between 1980 and 1989, the rate of growth had declined to only 0.7 percent. The statistics also disclose the relative consistency in the high rate of growth in urbanization, showing a slight increase from 5.8 percent to 6.0 percent between the period of 1965 to 1989.

Structure of Export Commodities. Table 5 reveals the composition of manufacturing exports for 1989. The high concentration of exports in the primary sector of the economy represents the difficulty that African countries are having in implementing strategies for industrial development. For example, 53 percent of exports derive from fuels, minerals, and metals, while another 36 percent comes from other primary commodities. This contrasts with only 1 percent in heavy industry and 10 percent in other areas of light industry. In comparison with the more economically developed countries in the Organization for Economic Cooperation, the situation is just the opposite. For these countries, exports primarily derive from the secondary sector of heavy industry and other value added categories of industry.

In light of the attractiveness of such recognized plans as the Organization of African's Unity's Lagos Plan of Action, where one principal course for reducing the stagnation and under development in industry was recognized to be changing traditional reliance on the export of a few raw materials (OAU, 1982), Table 5 suggests the need to understand the complexity of underlying conditions which are impeding industrial development in African countries. It is clear that the explanations will not be categorically the same for each country; however, it is clear that each explanation will involve economic relationships between African countries and the more developed countries as well as established policies internal to each country in terms of commitment to the formal plans for industrial development.

Conclusion

This study began with the assumption that many of the problems of development in African nations are associated with the rapid increase in urbanization and the lack of concomitant development in the modern economic sector. We stated, therefore, two objectives. The first was to examine urbanization in Sub-Saharan African countries in terms of conditions associated with the rise and distribution of big and large cities; the second was to examine the industrial sector as one of the prime forces for development. Findings, derived from an examination of indicators of changes in urbanization and industry and rates of the gross domestic product, emerge which lead to the pessimistic conclusion that Sub-Saharan countries are experiencing serious breakdowns in the modern economic sector. Data, for example, show that from 1965 to 1989 the urban population

Table 5: Export Commodities for Sub-Saharan Africa and World Regions, 1989				
Exports	Percentage Share of Commodity			
	Fuels, Minerals and Metals	Other Primary Commod.	Machinery, and Transp. Equipment	Other Manuf.
World Reg.				
World	12	14	35	39
Africa	53	36	1	10
East Asia	12	19	22	47
South Asia	6	24	56	5
Europe, M. East, and North Africa	34	12	20	33
Latin America and Carribean	33	33	12	24
OECD Countries	9	12	40	40

Source: *World Development Report, 1991: The Challenge of Development.*

in Sub-Saharan countries has continued to increase; on the other hand, these data reveal that the expected growth in industry has not occurred, but rather declined over the same period. This decline, coupled with the decline in agricultural productivity for these countries, has had a direct affect on the decreasing value of the GDP in these countries, which is in effect made more significant as the declining agricultural sector is now increasing in its proportionate share to the value of the GDP.

There are some caveats with respect to the foregoing discussion. One of the most important is that trends derived from the use of aggregate averages, such as provided in this work, do not disclose some of the critical dynamics associated with industrial development in the region or in particular countries. For example, the direction of change between the early years of industrial "take off" and the period beginning with the last decade has not been a direct descending movement. If we were to examine the growth of manufacturing between 1960 and 1975, we would observe that it advanced rapidly. However, since the early 1980s, manufacturing has declined in Sub-Saharan Africa, and considerably below the level of other world regions.

To fully understand changes in the developmental process for a particular country, it is necessary to gain a familiarity with a diverse array of essential elements which include: the stability of its political process, the impact of external forces on its economic system, its access to technical innovations, its geographic resources, and its advantageous adaptation to the changing global system. There are clear illustrations of this point which range from the effect of the decline in the petroleum industry that affected Nigeria's economy, the fluctuation of the cocoa market that affected Ghana, the international sanctions against South Africa that affected its economy, to the political crises in Zaire that affected the climate for development. The phenomenal growth of the urban population in Sub-Saharan Africa, which is a function of both natural increase and migration, has resulted in serious national problems in employment , housing, transportation, health, education, and the like. In view of their awareness of these problems, scholars have proposed different strategies and methods to address the urban pressure and the need for expanding industrial development. Among these proposals include arguments for shifting funds and resources from the large cities to smaller secondary cities as a way to relieve population pressures; advocacy for more equity in commercial exchanges of goods and capital in the international markets between African countries and the super powers in the world system; calls to refocus attention on education and technical sciences; and schemes for national leaders to pursue vertical planning between the intergovernmental structures of national, regional, state, and local levels for more integrated development.

Finally, the above proposals suggest the complexity of the problem of development, and it is becoming more complex as we face the reality of the continuing urban growth phenomenon in Sub-Saharan Africa. No extraordinary vision is required to recognize that new national strategies for development are needed, and, in some instances, so is greater commitment on the part of national leaders to implement them. Both innovation and commitment are necessary if in the future current problems are not to loom even more ominously in the Sub-Saharan region.

References

Reprinted from: *Journal of the Third World Spectrum*, Volume 2, Number 1, 1995, by permission of the author and the *Journal of the Third World Spectrum*, Washington, D.C.

Boswell, T. 1989. "Colonial Empires and the Capitalist World-Economy: A Time Series Analysis   of Colonization, 1640-1960." *American Sociological Review 54*: 180-196.

Dogan, M. and J. D. Kasarda. 1988. *The Metropolis Era: A World of Cities.* Newbury Park: Sage   Publications.

Europa. 1991. *Africa South of the Sahara.* London: Europa Publication Limited.

Federation of Nigeria. 1981. *Fourth National Development Plan, 1981-1985.* Lagos: The National Planning Office, Federal Ministry of National Planning.

Glickman, H. 1988. *The Crisis and Challenge of African Development.* New York: Greenwood Press.

Gugler, J. and W. G. Flanagan. 1978. *Urbanization and Social Change in West Africa.* Cambridge: Cambridge University Press.

Gulhati, R., and S. Yalamanchili. 1988. "Contemporary Policy Responses to Economic Decline in Africa." In H. Glickman (ed.), *The Crisis and Challenge of African Development.* New York:

Greenwood Press.

International Labor Organization. 1990. *Year Book of Labor Statistics*. Geneva: International Labor Office.

James, V. U . 1991. *Resource Management in Developing Countries: Africa's Ecological and Economic Problems*. New York: Bergin and Garvey.

Jarmon, C. 1988. Nigeria: *Reorganization and Development since the Mid-Twentieth Century*. Leiden: E. J. Brill.

Manning, P. 1988. *Francophone Sub-Saharan Africa: 1980-1985*. Cambridge: Cambridge University Press.

Mumford, L. 1961. *The City in History*. New York: Harcourt, Brace, and World.

Nyang'oro, J. 1989. *The State and Capitalist Development in Africa: Declining Political Economies*.
_____. 1990. *Demographic Yearbook 1988*, New York: United Nations.

Wickins, P. 1986. *Africa, 1880-1980: An Economic History*. Cape Town: Oxford University Press.

The World Bank (The International Bank for Reconstruction and Development). 1991a. *World Development Report, 1991: The Challenge of Development*. New York: Oxford University.
_____. 1985 *World Development Report, 1985*. New York: Oxford University.

The World Bank. 1991. *World Tables, 1991*. Baltimore: The John Hopkins University Press.

_____. 1991b. *Social Indicators of Development, 1990*. Baltimore: The John Hopkins University Press.
New York: Praeger.

Organization of African Unity. 1982. *Lagos Plan of Action for the Economic Development of Africa, 1980-2000*. 2nd rev. ed. Geneva: International Institute for Labor Studies.

Pellow, D., and N. Chazan. 1986. *Ghana: Coping with Uncertainty*. Boulder: Westview Press.

RAPID (Resources for the Awareness of Population Impacts on Development). 1985. *The Effects of Population Factors on Social and Economic Development*. Lagos: Federal Ministry of Health and the National Population Bureau.

Rodney, W., 1972. *How Europe Underdeveloped Africa*. Dar es Salaam: Tanzania Publishing House.

Rondinelli, D. A. "Giant and Secondary City Growth in Africa." In M. Dogan and J. D. Kasarda (eds.), *The Metropolis Era: A World of Cities*. Beverly Hills: Sage Publications.

Schatz, S. P. 1988. "African Capitalism and African Economic Performance," In H. Glickman (ed.), *The Crisis and Challenge of African Development*. New York: Greenwood Press.

Shaw, M., and O. Aluko. 1984. *The Political Economy of African Foreign Policy*. New York: St. Martin Press.

United Nations. 1969. *Growth of the World's Urban and Rural Population, 1920-2000*. New York: Department of Economic and Social Affairs.

United Nations. 1973. *Urban Land Policies and Land-Use Control Measures, Volume I Africa*, New York: Department of Economic and Social Affairs.

_____. 1975. *Demographic Handbook for Africa*. New York: Economic Commission for Africa.

Chapter III

The African Periphery in the World-System: Kondratieff Longwaves of Exports and Indebtedness

Dr. David Kowalewski

I n recent years a growing number of scholars have taken a world-system approach to significant global phenomena. In particular, studies of Kondratieff longwaves in the world economy have elicited appeals for a more historical-structural view of world dynamics within the disciplines. Speculation, however, has yet to be matched by empirical research.

The extent to which Africa can be shown to fit neatly into this global paradigm is especially problematic. The comparatively late integration of the African interior into European economies, its historical peculiarities (e.g., slave trade, tribalism), and sketchy historical data raise serious questions about the theoretical appropriateness and empirical utility of the world-system approach for understanding the region. Proponents of the historical-structural framework, however, seem convinced that longitudinal empirical analysis can demonstrate how the region's problems and prospects have been largely shaped by wider, transcontinental forces (Wallerstein, 1976b; Smaldone, 1976).

The present essay maps out and tests a number of propositions of world-system theory using historical African data on exports and foreign indebtedness in the last two centuries. If the world-system approach is correct, then the structural dependencies of the region on advanced capitalist nations should generate longwaves of exports and debt. In the following sections, the theoretical rationale for the study is laid out, hypotheses formulated, empirical tests conducted, and conclusions reached about the relevance of world-system theory for the study of Africa.

The World-System and the Kondratieff Longwave

According to world-system analysis, the roots of the international political economy of modern capitalism can be traced back five centuries to the search by European merchants for markets, gold and silver, and raw materials abroad (Wallerstein, 1976a; Hopkins and Wallerstein, 1980). Driven by a combination of technological innovation, surplus production, a cognitive reordering of priorities toward international profit- taking, the growing influence of the merchant classes, and stiff competition, the elites of advanced or "Core" economies began to lay the foundation of the contemporary international division of labor (Hall, 1986).

As Core nations made their inroads into underdeveloped or "Periphery" areas, the structures of their respective economies were correspondingly established. Core countries modernized and eventually attained industrial and then postindustrial status, to some degree on the basis of the wealth extracted from the Periphery. Periphery areas, in contrast, became locked into various dependencies (technology, finance, investment, trade) on Core countries. Consequently, they have continued to lag behind the latter. While the benefits of this international stratification system have largely accrued to the Core, the costs have been disproportionately shouldered by the Periphery.

As a capitalist political economy, the modern world-system has undergone several crises and comebacks in its 500-year history (Wallerstein, 1984a). One cycle of crisis and comeback has been the Kondratieff longwave (K-wave). While most observers acknowledge the existence of various short "business" and other cycles of boom and bust (Kitchin, Juglar, Kuznets), recently a growing amount of research has been devoted to the possibility of longer waves of 48-55 years in the industrial/postindustrial age (Kondratieff, 1973). The K-wave, a multivariate, international set of upswings and downswings experienced more or less synchronically in Core countries, apparently reflects not only the international integration, but also the structural contradictions, of the single capitalist world-system. As yet, however, little agreement on the existence, let alone the constituent elements, of the K-wave can be found (Garvy, 1943; Burns, 1968; Jewett, 1985; Rostow, 1978; Wallerstein, 1979).

World-system scholars also propose that the crises of the Core are ultimately solved to some degree through its domination of the Periphery (Wallerstein, 1984b). As Core nations experience systemic difficulties in profit-taking, they intensify the exploitation of existing Periphery nations and incorporate new Periphery regions into the world-system. They also extend their domination to new geographical "external arenas." As an integral part of the world-system, therefore, the Periphery is greatly affected by the crises and recoveries of the Core. Its fate is intimately related to Core upswings and downswings.

This proposition seems to imply that the K-waves of the Core are reflected in the political economies of the Periphery (Jacobsen, 1984).

Industrial/Postindustrial K-Waves in the Core

While still viewed skeptically by many, the K-wave notion has gained some credibility from current research on political and economic cycles (Dewey, 1971). The scores of studies on economic oscillations reveal that the vast majority of cycles have periods of a few weeks to 20 years. Beyond the 20-year wavelength, however, a number of more "macrowave" economic fluctuations have been catalogued. Yet the clear plurality of all these macrowaves have periods of about 50 years. And virtually all are synchronized more or less with the K-wave as proposed by world-system theorists (Alcock and Quittner, 1978). These studies suggest that the Kondratieff longwave may be an international phenomenon of systemic import (Dewey, 1964, 1972; Alcock, 1977).

Numerous theories have been offered to lend conceptual coherence to the suspected K-wave (for a concise summary, see Goldstein, 1985:412-3). Space disallows an elaboration of the many paradigms. Explanations range from meteorology (Georgelin, 1979; *Cycles,* 1979), sunspots (Robbins, 1984), and cycle harmonics (Herbst, 1982) to capital investment (Forrester, 1976; Day, 1976), war (Eklund, 1980; Vayrynen, 1983), capital-labor relations (Screpanti, 1984; Gordon, 1978), profit-fluctuation (Mandel, 1980), innovation (Ray, 1983), and hybrids of the above (Coombs, 1983; Steinherr, 1982; Schumpeter, 1939; Tylecote, 1984).

Recently, however, some scholars have begun to reach a consensus on the dynamics driving the longwave. Investment fluctuations in capital-goods industries, within a political context of minimal macro-level planning, appear to provide a plausible and coherent explanation (Kondratieff, 1984; van Duijn, 1983). Briefly, since orders for capital-stock (construction, equipment, steel, mining, and other basic industries) are far removed from final demand, they experience a high degree of fluctuation across time. Errors of under- and over-production are prevalent because of the long lag between the decision to produce and the appearance of the product. Frequently the production process is completed in a situation of demand far different from the one prevailing when the decision to produce was made. Further, the capitalist drive for profit-taking, inter-firm competition, and close connections among industries stimulate waves of optimism and pessimism which exaggerate the errors of production when they occur.

As a result of systemic errors of optimism, industries overexpand and unsold goods accumulate. Thus comes the turning point of the upswing and the initiation of stagnation. As the downswing runs its course, however, capital stock wears out, demand begins to grow, and unused capital begins to accumulate. In particular, new basic inventions (as opposed to minor innovations) begin to come on line as companies search for a way out of the stagnation. As a result, the beginnings of a "new technological paradigm" are established. The turning point of the downswing takes place (Perez, 1985).

The longwave's phase-length (on average 20-25 years) can be explained by the time needed to prepare for making new capital- goods investment and stimulate effective global demand, as well as the time it takes for capital stock eventually to wear out. Its international synchronicity can be explained by the connections of global trade and the crossborder diffusion of new technologies. Its multivariate dimensionality is due to the "entrainment" or coupling of many phenomena with the crucial capital-goods sector. Changes in economic and other variables tend to be more strongly tied to capital goods than to other sectors. Thus the fluctuations of this sector are notable for their powerful repercussions on other variables. Finally, the fact that capital-goods investment has occurred within a single capitalist framework throughout the past two centuries, as well as memory loss between generations of investors, help account for the K-wave's recurrence.

The Systems Dynamics Project at the Massachusetts Institute of Technology has successfully generated such a model of K-wave oscillations (Forrester, 1977). A recent paper (Kowalewski, 1986) has listed the several empirical studies demonstrating industrial/ postindustrial fluctuations of the approximate K- wavelength. Substantial agreement has been found among the many researchers, who have used a wide variety of methodologies and databases, that K-waves are manifest throughout the Core. The multivariate nature of the K-wave is evident. Upswings and downswings have been demonstrated for inventions, production, employment and wages, prices, finance, level of international trade and protectionism, battle deaths in Core-Core wars, sociopolitical values and other phenomena. The Core-wide scope of the cycle is clear. Longwaves have been evidenced for the Core region in the aggregate and for several Core nations in particular. Core countries appear to experience, more or less simultaneously, periodic crises and recoveries along several dimensions.

K-Waves in the Periphery?

Variables for the subordinate Periphery might be expected to rise and fall together with those for the dominant Core. The fates of Periphery nations have been locked to those of Core metropoles since colonial times. In particular the exports of Periphery commodities, highly dependent on Core markets, should rise and fall with expanding and contracting Core demand. Exports to the Core play a key role in Periphery economies (Chu and Morrison, 1984). Today some 75 percent of the trade of Periphery nations is with the Core; Periphery-Periphery trade is minimal (World Bank, 1984). Core economies have been found to have a "major impact" on Periphery exports (Dell and Lawrence, 1986).

During upswings, as Core production grows and the demand for raw materials increases, Periphery exports should surge accordingly. Rising employment and wages in the Core should enhance demand for imports from the Periphery. The clustering of inventions toward the beginning of upswings in the Core, and the subsequent development of new products, should stimulate the creation of new raw-material export industries in the Periphery. The decline in protectionism of Core markets should facilitate the entry of Periphery commodities. The greater intensity of Core-Core military conflict should enhance the demand for Periphery raw materials.

As the Core experiences downswings, however, and demand for foreign resources declines, Periphery exports should suffer accordingly. The decline of Core production should shrink demand for Periphery raw materials. Growing unemployment and falling wages imply a reduction in demand for imports from the Periphery. As Core investors become more risk-averse and reduce their inputs into research, the development of new raw material industries in the Periphery should wane. The growth of protectionism in downswings indicates shrinking opportunities for the entry of Periphery goods into Core markets. The lower intensity of Core- Core military conflict in downswings suggests a fall in demand for Periphery raw materials. Declining export revenues lead to even higher production of commodities across the Periphery, thereby increasing supply and further reducing prices for exported goods. Commodity prices, however, tend to fall even more than those for necessary manufactured goods imported from the Core. Serious balance-of-payments problems become evident (Wickins, 1986; Kleinknecht, 1989).

Downswings in Periphery exports should be associated with foreign indebtedness. As income declines, Periphery nations will turn to Core nations for loans to tide them over the export shortfalls. Yet the prolonged duration of the K-downswing implies that repayment will be extremely difficult. Additional loans will be taken out. The deepening of the downswing, moreover, and the eventual cessation of loans from exhausted and impatient Core creditors, lead ultimately to a wave of defaults.

After World War II, however, with the emergence of a new world-system hegemon, the United States, and its establishment of global countercyclical financial institutions (e.g., International Monetary Fund [IMF]), debts were rescheduled throughout the downswing. Thus, the waves of defaults which occurred in the past were substantially muted. Yet, according to many critics, the austerity programs imposed on the Periphery by Core creditors in return for the new loans have caused severe deprivation for Periphery peoples. Discontent with the hardships has been manifested in numerous "IMF riots" across the Periphery.

Kondratieffs in Africa?

This pattern appears to characterize African trade and indebtedness during the past two centuries. Prior to the 19th century, Core colonization of Africa was limited largely to the coastal areas and the slave-trade dominated Core-Periphery relations. After the Napoleonic Wars, however, the continent was increasingly incorporated into the world economy (Harris, 1914). The emergence of Great Britain as the world-system's hegemon brought the demise of the slave-trade. The world-leader emphasized free trade, a "new capitalist imperialism," secured by its global naval power (Oliver and Fage, 1962:158-

93). With growing stress on free trade came the Core's promotion of enhanced production of African commodities for export (Wallerstein, 1976b).

This process was accelerated by several factors. The trend toward home-rule and self-support in the colonies encouraged Periphery governors to gear their economies toward exports. The industrial revolution in Europe, with its mass production for global marketing, spurred the Core to encourage the Periphery to produce more raw materials. The Core also pressed for the enhancement of export revenues to finance the imports of manufactured goods into Periphery markets (Harris, 1914). Exports were largely controlled by Core expatriates, who were especially sensitive to Core demand. The rapid extension of railroad construction from coastal areas to the interior strengthened the ties of African production to Core markets. Trade with the Core eventually became a major proportion of the GNPs of African economies (Wickins, 1986).

By the 1980s, this historical structuring had left many African economies precariously dependent on few primary products subject to Core demand (Wickins, 1986). As the most underdeveloped part of the Periphery, Africa has few economies structurally differentiated enough to avoid the impact of fluctuating Core demand for its exports. Some statistical evidence suggests that African economic growth is much more affected by exogenous shocks than domestic policies (Helleiner, 1984). Most African polities, having only recently attained political independence, have historically enjoyed minimal autonomy and hence little bargaining power when negotiating with the Core on issues of trade and finance (Wolff, 1974; Gutkind and Wallerstein, 1976).

Some scattered evidence suggests a K-wave pattern in Africa. Lee (1987) has shown that railroad construction by Core investors fluctuated with K-wave periodicity. Scholars have documented certain export surges and declines across African economic history. Piecing these crests and valleys together, one begins to see a cyclical pattern following K-wave dating. Stagnation was observed after 1870 until recovery in 1890-1920, which was followed by depression until 1936. The latter downswing was succeeded by a two-decade postwar boom, after which arrived a serious deterioration in 1970-1990 (Wickins, 1986; Oliver and Fage, 1962; Wallerstein, 1976b).

Debt-problems in Africa have seemingly risen and fallen with export decline and growth. Colonial governments received most of their revenues from customs duties and export levies. Other types of taxes were minimal because of difficulties with currency variations, the low level of individual land-tenure and wage- labor, information and administration, and the logistics of collection in the interior. In periods of export declines, Core bankers, already geared toward lending to export-oriented producers, viewed loans to Periphery governments as especially profitable. The length of the downswings, however, made repayment difficult. In the postwar era, however, IMF austerity programs delayed the onset of Africa-wide defaults and initiated instead a wave of welfare protests (Cheru, 1989; Wickins, 1986; Oliver and Fage, 1962).

Data and Findings

These hypotheses can be tested with export and indebtedness data for African nations in the 19th and 20th centuries. Since Kondratieff's original work (1984) failed to give exact turning points for upswings and downswings, the present study uses the periodization from van Duijn's empirical results (1983) concerning growth waves in the Core, which deviates only slightly from those of other researchers (Goldstein, 1985; Martin, 1985). Although K-wave scholars usually start their research with the "first Kondratieff upswing" in the 1780s ("K-1-U"), this study begins with the "second" iteration of the wave (1837-65 or "K-2") and proceeds through the current "fourth" downswing (1966-present or "K-4-D"). Not only was Africa incorporated comparatively late into the world-system. Data is far sketchier for the early 19th century. Many scholars also question the applicability of K- waves to the pre-industrial era (Kleinknecht, 1989).

Table 1 presents the results on African exports. For each time-series of every country within each period-phase, an ordinary-least-squares regression was performed to find the best- fitting slope over time. Each slope was then standardized through division by the mean value of the variable during the period-phase. The mean-standardized slope for each variable, for each phase, is interpretable as the percentage annual increase of the trend line at the mean. Since Kondratieff "downswings" in economic variables are often in fact "stagnations" rather than actual declines, the *signs* of the slopes are less theoretically important than comparisons of *value differences* between periods. Hypothetically, slopes should have significantly lower values for downswing than for upswing phases. To test statistically for differences between the standardized slopes, paired t-tests were used. Slopes for all downswings were first paired with those for all following upswings. Then, in a separate test, those for all upswings were paired with those for all following downswings. The full sets of paired slopes for all phases, for all available countries in each phase, were the samples analyzed by the t-tests (Goldstein, 1985).[1]

The results tend to confirm the world-system supposition of alternating export currents in the African Periphery. In only one upswing (K-3), for example, was a negative slope (British Somaliland) evident, compared with 13 negative slopes in downswings (see also Kindleberger, 1975). Since world-system theory predicts substantial differences between phases, one- tailed significance levels were utilized for the phase comparisons. The matching of downswings with subsequent upswings yields a high significance level ($p =$ .001) for the t- test. Comparison of upswings with subsequent downswings produces a similar result ($p = .001$).

The findings offer some support for the logic of world-system analysis with its suggestion of a single integrated network of developed and underdeveloped capitalist economies oscillating in half-century cycles. Export-oriented African economies, highly dependent on Core markets, appear to rise and fall with fluctuating Core demand.

The oscillations should be inversely related to levels of external debt. Historical data

Table 1.: Kondratieffs in African Exports

Locale	K-2-U (1837-65)	K-2-D (1866-82)	K-3-U (1883-1920)	K-3-D (1921-36)	K-4-U (1937-66)	K-4-D (1967-)
Algeria	1029	0412	0604	0376	1462	
Angola			0177	0383	0803	1850
Benin			0675	-0232	0508	
British Somaliland			-0081	-0483	1185	
Cameroon				0425	1233	
					0970	1137
Cape of Good Hope	0752	0710	0730			
Central African R/E				0729	0361	
Chad				0536	0805	
Egypt	1393	0199	0549	-0426	0628	1062
Ethiopia					0724	1038
French Equatorial Africa			0755	0944	1577	
French Guinea		0477	0427	1445		
Gabon					1386	2819
Gambia	0029	0091	00706	-0411	0712	
Ghanna		0310	0824	0011	1769	
Ivory Coast			0701	0340	1019	
					1112	1475
Kenya			1464	0305	1131	
					0630	1522
Liberia				0917	2432	
					1044	1237
Libya					2143	1852
Madagascar			1129	0277	0988	
				0599	1094	
Malawi			1136	0242	0798	
Mali				0395	1702	
Mauritania				4684	1119	
Mauritius	0499	0348	0252	-1004	0666	2540
Middle Congo			1638	2277		
Morocco			1411	0365	1097	
				0838	1624	
Mozambique				0790	0636	
Natal	1367	0619	0591			
Niger			-0188	0062		
				1143	1153	
Nigeria			-0198	0844	2506	
Reunion	0312	-0046	0292	0198	3243	
				0634	0556	
Senegal	0873	0221	0820	-0052	1922	
				0715	1480	
Sierra Leone		-0801	0854	-0173	1301	
Somalia				0351	1227	
South Africa			0938	-0184	1251	
				0455	1425	
Sudan			1436	0349	0744	0870
Tanganyika/Tanzania			0371	0947		
				0738	0781	
Togo			0038	1384		
				0961	1778	
Tunisia	0296	0627	0126	2088		
				0334	1395	
Uganda				0332	0063	
Upper Volta				1230	0861	
Zaire		0769	0541	1056		
				1624	1050	
Zambia			1356	2075	0744	
				0725	0269	
Zanzibar		0259	-0691	0521		
Zimbabwe		2159	0199	0915		

Source: Mitchell (1982).
Note: Decimal points omitted. Double entries within a phase indicate currency changes; the first entry gives the first part of phase; the second, the second part. Empty entries are due to missing data or substantial database changes in terms of territory included or goods/   services exported. In cases of a few missing years for a series, figures were extrapolated from data for previous and subsequent years.

on indebtedness for seven North African and Near Eastern nations were gathered from the *London Times* and *New York Times* indices and 24 secondary historical sources. The nations were selected on the basis of length of time of incorporation into the world-system and data-availability. Thus the findings are only meant to be suggestive for the whole of Africa. Finer-grained studies using local sources for a wider range of nations should be conducted before definite conclusions are made.

Two time-series for each nation were constructed. Each nation for each year was coded with "1's" if its government was reported as (1) experiencing a debt-problem (including dafault), and (2) indicating default. It received "0's" in the absence of debt-problems and defaults. Some connection between exports and financial difficulties is apparent. Time-series measuring the annual percent of export growth for each nation (see Table 1) were correlated with its two indebtedness series. Limited data, low N's, and occasional lack of variation preclude a determination of correlations for low N's, and occasional lack of variation preclude a determination of correlations for all possible relationships. However, as expected, the Pearsonian r's are generally negative (four of five for debt-problems, and two of two for defaults). The findings for the individual nations do tend to conform to world-system logic.

From the several individual time-series, two aggregated or Africa-wide time-series were constructed for debt-problems and defaults. The seven individual time-series for debt-problems were added, then divided by the number of countries, to yield a single time-series for the percent of nations experiencing debt-problems in each year. The same procedure was followed defaults. Thus the two time-series indicate the extent to which the region experienced the two phenomena over time. Such summative measures are consistent with world-system theory's insistence on viewing Periphery nations as a single aggregate "zone within the international political economy. Note, however, that the indicators measure only the *scope* and not the *depth* (e.g., actual amount of debt) of external financial problems.

Debt-problems and defaults appear to follow the K-wave pattern. Figure 1 shows the seven-year moving-average time paths for the two series. Vertical axes mark the K-wave turning points. In each downswing, debt-problems rise. In each downswing, they fall. Defaults, however, only follow this pattern until K-4-D, when they rise only minimally. As suggested above, the global countercyclical policies of the new postwar hegemon have apparently succeeded in preventing, or at least postponing, the extensive defaults which occurred in previous downswings.

Table 2 presents analysis-of-variance results for the two time-series. The means-comparisons are significant above the .0001 level. Debt-problems and defaults are substantially higher in downswings than upswings. Debt-problems start to rise in K-D recessions, then become much more severe in the subsequent K-D depressions.

Figure 1.Seven-year moving avarages of percent of selected African nations with
debt-problems and defaults, 1837-1985.

Debt-Problems

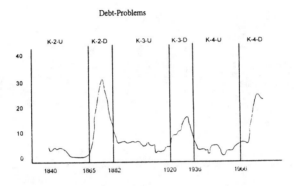

Defaults

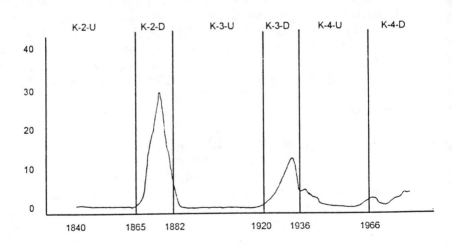

*Table 2 . : Kondratieff Longwaves and African Indebtedness

K-Phase	Debt-Problem %	Default %	N
K-2-U Recovery (1837-45)	3.17	0.00	9
Prosperity (1846-65)	1.43	0.00	20
K-2-D Recession (1866-73)	8.93	5.36	8
Depression (1874-82)	25.40	9.05	9
K-3-U Recovery (1883-92)	5.71	0.00	10
Prosperity (1893-1920)	4.08	0.00	28
K-3-D Recession (1921-29)	7.94	3.17	9
Depression (1930-36)	14.29	10.20	7
K-4-U Recovery (1937-48)	1.19	1.19	12
Prosperity (1949-66)	3.17	0.79	18
K-4-D Recession (1967-73)	4.08	0.00	7
Depression (1974-85)	21.42	3.57	12
	$F = 10.29$	$F = 7.91$	
	p .0001	p .0001	
N			149

Notable again, however, is the slow rise in defaults during the K-4-D depression as compared with prior depressions. The additional lending sponsored by Core nations, and guaranteed by IMF austerity programs, have staved off a cresting of defaults. Indeed, the seven nations of the study signed no fewer than 29 standby agreements with the IMF between 1966 and 1984 (author's calculation from IMF *Annual Reports)*. As noted above, however, several observers have suggested that the cuts in public subsidies required by these austerity programs have imposed severe hardships on African peoples (Onimode, 1989). Frequently the subsequent sharp increases in the prices of food, transportation, and utilities have provoked large-scale welfare protests with bloody repressive consequences. Debt-related rioting occurred, for example, in Egypt in 1977, Sudan in 1979, and Morocco in 1981 (Wilkins, 1986).

Conclusion

The world-system perspective posits a single global political economy dating from the 16th century. It also proposes that this world-system, as capitalist, is prone to serious periodic crises and comebacks, particularly in the form of K- longwaves. The international political economy is characterized by a single, highly structured and articulated, concatenation of nations with respect to major political and economic dimensions, which co-vary in oscillating fashion across space and time in half-century cycles. The tight integration of nations has made it highly difficult for any polity to escape from the systemic reverberations which result from the historical structuring.

The findings of this paper offer support for the world- system perspective. Numerous studies have discovered K-wave phenomena for Core countries in the industrial/ postindustrial era. Our export and indebtedness data indicate a systemic resonance in the

Periphery as well. The evidence suggests that the attention devoted to the notion of a single world-system, with its proposition of K-wave alternations, seems well placed. Despite its peculiarities, Africa seems an integral part of the Periphery-subsystem.

Yet at least three caveats are in order. First, the African findings only apply to the industrial/postindustrial era. Data- gathering and analysis of the preindustrial period should also be performed. Second, while exports and indebtedness are undoubtedly key elements of Periphery well-being, time-series for other economic and political phenomena should also be examined. Third, the African study should be complemented by analysis of other Periphery regions with an eye to similarities and differences. As both proponents and critics of the world-system perspective insist, the macro-level view of global structuring should not obscure the rich and varied historical concreteness manifest at lower levels of analysis.

Endnotes

Reprinted form: *Journal of the Third World Spectrum*, Volume I, Number 1, 1994, by permission of the author and the *Journal of the Third World Specturm*, Washington, D.C.

1. The use of linear slopes offers a view of each general *phase-tendency* rather than cumbersome year-by-year comparisons. Standardization by the mean effectively controls for upward trend of export values. The paired t-tests prevent acceptance of actually insubstantial results based on unsystematic comparisons of upswing-downswing variation. They provide a single, parsimonious historical-continental overview of oscillations for several nations (Goldstein, 1985).

2. The nations include Algeria, Egypt, Ethiopia, Iran, Liberia, Morocco, and Turkey. The sources and methodology are more fully explained in the author's (1989) study of Periphery- wide indebtedness. Here it might be noted that the African findings are consistent with those for the Periphery as a whole.

3. Limited data disallow any separate analyses for the two "Periphery" and "Semi-Periphery" subzones suggested by world- system analysis. With respect to the K-wave, to this writer's knowledge, no world-system literature suggests any significant differences between the two subzones.

•Note: Debt-problems are indicated by mention in the sources of foreign financing crisis; debt burden or debt problem; nonperforming Core loans; concern by private foreign creditors, such as condholders or bankers; urgent need for additional foreign loans; debt-related export or balance-of-payments or foreign-exchange crisis; national bankrptcy or financial panic in conjunction with loan repayment; debt-related austerity discussions or programs; debt-servicing difficulties; debt negotiations with Core lenders, reschedulings, refinancings, bridge loans, or consolidational suspensions of a country's bonds from Core stock exchanges; discussions of a Periphery nation's grants of monpolies or stock equity to Core lenders for the sake of repayment; imminent, threatening, or near default; and pleas for moratoriums. Defaults on interest or principal were also included. However, since Periphery borrowers often remained in default for decades after declaration, only the mentions of initiations of defaults, rather than continuations of the previous year's defaults, on separate loan issues were coded.

The default series included mentions of deferral; being behind on payments; postponement; payment in non gold currency or scrip; Core-lender calls or attempts to compel payment; debt-related Core seizures of Periphery customs facilities; repudiations of lender demands to repay because of financial reasons; forfeiture; arrears; suspensions; non repayment; failures to repay; delays; overdue payments; moratoriums; and extensions.

REFERENCES

Alcock, Norman. 1977. "Cyclical Analysis of Global Economics." *Cycles* 28, 4 (June):77-87.
_____, and J. Quittner. 1978. "The Prediction of Civil Violence to the Year 2001." *Journal of Interdisciplinary Cycle Research* 9, 4 (December):307-24.

Burns, A.F. 1968. "Business Cycles." *International Encyclopedia of the Social Sciences*. New York: Macmillan and Free Press.

Cheru, Fantu. 1989. *Silent Revolution in Africa: Debt, Development, and Democracy*. London: Zed.

Chu, Ke-Young, and Thomas Morrison. 1984. "The 1981-82 Recession and Non-Oil Primary Commodity Prices." *IMF* Staff Papers 31, 1 (March):93-140.

Coombs, Rod. 1983. "Innovation, Automation, and the Longwave Theory." Pp. 115-34 in Christopher Freeman, ed., *Longwaves in the World Economy*. London: Buttersworth.

Cycles. 1979. "About the Wheeler Cycles." 30,5 (June):117-18.

Day, Richard. 1976. "The Theory of the Long Cycle." *New Left Review* 99 (September-October):67-82.

Dell, Sidney, and Roger Lawrence. 1980. *The Balance of Payments Adjustment Process in Developing Countries*. New York: Pergamon.

Dewey, Edward. 1964. "A Count of Reported Economic Cycles Classified by Wavelength." *Cycles* 15, 3 (March):49-52.

Eklund, Klas. 1980. "Long Waves in the Development of Capitalism?" *Kyklos* 33:383-419.

Forrester, Jay. 1976. "Business Structure, Economic Cycles, and National Policy." *Cycles* 27, 2 (February):29-46.

_____. 1977. "Growth Cycle." *De Economist*, 125, 4:525-543.

Garvy, George. 1943. "Kondratieff's Theory of Long Cycles." *Review of Economic Statistics* 25, 4 (November):203-20.

Georgelin, Jean. 1979. "Les mouvements de longue duree des prix (Kondratieff): leurs liens avec la production agricole et les variations du climat en Europe occidentale—17e-20e siecles." *Bulletin d'Histoire Economique de l'Universite de Geneve* 4:mimeo.

Goldstein, Joshua. 1985. "Kondratieff Waves as War Cycles." *International Studies Quarterly* 29, 4 (December):411- 44.

Gordon, David. 1978. "Up and down the Long Roller Coaster." Pp. 22-35 in Union for Radical Political Economics ed., *U.S. Capitalism in Crisis*. New York.

Gutkind, Peter, and Immanuel Wallerstein. 1976. "Editors' Introduction." Pp. 7-29 in authors (eds.), *Political Economy of Contemporary Africa*. Beverly Hills, CA: Sage.

Hall, Thomas. 1986. "Incorporation in the World System." *American Sociological Review* 51, 3 (June):390-402.

Harris, Norman. 1914. *Intervention and Colonization in Africa*. Boston, MA: Houghton-

Mifflin.
  Helleiner, G. K. 1984. *Aid and Liquidity: The Neglect of the Poorest in the Emerging International Monetary System.* Toronto: Development Studies Programme, University of Toronto, Working Paper No. A-14.
  Herbst, Anthony. 1981. "A 54-Year Cycle in the Purchasing Power of Gold." *Cycles* 32, 2 (March):42.
  Hopkins, Terrance, and Immanuel Wallerstein. 1980. *Processes of the World System.* Beverly Hills, CA: Sage.
  International Monetary Fund. 1966-84. *Annual Report.* Washington, D.C.
  Jacobsen, Nils. 1984. *Cycles and Booms in Latin American Export Agriculture. Review* 7, 3 (Winter):443-507.
  Jewett, D.L. 1985. "Logic Flawed in Kondratieff Cycle Argument." *Futurist* 19, 3:6.
  Kindleberger, Charles. 1975. *World in Depression.* Berkeley, CA: University of California Press.
  Kleinknecht, Alfred. 1989. "Post-1945 Growth as a Schumpeter Boom." *Review* 12, 4 (Fall):437-56.
  Kondratieff, Nikolai. 1973. "Longwaves in Economic Life." *Cycles* 24, 11 (December):277-86.
  _____. 1984. *Long Wave Cycle.* New York, NY: Richardson and Snyder.
  Kowalewski, David. 1986. Kondratieffs in the Modern World- System. Paper prepared for the *International Studies Association Southwest*, San Antonio, TX, March.
  _____. 1989. "Global Debt Crises in Structural-Cyclical Perspective: 1791-1984." Pp. 57-84 in William Avery and David Rapkin, eds., *Markets, Politics, and Change in the Global Political Economy.* Boulder, CO: Lynne Rienner.
  Lee, Richard. 1987. "World-System Incorporation of West Africa: Core Expansion and the Railroads." Fernand Braudel Center, SUNY-Binghamton, xerox.
  Mandel, Ernest. 1980. *Longwaves of Capitalist Development.* London: Cambridge University Press.
  Martin, Bill. 1985. *Turning Points of the Kondratieff.* Binghamton, NY: Fernand Braudel Center, SUNY, xerox.
  Mitchell, B.R. 1982. *International Historical Statistics: Africa and Asia.* New York: New York University Press.
  Oliver, Roland, and J.D. Fage. 1962. *A Short History of Africa.* Baltimore, MD: Penguin.
  Onimode, Bade. 1989. *The IMF, World Bank, and the African Debt.* London: Zed.
  Perez, Carlota. 1985. "Microelectronics, Long Waves, and World Structural Change." *World Development* 13, 3:441-63
  Ray, George. 1983. "Energy and the Long Cycles." *Energy Economics* (January):3-8.
  Robbins, R.W. 1984. "Evidence of Solar and Lunar Influences on Economic Cycles." *Cycles* 35, 7 (September):189-94.
  Rostow, Walt. 1978. *Getting from Here to There.* New York: McGraw-Hill.
  Schumpeter, Joseph. 1939. *Business Cycles.* New York: McGraw-Hill.
  Screpanti, Ernesto. 1984. "Long Economic Cycles and Recurring Proletarian Insurgencies." *Review* 7, 2 (Winter):509- 48.   Smaldone, Joseph. 1976. "Quantitative Research in African History." *Historical Studies Newsletter* 10, 1 (December):20-29.
  Steinherr, Alfred. 1982. *The Great Depression: A Repeat in the 1980s?* Brussels: Commission of the European Communities, Economic Papers, No. 10 (November).

Tylecote, Andrew. 1984. "Towards an Explanation of the Longwave: 1780-2000." *Review* 7, 4 (Spring):703-17.

van Duijn, J.J. 1983. *The Longwave in Economic Life.* Boston: Allen and Unwin.

Vayrynen, Raimo. 1983. "Economic Cycles, Power Transitions, Political Management and Wars between Major Powers." *International Studies Quarterly* 27, 4 (December):389-418.

Wallerstein, Immanuel. 1976a. *The Modern World System.* New York: Academic.

_____. 1976b. "Three Stages of African Involvement in the World-Economy." Pp. 30-57 in Peter Gutkind and Immanuel Wallerstein, eds., *Political Economy of Contemporary Africa.* Beverly Hills, CA: Sage.

_____. 1979. "Kondratieff up or Kondratieff down?" *Review* 2, 4 (Spring):663-73.

_____. 1984a. "Longwaves as Capitalist Process." *Review* 7, 4 (Spring):557-76.

_____. 1984b. *Politics of the World Economy: States, Movements, and the Civilizations.* New York: Cambridge University Press.

Wickins, Peter. 1986. *Africa 1880-1980: An Economic History.* New York, NY: Oxford University Press.

Wolff, Richard. 1974. *Economics of Colonialism.* New Haven, CT: Yale University Press.

World Bank. 1984. *World Development Report.* Washington, D.C.

Chapter IV

Third World Political Economy and Foreign Policy in the Post-Cold War Era: Lessons from Africa

Dr. Timothy M. Shaw & Dr. Larry A. Swatuk

1. Overview

Approaches to and actualities of Third World, particularly African foreign policy are in flux, as the last decade of the 20th Century dawns.[1] Old assumptions about diplomacy and ideology are being reconsidered and revised, because both internal and international political economies are in transition, given dramatic changes throughout the 1980s, particularly in the decade's final months.[2] The combination of domestic crises and "reforms" and global shifts and realignments means that the African continent, more than any other region of the South, is more marginal and vulnerable, but also perhaps more flexible and fluid than ever before.[3] In short, the conjuncture of the early-1990s offers a unique opportunity for creative scholarship and statesmanship.

This overview attempts to define and advance such revisionism in the study of the Third World's internal as well as international relations. We have chosen Africa as our specific case, hoping, that others will find much here to compare and contrast with their own particular studies of Third World political economies. Special emphasis is given to the intermediate, regional level of analysis and interaction. This is so for a number or reasons.

First, the end of the Cold War has brought a concomitant lessening of super-power rivalry on the continent. This has led, on the one hand, toward limited, joint and largely cooperative American-Soviet "problem-solving" in a variety of regional conflicts. Namibian independence, achieved in March 1990, and subsequent moves toward conflict resolution in Angola and Mozambique, raised hopes that Cold War-fostered and exacerbated inter and intra-state conflicts might now be overcome.[4] Further, heightened political instability in Algeria, Kenya, Lesotho, Liberia, South Africa and Zaire, to name but a handful of states, as well as the specter of famine and continued conflict in the Sahel, the Horn, and Southern Africa, particularly Mozambique, raises the equally legitimate fear, that regional hegemons and new and renewed regional conflicts will arise in the wake of the superpowers' departure: Africa, too, may soon miss the Cold War.[5] Given the level of superpower supported, continent-wide militarization, these conflicts are likely to be increasingly bloody. Recent events in Ethiopia, Liberia, and South Africa are testimony in this regard.[6]

Second, acute economic difficulties in the form of accumulated debt made less bearable by the ubiquitous - some say pernicious - application of Bank/Fund-directed "adjustment reforms" has given new currency to old ideas about "regionalism" and "regional economic/ political integration."

Fostering regional formal economies of scale, is seen as one possible way out of the debt crisis. Made popular by the ECA, the OAU, as well as the UNDP,[7] it is an African variation on Schyumacher's theme that "small is beautiful" and regions are most likely of optimum size for realizing "self-sufficiency."[8] To some observers, this renewed focus on regionalism is not an option, but an imperative. In its absence, tiny, fragmented, state-based African economies remain hostage to Bank/Fund case-by-case reform packages whose emphasis on "export-led growth" suggests, to some, a return to colonial status. According to S.K.B Asante:

> [T]he implementation of structural adjustment programs has given rise to several concerns. Their objectives... are essentially of a short-term, and much less often of a medium-term nature. as such, they are more often than not sharply in contrast... with the objectives of more balanced long-term development... The programs fail to lay the foundations for long-term development or to re-orient African economies away from economic and bureaucratic structures inherited from the colonial era - structures that, because they were designed to benefit European economies, work tot he disadvantage of Africa.[9]

There is a cruel irony in the fact that many African and other developing world state-makers have found themselves before Bank/Fund officials, meekly accepting individual state-centered adjustment programs that counter the clearly, and regularly, articulated collective aspirations of the South, as first formulated at Bandung an din the deliberations of UNCTAD I nearly 30 years ago.[10] Moreover, standard Bank/Fund reform package conditionalities - e.g. deregulation, subsidization, devaluation, privatization - designed to alleviate the debt crisis via export-led growth have been undertaken amid rising protectionism in the North, declining commodity prices, and, since 1983, net capital outflows from the Third World to the core countries.[11]

Citing a 1987 article written by Clairmonte and Cavanagh, Ankie Hoogvelt states, flight capital and profit remittances:

> ...have lifted the total net financial transfers over the period 1981-86 to a figure well over $250 billion representing the total financial contribution of the Third World to the advanced, core countries over that period. This figure, in today's prices... is four times the one of the $13 billion Marshall aid with which the US financed the post-war recovery of Europe.[12]

Hoogvelt then adds, in rhetorical, but no less poignant fashion:

> Today the idea of the Marshall Plan is frequently invoked in connection with the need to reconstruct Central and Eastern Europe. It is generally acknowledged that the sums involved are truly awesome. If an when the core countries do decide on this most fraternal of gestures, we would do well to remember where the money is coming from.[13]

In light of this most frustrating scenario, Adebayo Adedeji, in 1989, was moved to ask:

> Has our over-preoccupation in the 1980s with achieving external and internal financing and monetary balances at the expense of long-term development and transformation objectives not exacerbated our economic plight and circumstances? Have orthodox SAPs not been more of a diversion, when in actual fact what we should be worrying about is how to truly transform our economies structurally and become self-reliant?...Should we forego the pursuit of the goal of self-reliance in preference to servicing our external debt and achieving balance of payments or budget equilibria - goals that the most developed industrialized economies have never been able to achieve on a sustained basis? Must we march backwards with our dependency syndrome fully intact?[14]

Yet, as African state-makers continue to lobby for collective responses to the debt crisis, the twin 'conditionalities" of economic reform and political liberalization have both contracted the state and embattled regimes. Ironically, at a time when some scholars are lobbying to bring the state "back in" as the center-piece of analysis, politico-economic realities, are stripping it of both power and purpose. Nevertheless, regimes cling tenaciously to the state, thereby ensuring it remains a central feature of African and international affairs, for the foreseeable future. But, its contraction has led to a number of interesting hypotheses about new forms of political economic cooperation, largely of a regional nature, led by ideas of expanding cross- national informal sectors and civil societies.[15]

In summary, then, our working hypothesis is that (a) changes in the New international Divisions of Labor and Power, have created/exacerbated acute crises in all African and most Third World political economies - crises of production and accumulation, of power and governance; (b) these crises, manifested most acutely at the national level, have led to all sorts of expectations about and for the future of African and other "developing" states and societies; and (c) the "region' will be the arena most likely to see these many pressures and expectations played out, if not resolved. Hence, our hypothesized salience of a new regionalism, in both analysis and praxis.[16]

However, before we turn to an elaboration of these themes and hypotheses, one caveat is in order. Given the failure of existing modes of analysis and their related models of development to either moderate, let alone alleviate, Africa's crisis or predict any of the cataclysmic changes in global political economy at the decade's end, we emphasize, that alternative modes of analysis, perhaps giving rise to new models and definitions of development, are in order for the 1990s. This overview, therefore, seeks, in a modest way, to help us move toward alternative analytical forms, in part by highlighting the content and potential impact of a new agenda for Africa's political economy in the 1990s. It is both our belief and hope, that this new agenda and approach holds relevance for other regions of the Third World.

II. Global Contexts: Changing International Divisions of Labour and Power

The end of the Cold War division of Europe relieves us of the great insecurity of living under the nuclear shadow. But the reordering of European and international relations does not guarantee us future stability or security. We are living in fear of the unknown. We cannot see clearly the character of the emerging international system. We do not know who will be the winners and losers. (Henry Gill, Permanent Secretary, Latin American Economic System.) We appeal to the European community, do not abandon your friends in the South, just because of your brothers in the North. (General Eyadema, on behalf of the ACP grouping of states). It's not a zero-sum game. We do not intend to rob [the developing world] to meet the demands in eastern Europe. (Barber Conable, President, World Bank).

Analysts of Third World affairs have been speculating on the character of economic and strategic rumblings in Europe and the ex-Soviet Union and their potential effects on peace, development, and security in the South. As is clearly indicated in the quotations from Gill and Eyadema, pessimism, apprehension, and uncertainty characterize much of the developing world's present point of departure. This is particularly so in Africa, where much of the continent has reeled from crisis for over a decade. And, in spite of Conable's positive remarks in the third quotation, many Third World leaders and sympathizers suspect that much of the developing world will become increasingly marginalized from the North-dominated global political economy, as events in the Soviet Union, in Eastern Europe, and in East-West relations generally, continue to dominate the North's global agenda. According to the lead article in the April 1990 issue of South magazine:

> [w]hile the fascination with Eastern Europe continues, Third World countries will find it increasingly difficult to attract political attention, funds and managerial resources from developed countries and institutions such as the Bank and the IMF. Africa is mainly worried about losing aid, while middle-income countries in Latin America and Asia fear

the loss of investment and trade.

These sentiments are echoed by Kivutha Kibwana in the December 1990 issue of the AAAPS Newsletter.

Without getting into elaborate economic analysis, it appears to us such fear by African leaders has justification. Any resources which the West mobilizes for overseas investment are necessarily limited. If a and Eastern Europe, they will consequently not be available to Africa and the Third World. Also the West is likely to adopt a strategy of saturating the East with Western finance to ensure a foothold and proper penetration of East European economies.

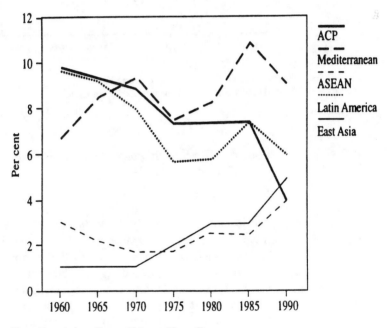

Note: East Asia = Korea, Taiwan, Hong Kong.
Source: Calculated from data supplied by Eurostat.

gure 1:   *EC imports from developing countries by region as a share of extra-EC imports, 1960-90*

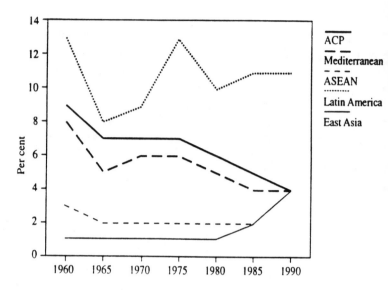

Note: East Asia = Korea, Taiwan, Hong Kong.
Source: Calculated from data supplied by Eurostat.

Figure 2:   EC exports to developing countries by region as a share
             of extra-EC imports, 1960-90

Despite the eloquent articulation of Third World fears and speculations, the accuracy and implications of such hypotheses are at the formative stage. Some scholars, for example, do not fear but rather welcome such developments, arguing that heightening political-economic contradictions will finally topple unjust and largely authoritarian regimes, regimes that Ihonvbere has labelled booty capitalist."[17] Other scholars contend that recent changes in the global division of power are themselves dependent variables, the result of more general shifts in the global division of labour: trends toward liberalization of state-based economies, increasing privatisation, expansion and internationalization of business and industry, etc.;i.e. in the creation of what since the mid-1970s has come to be called the New International Division of Labour (NIDL).[18] Finally, still other scholars point out that these "shifts" in the global divisions of labour and power have had sharply felt but uneven impacts upon the developing world over the last 15-20 years, an impact that is not uniformly negative.[19]

According to a recent study conducted by Dr. Christopher Stevens of the ODI, the increasing marginalization of ACP countries south of the Sahara from the mainstream of EC economic activity marks the continuation of a trend discernible prior to the end of the Cold War. The events of 1989-90 thereby exacerbate an existing trend. Stevens states:

> The share of all third parties in total EC imports and exports has fallen since 1960 as the creation of the Common Market has encouraged members to trade with each other. However, whilst non-EC developed countries were more severely affected by this decline than were LDCs in the period 1960-75, since then the reverse has been true. The LDC share of EC imports has continued to fall (from 23% in 1975 to only 13% by 1988) whilst the developed country share has stabilized (and was slightly higher in 1988, at imports from outside Community fell from 10% in 1960 to 4% by 1988, and a similar picture applies to EC exports. (see figures 1 and 2)[20]

To be sure, the waning of the Cold War and the dismantling of the Iron Curtain as discrete political events of 1989-90 have had forceful effects on many regions and regimes of the South. Two of the more salient effects bear elaboration: (i) the end of superpower competition on the continent; (ii) the economic and political liberalization.

First, the end of the Cold War has meant to the removal of an artificial, oppressive, Cold War-dictated "stability" in many Southern societies. In the face of growing domestic pressure fro multi-party democracy, authoritarian regimes now find themselves unable to turn to their "super-patron' for support. The removal of this Cold War option, therefore, has added, in many parts of the globe, political uncertainly to increasing economic instability. Less Cold War-style intervention is likely to mean less order, as domestic and regional conflicts take on indigenous rather than super-power-proxy characteristics. The violent turn of events in Ethiopia, Liberia, Sudan, and Somalia, among many other examples, offers eloquent testimony in this regard.[21] Nevertheless, forced, fractious "peace settlements", like those being pursued in Angola and Mozambique, are unlikely to create lasting peace in the face of continuing, and in many cases increasing economic adversity. They are likely to lead to political and, perhaps, regime change in the short term, however. Regimes increasingly dependent on external intervention for their own legitimacy and hegemony, as are those in Angola, Mozambique, Zambia, Zaire, and must of French West Africa stand to be toppled by war-and debt-weary populaces in free elections. The 26 March 1991 overthrow of Mali's Moussa Traore, the democratic election, two days earlier, of a new president, Micephore Soglo, in Benin, and, most recently, the resounding defeat handed Kenneth Kaunda and the long-ruling United National Independence Party (UNIP) of Zambia by Frederick Chiluba and his Movement for Multiparty Democracy (MMD)-the opposition party won more than 4/5 of the vote and garnered 125 of the 150 parliamentary seats - are suggestive in this regard.[22] But Mobutu's tenacious hold on power in Zaire, and the usurpation of the democratic process by well-entrenched elites, classes, fractions, and even families, elsewhere on the continent also suggests that many of Africa's long-standing autocrats are not going to bow out gracefully.[23]

Clearly, the drama of events in Europe culminating in a series of popular revolutions at decade's end led, understandably, to a sort of "premature triumphalism' in academic and popular analysis. Now that the initial euphoria has given way to harsh politico-economic reality, present speculations tends to be much more pessimistic.

Second, heightened Western pressure for similar political liberalizations as conditionality for continuing economic and political support will pose a serious threat not only to the continuing hegemony of authoritarian regimes, many of which are clients of the American "super-patron", but to more populist and/or socialist-oriented regimes, as in Mozambique and Tanzania, as well. Emboldened by the end of the Cold War, and hampered by slow economic growth, Western governments and Western-dominated multilateral organizations are more inclined than previously to attach political conditionalities to the extension of (declining) aid, loans, and investment. For example, in December 1989 at its annual meeting, the Development Assistance Committee of the OECD, citing the World Bank's recent report of Africa, declared that: "There is a vital connection, now more widely appreciated, between open, democratic and accountable political systems, individual fights and the effective and equitable of economic systems."[24]

Given the uniformity of this approach, one might anticipate serious obstacles to the successful simultaneous pursuit of political and economic liberalization. There may by lessons for Africa from recent Soviet and Chinese experience.

III. Implications for the Third World of Changing Global Divisions of Labour and Power
III.I Towards A "New" Political Economy for the South

As stated in our introduction, the new global context and continental condition have engendered a mood of revisionism in both analysis and praxis. Three closely interrelated factors have given rise to such a mood: i) frustration over the lack of analysis; ii) the near-universal application and serious impact of structural adjustment conditionalities upon African and other-Third World "stated" and "societies;" and iii) the rise of internal opposition to near ubiquitous one-party forms of governance in Africa, their resistance to authoritarian rule buoyed by the emergence of democratic forms of government in Eastern Europe and Latin America. A brief elaboration of these points is in order.

First, it seems to us, neither orthodox modernization nor orthodox materialism have been able to explain the causes and characters of the so-called "developing world's divergent political economies: from NICs to MSAs; from hitherto ubiquitous state "socialism" to contemporary state "capitalism."

Second, political economies under intense conditionalities and contradictions have compelled revisionist political economy approaches. In much of Africa, Central and Latin America, and the Caribbean, post-colonial state controls have been superseded by post-crisis structural adjustments, i.e. the familiar mix of devaluation, deregulation, desubsidization, and privatisation. These structural adjustment conditionalities have had significant impact upon both the character of the "state" and the nature of "state control", hence, the need to rethink state-centric explanations and approaches.

Third, internal opposition to adjustment deprivations have been buoyed by external examples of former-East bloc resistance to oppression. This has led to what appears to be an irreversible spread of demand for multi-party forms of participation, buttressed by freedoms to articulate and organize. As Third World elites continue to be exposed as little more than petty thieves, "state-socialism" is stripped of its ideological mantle now to be replaced by the market and the individual.[25]

To be sure, some continuities of assumption and condition remain, yet, it seems to us, the emerging analytic response must be both post-modernization and -materialism, now reinforced by the series of democratic transformations and /or aspirations in Eastern Europe and the ex-Soviet Union. The new contexts confronting academic analysts and policy-makers alike, mean that established explanations and prescription are no longer valid. In particular, the orthodox paradigm of modernization and orthodox policy of one-party state control are being seriously challenged by i) more radical approaches which treat gender,[26] ecology[27] culture, and informal sectors[28] as well as constitutions, organizations, classes and formal sectors; and ii) more pragmatic ideologies which advance agriculture, innovation, and accumulation rather than industry, conformity,and consumption.[29]

If both indigenous and international scholars, many of whom were writing in the wake of African independence, facilitated the initial nationalist, state-based and one-party state-dominated programmes for "development," then external and externally-directed police-makers have since advocated and advanced the post-nationalist programme espoused most notably by the World Bank and other international financial institutions, writing in the wake of the international financial institutions, writing int he wake of the international debt crisis. It the motif of the 1960s was the familiar claim of African nationalist Kwame Nkrumah to "[s]eek ye first the political kingdom," then that of the 1980s, dominated as it was by the Berg report, was "seek ye first and open economy" and all else will follow in its place. "Deregulation" replaced "nationalism" as the panacea of Third World underdevelopment.

At the very least, deregulation helped foster a new openness for expression - albeit quite unintentional - leading in some instances toward a new toleration of pluralism, and even a "back to the barracks" trend in Latin America; elsewhere, but particularly in Africa, endangered states and domestic repression in a last-ditch effort to reverse the indigenous "winds of change" blowing across the African continent.[30] It is our hope that this "second revolution" is less likely to be high-jacked than the first because of changed international as well as internal conditions and expectations; this, of course, remains to be both demonstrated and proven.

In contrast to the dominance of American political science and agendas over the course of the last three decades, and inadequate, often hopelessly idealistic Third World intellectual responses, the "new" political economy for the south attempts to go beyond these two solitudes toward a mix of both materialist and non-materialist perspectives, combining policy with production, ideology with interest, and national with global interactions.

II. ii.   Towards a Rethinking to Third World "Foreign Policy": The African Case

If national and global political economies have been transformed during the 1980s so too have foreign relations among international actors. The established assumptions and positions of Third World, Less Developed Countries towards the super-and major-powers on the one hand and towards international and transactional organizations on the other hand - from non - alignment to counter-dependence - have of necessity been superseded by notions of cross- conditionalities and marginality. Much of the African continent has slipped form the Third to Fourth World of the Least Developed, while a few regional powers have exercised a limited post-bipolarity hegemony: Cote d'Ivoire, Egypt, Kenya, Nigeria, Zimbabwe and, most unambiguously, South Africa.[31]

Given the exponential impacts of, first, crises, and then conditionalities, most African states have experienced a precipitous decline in their national attributes and rank order. A few were able to exploit the opportunities of the series of "oil shocks" in the 1970s, but hardly, any have been able to adapt positively to the "high-tech" computer-chip decade of the 1980s. So, Africa is the none Southern continent with no NIC, by contrast to Asia (the four "dragons" of Hong Kong, Singapore, South Korea, Taiwan) and Latin America (Brazil, Mexico). Indeed, it has no apparent near - NICs like Malaysia or Thailand, nor good future prospects like one to two of the ex-East European states. South Africa, is the most plausible candidate for such upward-mobility, although its claims to "graduation" will depend on the speed and style of the transition beyond apartheid. The overwhelming 68.2% "yes" vote in RSA's recent white-only referendum on continued negotiations toward a fairer political dispensation is almost certainly a positive step.[32] Recent studies, however, suggest that apartheid notwithstanding, South Africa faces serious structural problems which are much more likely to create havoc than wealth.[33] The purported aspirations of other African states - Algeria, Cote d'Ivoire, Egypt, Kenya, Nigeria, and Zimbabwe - are really quite fanciful or premature. In addition, as the rest of the world moves toward three giant free trading zones (Dollar, ECUs, Yen), moves that are bound to increase the fortunes of a number of previously trade-discriminated developing countries in addition to those NICs and near-NICs mentioned above, Africa stands to be further marginalized in this rapidly transformed global division of labour.[34] In short, African will remain the most peripheral of the Southern continents for the foreseeable future, i.e. well into the next century.[35]

If such is our substructural definition of the African continent in the New International Division of Labor, symbolized by new technologies and NICs, its superstructural assumptions and articulations have yet to recognize or internalize such constraints. Africa's collective nationalism, within the context of the NAM, the G77, and the OAU enabled it to play a larger than life role on the international stage at the height of the Cold War. In addition, it roughly 50 votes in UN fora gave it a voice out of proportion to any objective measure of its "power," and its anti-imperialist, especially anti-apartheid, collective stance gave it an artificial unity easily denied by the most cursory examination of individual state foreign policies. Unstated, of course, was the utility these foreign policies held in legitimating the continuation, indeed proliferation, of one-party rule in virtually all African states.

The transition to harsh economic, rather than diplomatic or strategic, realpolitik in the 1990s, exposed African unity and power as both hollow and obfuscatory. Its hollowness is best exemplified in contrasting African states' almost negligible "weighted" voting power in the IMF/IBRD system with that "wielded" in UN and other international fora. Its obfuscatory nature was exposed when "post-Cold War" brought an end to nonaligned and individual regime bargaining and "blackmail" power. Coinciding as it did, with an emergent donor state emphasis on not only debt, but also democracy, and environment, many established regimes and values found themselves increasingly threatened and, given declining resources, decreasingly able to do anything about it.[36]

Transformations in African foreign policy in the 1990s, can be abstracted at three different levels. First, at the global level, as already indicated, Africa has been affected negatively by shifts in the New International Divisions of Labor and Power. The preoccupations of African leaders with debt, structural economic adjustment, and now the cross-conditionality of movement toward multi-partyism, have combined to reign in even the most modest of African aspirations, let alone external adventurism. Thus African foreign policy makers face a new type of realism: optimistic assumptions about economic and strategic expansion have yielded to pessimistic anticipations of incremental decline at worst, stagnation at best, and regime survival at all cost.[37]

The continuing tension between collective aspiration and individual reality (what E.H. Carr, some 50 years ago identified as the tension between the "ought" and the "is) was eloquently demonstrated at the recent, May 1991, Kampala forum on Security, Stability, Development an cooperation in Africa. According to one observer, "while acknowledging that 'every African state is sovereign', CSSDCA's general principles state that 'the security, stability, and development of every African country is inseparably linked with those of other African countries. Consequently, instability in one African country reduces the stability of all other African countries."[38] Recognizing the tension between individual sovereignty and mutual vulnerability, Adebayo Adedeji, in his own address to the conference suggested that the proliferation of small, micro-states based on colonial boundaries must be overcome in trade and policy-making, if not in juridical and territorial reality.[39]

Second, at the regional level, established nationalisms and hierarchies have continued to generate antagonisms, even conflicts. Increased informal sector exchanges have compensated for the stagnation or contraction in official trade and they typically include money and labor as well as goods and services. By contrast to burgeoning informal sector regionalism, few top-down formal organizations have survived since independence as regional inequalities and tensions have been hard to contain. The proliferation of structural adjustment projects, has served to undermine formal economic regionalism, even further, with its emphasis on extra-continental externalization and single-country individuation. While a recent Bank report at last recognizes the potential of such regionalism, and the contribution to be made to it by nurturing already expanding informal sectors, the major problem remains: how to move toward regional economies of scale, regional divisions of labor, and South-South exchange if Bank/Fund conditionalities assign individual states "colonial' status as primary product producers under the ruse of "comparative advantage' and "export-led growth"?[40] A burgeoning informal sector, after all, is not a panacea but an indication of fundamental structural problems, i.e. bankrupt formal sectors. Bank support for Africa's informal sector suggests exasperation with the problem; it is a poor doctor that locates the cure for disease in the symptoms themselves!

Meanwhile, the withdrawal of super power competition suggest, that while African "middle power" lose their patrons they simultaneously gain more freedom of action, thereby moving from "proxies" to "regional powers" in their own right. so, we may anticipate less capacity (given economic constraints) but, more capability (given an absence of super power agendas) amongst hitherto 'sub-imperial" actors. And given increasing politico-economic tensions and contradictions at both national and regional levels, we may speculate that continuing economic difficulty and differentiation might lead to further, but more confined, "border' conflicts. Ultimately, a new "post-adjustment" hierarchy may emerge of so called "strong" and "weak," even "ex," reformers. In light of the above, and to reiterate our central working hypothesis, it is clear that African foreign policies will be much concerned with and affected by this new regionalism.

Finally, at the national level, a new generation of post crisis and - adjustment African, is moving towards power, encouraged by dramatic regime change elsewhere. In Uganda we have an indication of the mode of transition to post-neocolonial regime: Museveni's guerrilla force, applying a classic strategy gradually, seizing the country from a series of unacceptable regimes. But, from Liberia and Somalia, we have indications that the transition process, while equally successful in removing a despot from power, is more likely to be messy and inconclusive. From both types of case, however, we can see, that success in the post-revolutionary period is difficult at best. Old assumptions about nationalism and socialism, state sectors and universal welfare, while the necessary rallying cry of guerrilla movements, quickly give way to revisionist notions of African capitalism and user-pay fees.[41] Other post-revolutionary regimes, e.g. those in former Lusophone Africa, are learning similar lessons; those recently coming to power, as in Ethiopia, need to be reminded of them. Still other, and here we are thinking primarily of Algeria, still suffer under neo-colonial hegemony; that state's transition to democracy having been overturned by the military and accepted, even condoned, by the West. James Mittelman highlights this global phenomenon:

> Notwithstanding the tenacity of the Shining Path and some other leftist organizations in Latin America, globalization has helped deprive revolutionary forces of their strength.

The remaining bastions of socialism - Vietnam, North Korea, Cuba - are isolated and under intense pressure to join the globalization trend. Plugged into modern communications with their faxlike speed, the masses in post-revolutionary societies want the material benefits of globalization...At the end of this millennium, liberating movements appear to be dead letter, a relic of another era.[42]

Nevertheless, resistance and response to adjustment measures, have strengthened popular organizations, including cooperative, female, religious, and youth institutions, which have seized some of the "space vacated by the shrinking state. "Civil society" has begun to flourish in some political economies, compelled by structural adjustments and emboldened by East European examples.[43] To James Mittelman, however, this is a trend to be regarded with caution: "[N]ew social movements can have a repressive side - e.g. the resurgence of anti-Semitism in the Soviet Union and Eastern Europe."[44] Mittelman discusses a further reason for caution:

[O]bservers have been quick to celebrate the formation of autonomous movements within civil society. Relatively little attention has been given to the coalescence of these movements. Coordination is a crucial matter precisely because the proliferation of new social movements can splinter civil society, perhaps culminating in the Lebanonisation of political life. the push for regional autonomy in areas such as Kurdistan has the potential to open a global Pandora's box.[45]

So, new social relations have begun to emerge as social formation continue to change. For example, structural adjustment reforms have included streamlining state bureaucracies, which in turn, have collapsed much of the middle class with is foundation in state-salaries rather than indigenous production. Further, structural adjustment in many states, has led to both a smaller and more fractionalized bourgeoisie (partly because of bureaucratic buts, but also partly because of declining sources of new foreign investment), a rising petit-bourgeoisie, both merchant-capital (with its roots in forex and the informal sector) and kilak (with its roots in the emergent IFI emphasis on strengthening agriculture), a threatened proletariat (due in part to decreasing industrialization, itself due to the selling off of para-statals and other moves toward privatization), and expanded peasantry (as many urbanites return to the land and states place increasing emphasis on agriculture and food self-sufficiency), and, perhaps most obviously, vast number of un- and under-employed. These factors, combined with a novel foreign policy agenda - debet, environment, gender, investment, technology -have encouraged new debates and directions.
These revisionist discourses embrace basic nations of political economy, national interest, and state security - all of which are threatened in the New International Divisions of Labor and Power. In particular, as the state contracts so security is being redefined: from territory to presidency? from party to military? from economy to ecology? And in the absence of increased foreign assistance, exchange, investment, and technology, self-reliance may become an inevitability rather than a desiderata. Its regional, rather than national or

continental possibilities are promising if informal sectors are liberated and encouraged s(that small-scale, female-dominated exchange rather than large-scale, state or corporat(trade becomes the center-piece.[46] In short, a variety of African capitalism and corporatism: may flourish as old restraints disappear and new conditionalities are effected.[47] Together then, the New International Divisions of Labor and Power constitute a new context for ar powerful impact upon African studies, African states, and African societies.

Endnotes

Reprinted from: *Journal of Asian and African Affairs*, Volume V, Number 1, 1993, by permissior of the authors and the *Journal of Asian and African Affairs*. Washington, D.C.

1. Cf. Timothy M. Shaw & Olajide Aluko, eds., *The Political Economy of African Foreign Policy* (Aldershot: Gower, 1984); T.M. Show and Julius Okolo, eds., *The Political Economy of Foreigr Policy in ECOWAS States*, (London: Macmillan, 1991); David Wurfel & Bruce Burton, eds., *Th(Political Economy of Foreign Policy in Southeast Asia*, (London: Macmillan, 1990); and Anthony T Bryan, et al, des., *Peace, Development and Security in the Caribbean, perspectives to the Year 2000* (London: Macmillan, 1990); Carmen Diana Deere, et al, *In the Shadows of the Sun*, (Boulder Westview, 1990); and Clark D. Neher, *Southeast Asia in the New International Era*, (Boulder Westview, 1991).

2. Cf. Timothy M. Shaw & E John Inegbedion, "Africa in the New Global Political Ecomy' comparative foreign policy at the periphery in the 1900s" and Bahgat Korany, "The Multiple Face of National Security: Reformulating a Basic concept", in Bahgat Korany, et al, eds., *The new Fac(of National Security in the Arab World: Dilemmas of security and development*, (London: Macmilan 1991); Timothy M. Shaw, "Foreign Policy in the New International Division of Labour in the Lat(1980s: the African dimension", in Wurdel & Burton, eds., *The Political Economy of Foreigr Policy in Southeast Asia;* and Richard F. Weisfelder, "Collective Foreign Policy Decision-Making within SADCC: Do Regional Objectives Alter National Policies? " Africa Today, 38:1 (1991): 5- 17; and Yezid Sayigh, *Confronting the 1990s: Security in the Developing Countries*, Adelph Papers 251 (London" IISS, 1990).

3. For an informed general discussion of recent changes in the global divisions of labour anc power, see James H. Mittelman, "The End of a Millenium: Changing Structures of World Ordei and the Challenges of Globalisation". *On Africa's power*, see. for example, Julius O. Ihonvbere' Political Conditionality and Prospects for Recovery in Sub-Saharan Africa," and Julius E. Nyang oro, "Reflections on the Sate, Democracy and NGOs in Africa." For an empirical exploration of th(North's disengagement from the South, see, Christopher Stevens, "Europe and the south in th(1990s: Disengagement to the South and Integration to the North of the Sahara". For a comparative Caribbean case including strategies for increasing integration, see, Aaron Segal, "Preferential Trade Leg-up Hand-me-Down: The Caribbean, the EC and the Caribbean Basin Initiative". All paper: presented at the March and September 1991 Dalhousie University international symposiums or "Surviving at the Margins: *Political Economy and Foreign Policy in the South in the 1990s"*.

4. For contrasting perspectives on the role of the US in post-Cold War conflict resolutior in the south, see, for example: Frances M. Deng & I.W. Zartman, eds., *Conflict Resolution in Africa* (Washington: Brooking Institute, 1991); Kenneth Oye, Robert Liever & Donald Rothschild, eds. Eagle in a New order: American Grand Strategy in the Post-Cold War Era, (New York HarperCollins 1992); and The Stanley Foundation, Foreign Aid: Beyond the Cold War, report of the 31st "Strategy

for Peace" US foreign policy conference, (Iowa: the Stanley Foundation, 1991).

5. Some of these hopes now appear premature, however. While the "peace divided" may bring with it unexpected debt relief to Angola and Ethiopia " who, along with Vietnam, are lobbying for a Union: to whom, they ask, do we owe these debts now that the Soviet Union itself has collapsed?), Mozambique's Renamo rebels continue to foot drag over the Rome peace talks with Frelimo. In the meantime, "the war which has claimed one million lives and displaced almost a quarter of the country's population of 16 million - shows no signs of abating." (Michael Wang,"Disturbing the Peace," The Globe and Mail, 4 March 1992). Cf John J. Mearsheimer, "Why we will Soon Miss the cold War," *The Atlantic*, 266:2 (August 1990). A longer version of this article is to be found in the Summer 1990 issue of *International Security*.

6. While the developed market economies continue to decrease levels of military expenditure, the arming of the south continues unabated, most alarmingly in Africa and the Middle East. in 1960 Africa as a whole spent 1.2% of its total GNP on the military. In 1987 the figure had risen to 4.4%. Except for the Middle East, this is the most marked rise in military expenditue anywhere in the world: comparative figures re. military spending as a percentage of GNP for the years 1960 and 1987 are as follows: OECD: 6.5%, 5.1%; Latin America: 1.9%, 1.6%, Middle East: 5.6, 16.9% (at the height of the Iran-Iraq war; one can spculate that post-Gulf War figures would be even higher); South Asia: 2.2%, 4.2%; Far East: 5.9%, 1.8%; Oceaning: 2.2%, 2.7%. Source Ruth L. Sivard, *World Military and Social Expenditures 1991*, 14th edition, (Washington: World Priorities Inc., 1991). Mahbub ul Hag points to the possible economic benefits of a freeze on Third World arms spending when he states: "If we succeed in that, the potential dividend is $10 billion in 1990, growing to $180 billion by the year 2000." (See, Mahbub ul Haq, "Focus on people and security precondition for development," *Development Foru*, 19:1 (Jan-Feb 1991): 4. Hopeful signs pointing toward demilitarization have come from Germany which in 1991, threatened to withhold 25% of its aid to India, if India did not agree to cut military spending. (See, John Stackhouse, "Third World pays for Soviet collapse," *The Globe and Mail*, 3 February 1992).

7. See, for example, the numerous reports over the 1980s following the general theme of sustainable, self-reliant, people-centred development: e.g., ECA/OAU, *Lagos Plan of Action* (1980); OAU, *Africa's Priority Programme for Economic Recovery* (APPER), 1985; *UN Programme of Action for African Economic Recovery and to Structural Adjustment Programmes for Socio-Economic Recovery and Transformation* (AFF-SAP), 1989; UNDP, *Human Development Report 1990; ECA, Arusha Declaration on Popular Participation in the Recovery and Development Process in Africa, 1990*; and, the *ECA/OAU Conference on Security, Stability, Development and Cooperation in Africa*, (CSSDACA), 1991.

8. See E.F. Schumacher, *Small is Beautiful*, (London: Abacus Press, 1974); and George McRobie, *Small is Possible* (London: Abacus, 1981). For an excellent overview of Third World experiences with "appropriate technology", see, Ian Smillie, *Mastering the Machine*, (Peterboroug: Broadview, 1992). On the african case, see the contribution by Goran Hyden in *World Bank, Long-Term Perspective Study of Sub-Saharan Africa: Background Papers*, (Washington, June, 1990) "the Changing Context of Institutional and Sociopolitical Issues.

9. S.K.B Asante, *African Development: Adebayo Adedeji's Alternative Strategies*, (London Hanszell 1991): 171.

10. See, Gwyneth Williams, *Third World Political Organizations*, 2nd ed., (London: Macmillan, 1987).

11. Reaching, according to one estimate from roy culpepper of the Ottwa-based North-South Institute, $12 billion in 1984 and $29 billion two years later. (See, for example, John Kohut,

"Which Way Out?", *The Globe and Mail*, 6 June 1987; and *UNCTAD, Trade Development Report 1989*, p. 38). On declining commodity prices, Chris Stevens states: "In all cases, except crude petroleum, dollar prices, in 1987 for the ACP's most important exports were 20-30% below their 1980 level." (cited by Trevor Parfit, "Lies and Statistics: the World Bank/ ECA Strutural Adjustment Controversy," *Review of African Political* Economy, 47 (Spring 1990): 133. Parfitt goes on to state, "[T]he situation for petroleum was even worse, its price having been halved. The ecports concerned include coffee, cocoa, wood, copper, and iron." (Ibid).

12. See, Hoogvelt, in the "Debates" section of *Review of African Political Economy*, 47 (spring 1990): 118.

13. *Ibid.*

14. Statement by Adedeji, made at the 25th assembly of heads of State and Government of the OAU, Addis Ababa, 25 July 1989. This kind of rhetoric holds very little water with IFIs, however, Commercial banks were initially very critical of the Brady plan. One reason they are skeptical of making new loans to highly-indebted countries in the past decade fled quickly abroad, by Telex or bulging suitcase. Flight capital is hard to measure, but economists at J.P. Morgan & Co., a New York bank, estimate that the stock of such wealth (assets held abroad by non-bank private sector residents of the 15 big debors) amounted to $300 billion at the end of 1987 - more than half their total foreign debt; Argentina's $46 billion is about three-quarters its debt. If a country's own residents have no confidence in their economy, foreign creditors get the message." ("New debt plans offer uncertain relief", *The Economist*, August 13-20, 1989).

15. According to German economist Winrich Kuhne, Africa is being marginalizedt from the global economy. For example, "Africa's share of global foreign investment has fallen below 2% from 5.5% in 1960. Africa, unable to compete successfully on the world market, is undergoing a process of deindustrialization." Solutions, he says, must be found by Africans "mobilizing their own resources and creativity." A new consensus, kuhne states, has evolved which "identifies the authoritarian bureaucratic state and party structures." Given present inabilities to act a facilitators in devlopment, the black market has risen to "highlight Africa's Creative entrepreneurial potential." But he informal sector is not a panacea. For Kuhyne, "There is a danger that in Africa, after a phase of too much state intervention in the economy, the debate will concentrate on the withdrawal of the state, believing that the rest can be left to market forces. But... the secret successful market economies is a state providing and efficient framework and infrastructure, as well as the planning and promoting of exports." According to Kuhne, "Africa needs a much more explicit debate on the transformation of the state and not just on its withdrawal." As quoted in Philip van Niekerk, 'out of Africa. But in may halt cycle of despair, The Weekly Mail (Johannesburg), 18-24.1.91:9.

16. See, for example, the annual review of the North-South Institute entitle "A whole new World, Regionalism as Building Block not a Barrier," *Review* '90 Outlook '91, (Ottawa, 1991); Timothy M. Shaw, "The Revival of Regionalism in Africa: cure for crisis or prescrioption for conflict?", *Jerusalem Journal of International Relations*, 11 (1989): 79-105; Ralph Onwuka a & amadu Sesay, eds., *The Future of Regionalism in Africa* , (London: Macmillan, 1985); the issue on "Managing Regional Conflict" of *International Journal*, 45:2 (Spring 1990); and Volume 4 of the World Bank published the *Long-Term Perspective Study of Sub-Saharan Africa*, (Washington, June 1990) entitled Proceedings of a Workshop in Regional Integration and Cooperation. For some observers, the move toward regional integration is a matter of urgency. For example, after making the case for increased integration and Cooperation. For some example, after making the case for increased integration among SADCC, including South Africa, states, Johan C. van Zyl states: "The above interactions would also be vitally important if in de- linked from international trade and finance."

(Southern Africa: towards closer economic cooperation in the 1990s", a discussion paper Development bank closer economic cooperation in the 1990s", a discussion paper Development bank of South Africa, November 1990). On the other hand, a widely-accepte caveat heard at the recent ASA meetings in St. Lois (November 1991) was that there seems to be a trend toward pushing "regionalism for regionalism's sake", i.e. without first having though some specifics: e.g. formal v. informal sectors and approaches; state sovereignty v. informal sectors and approachers; state sovereignty v. collective security, etc.

17. See, Julious O. Ihonvbere, "Africa's Political' Crisis: lessons and suggestions from the Nigerian case," and maria Nzomo, "Beyond the Structural Adjustments Programs: Democracy, Gender Equity and Development in Africa," papers presented to the symposium on *Surviving at the Margins: Africa in the New International Divisions of Labor and power, Halifax,* 26-28 March 1991. See also, Kivutha Kibwana, "Democracy and Constitutionalism in Africa," *AAPS Newsletter, (December 1990):* 4-9.

18. See, for example, James A. Caporaso, ed., *A Changing International Division of Labor,* (New York: Homes & Meier, 1985).

19. See, for example, Nigel Harris, *The End of the Third World,* (Harmondworth: penguin, 1986). That taiwan itself is reported to have invested $1 billion in Thailand in 1991 alone (up form $23 million in 1982) seems testimony enough to the uneven impacts of and responses to the various oil, and interest rate shocks and general recession of the post-Bretton Woods era. (See, *The Economist,* 14-21 February 1992).

20. See, Christopher Stevens, "Europe and the South in the 1990s", *op cit,* pp. 6-8.

21. See, for example, the voer satires on "Liberia, To the Victors, What Spils?" and 'Somalia After the Fall", in *Africa Report,* respectively the November-December 1990 and march-April 1991 issues.

22. See, "Africa: th new order", *Africa Confidential,* 5 Ap ril 1991, vol. 32, no. 7.

23. See, "Zambia: In the end, a graceful exit," *The Economist,* (Nov9, 1991): 44-45. A recent Africa Confidential report suggests that where "democratization" means the emergence of truly people-centered movements - e.g. Mali, Ethiopia, Zambia, RSA - these may be the exceptions that prove the rule: "It has become directly involved many citizens from outside the existing political elite, and particularly not in the rural areas." AC's correspondent labels this the "Senegalese model of democratic politics." ("Africa: democracy is not enough", *Africa Confidential,* 33:1 (10 January 1992).24 As reported in the *Business Day* (Johannesburg) article entitled "Donor nations link aid to democratic systems", 8 December 1989.

24. As reported in the *Business Day* (Johannesburg) article entitled "Donor nations link aid to democratic systems", 8 December 1989.

25. See, for example, Maria Nzomo, "Adjustment, Gender, and Democracy in Africa: the kenyan Case", and the papers by Julious Ihonvbere, and Julius Nyang'oro cited supra note 3, all three from the *Dalhousie International Symposia* on "Surviving at the Margins".

26. See, for example, Ingrid Palmer, *Gender and population in the adjustment of African Economies: Planning for Change, Women, Work, and Development 19,* (Geneva: ILO, 1991); and Eva M. Rathgeber. "Operationalizing Gender and Development", IDRC, Ottawa, March 1992.

27. See, for example, the numerous discussion papers produced by the UNRISD research program, *Sustainable Development through People's Participation in Resource Management,* under the direction of Jessica Vivien; Thomas FL Home-Dixon, "on the Threshold: Environmental Changes as Causes of Acute Conflict," *International Security,* 16:2 (Fall 1991); Alan B. Durning, *Apartheid's Environmental Toll,* Worldwatch Paper 95, (May 1990); and Jessica Tuchaman Matthews,

"Redefining Security," *Foreign Affairs*, 68:2 (Spring 1989).

28. See, for example, Atiq Rathman, "The Informal Sector in Bangladesh: an appraisal of its role in development," *Development and Change*, (January 1992); and Louis A. Ferman, "The Informal Economy," *The Annals*, (September 1988).

29. See, for example *UNDP, Human Development Report*, (New York: Oxford University Press, 1990). Cf the following from Adebayo Adedeji: "It is only people who make development possible. Unless they participate fully in policy-making they are not likely to be enthusiastic in their implementation...[O] or future development must be human-centered and must be dedicated to the goal of ensuring the overall well-being of the people through the equitable distribution of the fruits of development." (in S.K.B Asangte. *African Development*, 206).

30. See, for example, "Africa: the new order," *Africa Confidential*, 32:7 (5 April 1991); and the series of reports under the general heading, "The Decline of the Dictator", in *Africa Report*, (July-August 1991).

31. On stratification in African political economies see, for example, Adebayo Adedeji & Timothy M. Shaw, eds., *Economic crisis in Africa*, (Boulder: Lynne Rienner, 1985); Bonnie Campbell & John Loxley, eds., *Structural Adjustment in Africa*, (London: Macmillan, 1989); Trevor Parfitt & Setphen Riley, *The African Debt Crisis*, (London: Routledge, 1989). For an earlier assessment of the potential rise of regional powers, see, Timothy M. Shaw, "Kenya and South Africa: "sub-imperialist" states," *Orbis*, 21:2 (Summer 1977): 357-394.

32. See, Allister Sparks, "The Miracle that happened in South Africa," a Washington Post article reprinted in the Windsor Star, 25 March 1992.

33. See, for example, Auret van Heeren, "?Recent Trends in South Africa's Economy", unpublished paper, (ILO: Geneva, August 1991). Cf Timothy M. Shaw, "South and southern Africa in the New International Division of Labour: prospects for the 1990s", in larry A. Swatuk & Timothy M. Shaw, eds., *Prospects for Peace and Development in Southern Africa in the 1990s: Canadian and Comparative Perspectives*, (Lanham, Md: UPA, 991): 3-20; and SADCC position paper, SADCC: toward economic integration, (Gaborone, 1992).

34. See Christopher Stevens, "Europe and the South in the 1990s", *op cit.*

35. Cf, Owodunni Teriba & Jeggan C. Senghor, eds., Adebayo Adedeji at 60:   *Issues in African Development and Future prospects*, (forthcoming);   and Timothy M. Shaw, "The Future of the fourth World: Choices of and Constraints on the Very Poor in the 1980s," in Dennis Pirages & Christine Sylvester, eds., *Transformation in the Global Political Economy*, (London: Macmillan 1990): 195-229.

36. Commenting on the simultaneous imposition of the "crossconditionalities" of economic liberalism and political democracy, Kivuthu Kibwana states, "if a revolution has occurred in the East recently, the real revolution will occur whyen the west consciously disabuses herself (sic) of present economic advantage and hegemony in order to ensure that the basic conditions for the realization of freedom and democracy for all making are realized globally. Where countries are extremely poor and acquisition of political power is the most critical asset in ensuring economic survival, leaders cannot, logically, wish to willingly give up power or be very civil to those who pose challenge to their power. To condemn African countries to abject poverty and then simultaneously democracy which demands a high level of economic well-being is contradictory." ("Democracy and Constitutionalism in Africa," *AAPS Newsletter*, December 1990, 4).

37. See, for example, Timothy M. Shaw, "Dependent Development in the New International Division of Labour; prospects ofr Africa's political economy," in David Haglund & Michael Hawes, eds., *World Politics: Power, Interdependence, and Dependence*, (Toronto: HBJ, 1990): 333-360;

and Ralph Onwuka & Timothy M. Shaw, eds., *Africa in World Politics: into the 1990s*, (London: Macmillan, 1989).

38. "Africans Seek Homespun Remedies in Kampala," *Africa Report*, (July-Augus 1991): 8-9.

39. Ibid; cf, SADCC: SADCC. Towards Economic Integration and Johan C. van Zyl, Southern Africa: towards closer economic cooperation in the 1990s". Clearly, Capability is further hampered by debt; and colloective security is hampered by structural adjustment uniformities which inhibits regional actors from working toward regional complementarities.

40. See, for example, Naomi Chazan, "Ideology, Policy and the Crisis of Poverty: the African case," *Jerusalelm Journal of International Relations*, 10 (1988): 1-30. See, also, ROAPE 47 (Spring 1990), devoted to structural adjustment in Africa, entitled "What price economic reform?"

41. See, Timothy M. Shaw, "Africa After the Crisis of the 1980s" the dialectics of adjustment," in mary Hawkesworth & Maurice Kegan, eds., *Routledge Encyclopedia of Government and Politics*, (London: Routledge, 1991); and Paul Kennedy, *African Capitalism*, (Cambridge University Press, 1988).

42. James H. Mittleman, "The End of a Millenium" supra notes 3, pp. 16, 17.

43. See Richard Joseph, *Perstroika without Glasnost in Africa*, (Atlanta: the Carter Center, 1989); Timothy M. Shaw, "External Impediments to Effective Popular Participation: Towards Democratic Development in the 1990s, "ECA Conferene on Putting People First: Popular Participation in the Recovery and Development Process in Africa, (Arusha, February 1990); Peter Anyang Noyong'o, ed., *Popular Strudggles for Democracy in Africa*, (London: Zed, 1987); and Michael Bratton, "Beyond the State: Civil Society and Associational Life in Africa," *World Politics*, 41 (1989): 407-430.

44. James H. Mittleman, "The End of a Millenium", 15.

45. Mittelman, "The End of a Millennium", pp. 14-15.

46. See, for example, Jane L. parpart & Kathleen A. Staudt, eds., *Women and the State in Africa*, (Boulder: Lynne Rienner, 1989); and Maria Nzomo, "The Impact of the Women's Decade on Policies, Programmes and Empowerment in Kenya," *Issue*, 17:2 (1989).

47. See, Julius Nyan'oro &Timothy M. Shaw, eds., *Corporatism in Africa*, (Boulder: Westview, 1990); also World Bank, *The Long-Term Study of Sub-Saharan Africa, Background papers*, (Washington, June 1990, volumes 1 to 4.

Chapter V

Prospects for Regional Integration in Post-Apartheid Southern Africa

Dr. Larry A. Swatuk

Introduction

This paper examines the prospects for increasing formal regional, particularly economic, integration in post-*apartheid* Southern Africa. Southern Africa, it appears to some, is poised to move toward a new era of economic growth and sustainable development. Numerous voices and schemes for regional integration have been put forward: an enlarged South African Customs Union (SACU), a reformed Southern African Development Community (SADC; formerly the Southern African Development Coordination Conference or SADCC) which would *include* South Africa, a revived Constellation of Southern African States (CONSAS) *headed* by South Africa, and an enlarged and invigorated Preferential Trade Area for Eastern and Southern Africa (PTA; now known as the Common Market of Eastern and Southern African States or COMESA) working in coordination with some or all of the above. In most of these scenarios, South Africa is to be the "engine of growth", and the "SADC experience" is to provide the facilitative mechanism for cooperative state behaviour (*cf* Davies, 1992).

To be sure, a restructuring of regional relations and organisations is imperative if Southern Africa is to have any chance at a hopeful future beyond debt and destabilisation. The majority of Southern Africa's states, as juridically and empirically constituted, are unviable political economies (Jackson, 1992). They will never provide to the region's peoples the twin public goods of political security and economic prosperity — i.e. the traditional rationale for state formation in the post-Westphalian context — unless they can overcome the externalization of their economies and the tenacious hold by their political classes upon sovereignty (Saul, 1976). And, most certainly, as a "collection" of fragmented, indebted and unstable political economies, the region will neither be able to compete with nor integrate into one of the three emerging global trade blocs — be it European, North American or Pacific — in the New International Division of Labour (NIDL).

So, notwithstanding the continuing difficulty of moving successfully toward multipartyism in South Africa, this paper argues that optimistic scenarios for the region are premature at best. Given the ubiquity of debt and state-by-state negotiated structural adjustment programmes in the region, the prospects for state-initiated, *de jure* regional integration remain limited. *Status quo* and stagnation, if not decline, are therefore more likely scenarios at the end of the 1990s in Southern Africa (*cf* Saul, 1991; and Martin, 1991).

In support of this hypothesis, this essay proceeds as follows. First, I examine South Africa's emergence as the regional hegemon. This discussion highlights the *divisiveness* inherent in the extension and unequal consolidation of capitalism and race-based oppression to Southern Africa. Second, I examine the emergence and performance of the Southern African Development Coordination Conference (SADCC) as a proposed counterweight to the economic and political power of South Africa. And third, I look at the changing character of South Africa's economy over the last thirty or so years. In this way I seek to demonstrate that two basic assumptions fuelling speculation about Southern Africa as a potential "economic giant" in the post-*apartheid* era are flawed: (i) SADCC member-states have yet to develop a *regional* identity which transcends more narrowly-defined state interests; and (ii) far from a potential "engine of growth", post-*apartheid* South Africa faces innumerable problems of its own. Debt not strategic minerals will mark South Africa's major link to the North in the post-Cold War and -*apartheid* eras.

South Africa and the Evolving Global Division of Labour

South Africa's hegemonic position in the region derives from its great economic wealth — particularly, diamonds, gold, and a wide variety of other minerals, including uranium — and the method by which these abundant resources were exploited. Following the mineral revolution of the 1860s and onward, lines of transportation and communication that had been developing slowly and haphazardly into the interior were strengthened and streamlined along a settler/colonial-axis. South Africa became a wide basin into which much of the region's wealth, and human and natural resources drained. What emerged, over time, was a white-dominated South Africa whose powerful position in the regional political economy has been described as "sub-imperial" (Shaw, 1977). This position derived not from the workings of a free market economy but from, initially, international and, later also, national capital's overt manipulation of the regional environment. Clearly, white South Africa benefited disproportionately from this and other unequal regional relationships. With the ascendance of the Afrikaner-dominated Nationalist Party to power in the post-World War II period, much of this surplus capital was turned toward social reconstruction on a massive scale, i.e. *apartheid*.

Today, South Africa is the overwhelmingly dominant actor in the "regional subsystem":

> South Africa dominates the region economically. With under 30% of the population, South Africa produces nearly 3/4 of the region's GDP; and 2/3 of its exports (roughly $18 to $24 billion in 1984); about half the South African total is gold, and nearly 7% are exports to countries in the SACU. The majority of income arising in South Africa accrues to or is controlled by the minority white population of some 4.8 million. Thus, the 4 to 5% of the region's population comprising white South Africans receive or control at least half of the region's income -something of obvious importance in discussing the present realities and the future prospects of the region. (Lewis, 1988: 41; *cf* Bowman, 1968; and Stoneman & Thompson, 1991)

Despite this continually expanding economic domination, minority-rule came increasingly under threat throughout the post-"winds of change" period. As both domestic and external opposition to *apartheid* and continued settler/colonial rule in the region increased, the racist regime turned first toward cooptation of neighbours and "allies" and, only secondarily, toward "destabilisation" as the preferred method for continued national and regional hegemony (Barber & Barratt, 1990; Grundy, 1986; Hanlon, 1986; Johnson & Martin, 1986).

SADCC and Increasing Destabilisation

It was not until shortly after 1980 that the use of coercive measures came to dominate total strategy. 1980 was a watershed year in regional relations for three interrelated reasons. First, Zimbabwe came to independence under the leadership of an avowed Marxist, Robert Mugabe. South Africa's preferred candidate, Bishop Abel Muzorewa, had been soundly deafeated in pre-independence elections. Second, the independence of Zimbabwe marked the culmination of five years of activity on the part of the Frontline States coalition. At independence, Zimbabwe became yet another radical member of that group — with Botswana the lone democratic and capitalist state — whose activities now turned to the liberation of South Africa.

Third, the nine majority-ruled states of the region formed SADCC[1], clearly rejecting

Pretoria's CONSAS proposal. According to the 1980 Lusaka declaration, SADCC's mandate was fourfold: (i) reduce economic dependence particularly, but not only, on South Africa: (ii) forge links to create genuine, equitable regional integration: (iii) mobilise resources to promote the implementation of national, inter-state, and regional policies; and (iv) coordinate action to secure international cooperation within a framework of "strategy for economic liberation" (Anglin, 1986).

Zimbabwe's independence was key to the future of the SADCC states. It gave to the idea of regional economic cooperation beyond South Africa "a new kiss of life because of the strategic importance of Zimbabwe for countries like Botswana and Zambia" (Tsie, 1989: 8). Not only was SADCC to centre around the industrial power of Zimbabwe — thus posing a threat, at least theoretically, to South Africa's economic hegemony in the region — it also included as members those states previously considered most dependent upon and/or aligned with Pretoria (i.e. Lesotho, Malawi and Swaziland) — thus giving the impression that Pretoria was losing control of its destiny.

For South African policy-makers, SADCC's mandate, though couched in economic terms, was clearly political. Thus, in light of the extended nature of this perceived threat, South Africa's military-oriented policy-makers saw regional destabilisation as, quite possibly, their last resort.

The point to be drawn from this discussion of regional organisation and political response is that both the RSA and the SADCC states defined the major threats to their respective securities as each other.

Toward Post-Cold War and Post-apartheid

The end of the Cold War brought this confrontation to a crashing halt. With it went what little was left of white South Africa's sense of regional security. In the end, neither SADCC nor South Africa was made more secure. Almost every step of the way the basis for future inter-state cooperation was undermined. Regional schemes (e.g. CONSAS) and institutions (e.g. SADCC) were created not with co-prosperity in mind, but out of the need for survival defined in terms of state-makers' self-interests.

Today, therefore, the entire region stands divided and in dire straits; military "solutions" not only killed thousands and displaced millions, they also served to exacerbate the structural deformities of these countries' political economies entrenched since colonial times. In other words, the focus on *regional military confrontation* has virtually sapped the capacities of Southern Africa's states to deal with continuing crises brought on by the region's declining importance in the *global economic system*; in Mozambique and Angola, for example, military spending was absorbing as much as 40% of total state expenditure by the end of the 1980s" (SADCC, 1991: 13): a diversion of scarce resources that could clearly have been better used elsewhere (see Table 1). This has, in turn, heightened the *domestic sources* of instability. And now, Bank/Fund "rescue missions" have entered to squeeze them further.

The "African Condition" and Southern Africa

The Southern African region has not been exempt from the general crisis facing the continent (Shaw, 1988; 1993). Africa has always been a marginal force in the global economy (Swatuk & Shaw, 1993 and 1994). For example, in 1983, with roughly 500 million people (i.e. 10% of world

Table 1: SADCC and South African Military Expenditures

Country	Military Spending		% of GNP	
	1960	1987	1960	1987
Angola	---	2,040	---	20.0
Botswana	---	82	---	6.0
Lesotho	---	20	---	2.9
Malawi	---	21	---	1.8
Mozambique	---	102	---	8.0
South Africa	**243**	**3,292**	**0.9**	**4.2**
Swaziland	---	8	---	1.3
Tanzania	2	171	0.1	5.3
Zambia	11	63	1.1	3.6
Zimbabwe	---	390	---	8.1
SADCC	**13**	**2,897**	**0.13**	**6.3**

Source: Ruth Sivard, *World Military and Social Expenditures*, 1989.

total), Africa's gross continental product was merely three per cent of total world output. By the end of 1989 that had declined to less than one per cent. In comparison, the US, with five per cent of the world's population, produced roughly 35% of world output; and the EC, with a similar population, accounted for approximately 20% (Bing, 1991: 63).

Given this existing economic marginality, Kuhne suggests that Africa is being further marginalised from the global economy. For example, "Africa's share of global foreign investment has fallen below 2% from 5.5% in 1960. Africa, unable to compete successfully on the world market, is undergoing a process of de-industrialisation" (*Weekly Mail*, 18-24 January 1991: 9). This continuing marginalisation is due to a number of factors: uncompetitive production structures; debt; political instability; low investment and capital flight; and unstable export earnings, to name some of the more important variables. Africa's economic crisis is well known and need not be discussed further here (Shaw, 1988; 1993). The point to be made, however, is that Southern Africa, no less than the rest of the continent, has suffered from this changing international division of labour. Moreover, South Africa's policy of destabilisation has exacerbated the region's decline (World Bank, 1989: 23).

If Africa is marginal to the global economy, then Southern Africa, as a subregional grouping, is even more marginal. As can be seen in Table 2, "Southern Africa is responsible for a major part of the African continent's productive activity," with SADCC (7.3%) and South Africa (21.5%) combining for approximately 28.8% of continental GDP (SADCC, 1991: 8-9). In global terms, however, the contribution of the region is relatively insignificant, with SADCC/South Africa combined output approximating that of Finland (see Table 3). Given this relative economic marginality, both SADCC and South Africa manipulated largely Cold War-influenced interests to attract a disproportionate amount of international attention and assistance, albeit largely to destructive ends.

Table 2: Gross Domestic Product, 1989: selected comparisons

Country/Region	US$ millions	% of total African GDP	% of African GDP (excluding RSA)
SADCC countries	27,210	7.3	9.3
South Africa	80,370	21.5	
SADCC & RSA	107,580	28.8	
Rest of Africa	266,130	71.2	
Africa excluding South Africa	293,340		
Total	373,710		

Source: SADCC, *SADCC: Towards Economic Integration*, (1991): 9.

SADCC, as mentioned above, sought above all else to reduce its economic dependency upon both South Africa and the world system; to diversify SADCC state economies, particularly toward coordinated industrialisation and complementary structures of production; and to forge a regional mentality and economy that would help move the SADCC states

Table 3: Southern Africa Combined GDP in Comparison
     with Other Countries' and World GDP (1989)
Country/Region   GDP (US$ million)   %
World GDP

SADCC	27,210	0.14
South Africa	80,370	0.40
SADCC & RSA	107,580	0.54
Nigeria	28,920	0.15
Hungary	29,060	0.15
Finland	100,860	0.51
Brazil	319,150	1.60
World	19,981,540	

Source: **SADCC,** *SADCC: Towards Economic Integration,*
(1991): 9.

toward self-reliance. I will look briefly at SADCC's economic performance in terms of these strategies.

Decreased Dependence Upon South Africa

Intra-SADCC trade steadily declined in the 1981-86 period (SADCC, 1991: 15). Comparative PTA data suggests similar trends. According to Ncube, intra-PTA trade declined in the course of the 1980s from a total of US $640.6 million in 1980 to approximately US $579.2 million in 1989 (cited in *ibid*).

And while SADCC state exports have increased over the same time period, these exports have not been with each other, but have remained, and indeed are increasingly extra-continental (Stoneman & Thompson, 1991: 7). The reasons behind this increased dependence on external markets stem largely from the provisions of the structural adjustment policies that are rife throughout the region. Stressing "comparative advantage", SAPs have encouraged agricultural and raw material exports from each of the SADCC states. And, as can be seen in Table 4, SADCC state exports remain overwhelmingly "unfinished".

Table 4: Southern African Exports, latest available year

Country	Exports (US$ mn)	Leading Exports (% share)
Angola	3,000	oil (86), coffee (4)
Botswana	1,266	diamonds (80)
Lesotho	69	wool, mohair (n.a.)
Malawi	457	tobacco (50), tea (19), sugar (11)
Mozambique	101	fish (44), nuts, fruits & vegetables (38)
Swaziland	452	sugar (36)
Tanzania	407	coffee (26), cotton (24)
Zambia	1,370	copper (86)
Zimbabwe	1,620	gold (19), tobacco (18), ferroalloys (11)
South Africa	23,816	gold (40), manufactures (23)

Source: Stoneman & Thompson (1991): 10.

So, intra-SADCC trade remains at approximately 4% of SADCC state totals, and has been declining throughout the decade. Moreover, if one excludes Zimbabwe from these totals, intra-SADCC trade drops to approximately one per cent (Stoneman & Hutchence, 1991: 3).

Industrialisation and Manufacturing

However, SADCC was never intended to be trade-driven a la the PTA. To the contrary, in 1988 SADCC Executive Secretary Simba Makoni stated, "[T]he greatest single barrier to trade is lack of production. Hence our motto: Let production push trade rather than trade pull production" (Stoneman & Thompson, 1991: 8). Yet, as Stoneman and Hutchence clearly demonstrate, SADCC has failed to diversify into manufacturing. Of the US $3 billion in donor funds secured by 1990, fully $2.46 billion has gone into transportation rehabilitation and communications. Granted, these are indispensible infrastructural developments, without which SADCC stands no chance whatsoever of developing formal economies along regional lines. With regard to manufacturing and industry, however, by February 1989 SADCC's industrial programme had managed to secure a mere $317 million of its proposed $1.5 billion programme; $187 million of which was destined for a single project, the Mufindi pulp and paper mill in Tanzania (Stoneman & Hutchence, 1991: 2).

In the face of such disappointment, SADCC was forced to "rethink" its industrial policy along *private sector* lines, effectively fitting it to the prevailing global orthodoxy. Yet, even with this new focus on private sector involvement, of the 16 projects proposed in 1990 totalling $23 million, only $6.5 million in funding has been secured, and all projects are in the trade promotion and support service areas. Moreover, none of these projects, nor the proposed Export Pre-Financing Revolving Funds (EPRFs) have explicit regional components. The reasoning here is clear: "any EPRF which was limited to exporting *inside* the region would have much greater difficulty raising financing from *outside* the region" (Stoneman & Hutchence, 1991: 4).

Throughout the region, small internal markets and unequal income distributions have further limited competitive production for wider regional and global markets: highly subsidised and inefficient industries have long been producing for constricted markets (Stoneman, 1991: 2). And, even here, SADCC itself is skeptical of aiming at regional economies of scale designed to satisfy the *regional* market:

> [A]n integrated SADCC, even including South Africa, would constitute a small unit by global standards. Integration within Southern Africa cannot, therefore, be seen as a basis for inward looking policies; but rather in terms of enhancing capacity to become more competitive in an outward looking growth and development strategy. (1991: 28)

Forging A Regional Identity

In a recent position paper SADCC itself recognised that "Southern African countries, including South Africa already constitute a coherent and appreciably interconnected grouping, with a history of inter-relations and strong cultural and ethnic linkages" (1991: 35). Moreover, the SADCC study forcefully declares: "[C]hanging domestic, regional and global circumstances have made closer economic cooperation and integration an imperative for SADCC member countries" (1991: 1). The paper then highlights a number of areas for cooperation, with macro-economic policy coordination perhaps the most important.

At the same time, however, SADCC planners recognise the numerous barriers to cooperation at both formal and non-formal levels. Chief among the non-formal barriers to cooperation are the legacies of colonialism and *apartheid*, which have led, according to SADCC (1991), Stoneman and Thompson (1991), and Stoneman (1991) among others, to embedded inequalities in the structures of production, in the terms of trade, and in income distributions at the regional and global levels. SADCC also includes "poor governance" as a "major non-economic barrier to development in Southern Africa" (1991: 34; 11). Stoneman and Thompson (1991: 4) also point to policy failures, not merely at the SADCC state level, but on the part of "international agencies and other aid donors, which

have been involved in the region for almost three decades and thus must share the blame."
Given the above-mentioned and other (e.g. drought, domestic political instability) numerous constraints, it is little surprise that the region has fared so poorly over the course of the 1980s and into the 1990s:

> Regionally, the overall growth rate in the 1980s has been negative in per capita terms, with only Botswana and (marginally) Swaziland and Zimbabwe showing positive figures... All countries in the region ... are heavily dependent on primary commodity exports. The failure of most of their industrialisation plans, caused by uncertain demand and protectionism in Northern markets, the debt crisis, destabilisation ... and by poor or over-ambitious planning, has led to a renewed emphasis on primary commodity production, urged on by the World Bank and the IMF. Yet the terms of trade for African commodities have been falling... Most countries in Southern Africa are heavily in debt, with the regional total around $50 billion, of which South Africa accounts for nearly half. This is a small figure on the world scale, but it is large in relation to population or economic capacity to repay or service (Stoneman & Thompson, 1991: 2,3).

Nevertheless, Weisfelder (1991: 6-7) suggests that we should not lose sight of SADCC's successes. On this score, he highlights six elements: (i) promoted the emergence of a SADCC mentality; (ii) encouraged diversification of substantive bilateral linkages among members; (iii) solicited cnsiderable additional aid from external donors; (iv) improved regional communications and transportation networks; (v) created especially deep linkages with Nordic states; and (vi) established itself as an essential participant in international deliberations regarding the political and economic future of Southern Africa.

These successes are not to be denied, but, as SADCC itself, and others have pointed out, the regional "mentality" remains merely convenient to state-centric development policies:

> Member states' political commitment to mobilising regional resources for development is not in question. Indeed, the region's record in sustaining its common institutions is unparalleled, at least, on the African continent. The challenge, however, is in respect of the capacity and institutions for mobilising resources for regional development projects... As long as national and regional programmes are seen to be separate, the latter will come last in the allocation of scarce resources (SADCC, 1991: 31,32).

Of central importance to the SADCC project is the emergence of structural adjustment, both *de facto* and *de jure*, as the primary consideration in all SADCC state development policies. In spite of SADCC's stated objection to *laissez-faire* economics (1991: 1), the market has come to be regarded as the panacea to Southern Africa's persistent economic problems. According to Stoneman, in the South Africa case,

> [a]lready the market is being seen as the 'answer' to the market intervention of *apartheid*,
> but with no appreciation that markets deliver different results determined by the income
> and wealth distributions that they find, and that insofar as they change these distributions
> it is usually in the direction of greater inequality (1991: 4).

Market driven economic policies serve to heighten existing domestic contradictions,
and to pit ostensibly cooperative states against each other in the search for foreign investment. Again, according to Stoneman:

> [M]ost black people will remain miserably poor for the foreseeable future under orthodox
> economic policies, unless a sustained growth rate of the order of 10% per annum can be
> achieved - a very unlikely possibility ... Orthodox policies will thus prove disastrous for
> all but the elites. To make a real impact on South Africa's problems requires imaginative
> and radical solutions ... [However], the new international dispensation, which seems likely
> to deny developing countries any freedom to experiment (or even to follow tested protec-
> tionist industrialisation policies), could result in [South Africa's] integration into a world
> market as a marginal and essentially stagnant supplier of primary commodities
> (1991: 1).

In summary then, what SADCC and the world have seen with regard to Southern
African regional development since 1980 has been disheartening. Energy remains a serious drain on already weak economies; intra-SADCC trade remains virtually non-existent,
while individual SADCC state trade remains tied to the export of primary or only mini-
mally-processed products; and material and capital investment in transportation and
communication remains a battle to recover seriously deteriorated extant infrastructure —
despite an incredible infusion of foreign capital, and technical and material assistance.
The imposition of structural adjustment policies, coupled with the coming end of *apartheid* means that aid will still be forthcoming, but under increasingly stringent conditions.
As Stoneman notes,

> [T]he conditionality associated with the aid will be strong, aimed at preventing a search
> for alternative solutions which if successful might set unwelcome precedents; most Afri-
> can countries now have so weak a bargaining position that a little aid will command a lot
> of conditionality (*ibid*).

South Africa: An Engine of Growth?

If such is the SADCC case, what then of the RSA? To some observers, a post-*apartheid* South Africa would serve as the regional engine of growth. No doubt South Africa's economy will be considerably stronger than when it labored under domestic and international pressure, and the folly of *apartheid* legislation. But to think that an end to *apartheid* will lead to NIC status and provide immediate region-wide economic growth is to seriously under-estimate the structural crises facing the South African economy with or without the added burden of international sanctions (*cf* Davies, 1992). To highlight this embedded structural crisis I will look at South Africa's economy in terms of recent macroeconomic trends, minerals, manufactures, and money.

Recent Trends in South Africa's Economic Performance

James Cobbe (1992: 9) provides a succinct overview of recent trends in South Africa's economic performance:

South Africa's economy has been performing poorly in overall growth terms throughout the eighties, with only brief spurts of growth around 1981, 1983 and 1988. The long-term trend in South Africa's growth record is distinctly downward: the average growth rate of output fell from 6% per annum in the 1960s to 3% per annum in the 1970s to only 1% per annum (implying declining output per person) in the 1980s to actual declines in the 1990s so far. (Standard Bank, 1992: 1) Real GDP has been falling since 1989, at about 0.5% per annum in 1990 and 1991. In 1992, output will probably fall by another half to one per cent, and the South African business community seems to believe that general economic weakness may well persist through 1993. (First National Bank, 1992: 1).

Exploding the Myth of Post-apartheid Economic Growth

Unfortunately, at a time when much the rest of the world was restructuring in the attempt to cope with rapid changes in the NIDL, South African policy-makers were pursuing misguided policies dependent on twin myths: one, South Africa's economy is a strong one, in fact the richest on the continent, and is hampered only by "total onslaught" — i.e. from regional terrorism and international sanctions. Two, post-*apartheid* South Africa will achieve NIC status in short order.

Preoccupation with destabilisation further reinforced these myths. As we will see, it was not, in the main, militarisation nor was it sanctions that created South Africa's economic problems; rather, it was an over-reliance on raw materials as the central wealth creator in the economy.

Minerals

To use a rather tired cliche, "[m]ining is the bedrock on which the South African economy rests" (van Heerden, 1991: 18). In spite of the fact that manufacturing now accounts for a greater share of GDP (24.2% in 1989 versus 12.3% mining and 5.8% agriculture: van Heerden, 1991: 11), mining exports bring in approximately 70% of South Africa's total export earnings. According to van Heerden (1991: 18), "Gold alone used to make up 40% of total merchandise export earnings, but its exports have slowly shrunk and it now accounts for about 33% of all export earnings — worth R19.2bn in 1989. Gold mines generated 53% of total mineral revenues in 1989."

However, to Ovenden and Cole, "South African gold is of increasing insignificance in the world economy" (1990: 6). This is due to a number of factors: (i) increasing costs due to deeper mines, higher wages, work stoppages, and lower yields (from 106 tonnes in 1970 to 681t in 1985 and 606t in 1989); (ii) grades are only 40% of their levels of 20 years ago; (iii) many other mines have been opened around the world, dropping South Africa's share of the non-communist world's gold production from a high of 79.1% in 1971 to 44.15% today; (iv) the price of gold has steadily declined since 1980 when it touched US $800/ounce to less than US $400/ounce; and therefore (v) gold has lost its unique role of hedge investment in times of crisis or inflation.

> It is obviously too early to write an epitaph for gold, but its lacklustre performance in recent years suggests that the nature of the world financial system has changed. A wider range of very stable, interest bearing financial instruments now exists, and institutional investors are consequently holding less and less of their funds in purely speculative commodities like gold (van Heerden, 1991).

These trends, should they continue into the longer term, suggest massive retrenchment of mineworkers, expatriate *and* South African, as many mines reach the end of their economic shelf-life.

Manufacturing

And whereas exports of coal, ferrochrome, manganese, vanadium, and platinum, but less so diamonds, "have improved strongly in recent years" the fact remains, these are all raw materials whose prices are subject to wide fluctuations. Given gold's central importance as a forex earner, and the unpredictability of other mineral export contributions, then manufacturing exports must increase if South Africa is going to be able to service its debt (the interest payments of which total approximately R4bn/year or 10% of export earnings: Shaw, 1991: 7) and maintain a surplus on the current account of its balance of payments.

But South Africa's manufacturing production is heavily import dependent, and the country cannot afford these imports if it is to be able to meet its debt commitments (van Heerden, 1991: 9).

According to Gelb, during the 1950s and 1960s, it was mineral wealth which made it possible to pay for the necessary machinery imports (*Weekly Mail*, 30 Mar - 4 Apr, 1990). While this growth model was successful for some 20 years (what he calls "racial fordism"), by the first oil shock, the long-term trend in South Africa's GNP had already been downward. According to Gelb,

> The result has been stagnation, declining investment and productivity growth. One index of this is the transformation of the South African economy from one where "super-exploitation" yielded "super-profits" to one increasingly being abandoned as a locus of operations by multinational corporations, foreign and South African, because of poor profitability prospects (*ibid*).

This situation was helped along by the onset of international sanctions and massive capital outflows following on domestic political unrest and events in the mid-1970s and again in the mid-1980s. Hermele and Oden estimate that circumventing international sanctions cost the *apartheid* Republic US $3 billion annually until the late-1980s: i.e. $1 billion each to circumvent oil blockade, arms embargo, and trade boycotts (1988: 25).

Solutions to these economic problems were sought in three directions: first, via the creation of a Southern African co-prosperity sphere, the Constellation of Southern African States (CONSAS); second, via production for export, i.e. the NIC option; and third, "inward industrialisation", or what some South African economists have labelled the "basic needs approach" to economic recovery (not to be confused with Basic Human Needs or BHN). As stated above, the CONSAS option became a dead letter with the creation of SADCC. Nevertheless, for van Heerden potential still exists with each of the other two options. One serious constraint to the NIC option, however, lies in a "continuing raw materials mentality in the South African mining industry that has restricted creative thinking about alternatives to traditional mineral and metal exports" (van Heerden, 1991: 16).

Inward industrialisation places heavy emphasis on the provision of low-cost housing. These houses, for which there is massive need, would be constructed with labour-intensive methods and so would stimulate manufacturing output without increasing imports and so adding to South Africa's debt burden. It would be a kind of "trickle-up" approach.

In many ways, the formation of the basic needs approach marked a desperate reaction to the dual crises of international debt (and therefore lack of investment capital and new money) and domestic unrest (i.e. appeasement through shelter) that peaked in the mid-1980s (McCarthy, 1988: 20). But inward industrialisation, like import substitution, is strewn with many pitfalls, especially at a time when the major trends in the global economy are toward aggressive export-orientation.

For at least one observer, South Africa's salvation may lie in a combination of these two strategies, with South Africa's export market being the African continent itself. For Rob Davies, "[t]he markets of Africa will be of considerable importance to a future democratic, non-racial South Africa's efforts to become a significant exporter of manufactured goods" (in the *Weekly Mail*, 30 Nov - 6 Dec, 1990). At present, Africa absorbs 10% of total South African exports but 32% of its manufactured exports (van Heerden, 1991: 24). Given the high value-added on end products, Africa, in the absence of sanctions, clearly holds great potential as a market for South African goods.

This, however, suggests a hardening of present neocolonial relationships; something likely to be less easily resisted by other African states in the absence of *apartheid* and in the presence of debt and Bank/Fund ultimatums, but hardly a development that would foster more equitable regional economic growth.

Financial Factors

De facto sanctions imposed by the international financial and corporate communities in response to heightening regional instability were fundamental in bringing about the present move toward constitutional reform, perhaps moreso than were the politically-motivated sanctions imposed, often haphazardly, by Western states both unilaterally and via international fora. One-fifth of all US-based MNCs divested or pulled out of South Africa altogether in the post-1985 period. More important, however, was capital flight. As testimony to the volatility and high-risk nature of the *apartheid* Republic, in spite of the Rand's free fall, South Africa remained a net exporter of capital throughout the latter half of the 1980s. By the end of 1988, South Africa's outstanding debt was US $20.6bn (or approximately 25% of GNP), down from $23bn in 1985, but in spite of having repaid $6bn between 1985-88. Inflation remains high (with the consumer price index at 15.3% in 1989 and 13.5% in 1990), government deficits hover around $5bn per year, security still gobbles up 20.2% of the government's budget (this in spite of a 10% cut in real terms in the defence budget; the balance going, instead, to internal security — van Heerden, 1991: 21), and the 1980s was the first decade in which South Africa's per capita GDP actually declined. According to Shaw (1991:8):

> In short, the *apartheid* economy is in structural crisis which liberalisation
> may exacerbate rather than resolve in part because of an inefficient and
> outdated manufacturing sector as well as moribund gold industry.

Conclusion: Prospects for Regional Integration

By focusing on the paramount nature of the regional economic crisis and its relationship to both historical patterns of inequality and more contemporary forms of conflict, there seems to be a fairly persuasive case toward rethinking the possibilities of (especially economic) integration in the region. Given the end of the Cold War and the gradual emergence of three massive trading blocs — all of which will likely exclude Sub-Saharan Africa (forcing the latter into de facto self-reliance) — it is incumbent upon political leaders and members of civil society to move beyond the limitations of state-centric concepts of security toward a reconception which rests on a new regionalism and novel forms of South-South cooperation and exchange, particularly at the regional and/or continental level. Standing in the way of such schemes, however, are the myriad destabilizing factors highlighted above: (i) the historical incorporation of the region into the global capitalist system and South Africa's dominant place therein; (ii) South African military aggression and its post-*apartheid* residuals in the region; and (iii) South(ern) Africa's increasing marginalisation in the new international divisions of labour and power, best symbolised by debt and structural adjustment. Taken together, these factors serve to divide rather than unite the region, to perpetuate neocolonial relations of production, and to enhance rather than alleviate regional inequalities and problems of economic underdevelopment. In short, they constitute a very weak base upon which to build a regional identity.

References

Africa Confidential, various issues.

Anglin, Douglas G. (1986), "SADCC in the Aftermath of the Nkomati Accord," in Ibrahim S.R. Msabaha & Timothy M. Shaw, eds., *Confrontation and Liberation in Southern Africa: regional directions after the Nkomati Accord*, (Boulder: Westview).

Barber, James & John Barratt (1990), *South Africa's Foreign Policy: the Search for Status and Security, 1945-1988*, (Cambridge: Cambridge University Press).

Bing, Adotey (1991), "Salim A. Salim on the OAU and the African Agenda," *Review of African Political Economy*, 50 (March): 60-69.

Bond, Patrick (1991), "Selling Structural Adjustment in South Africa," *Southern Africa Report*, (July): 18-21.

Bowman, Larry (1968), "The Subordinate State System of Southern Africa," *International Studies Quarterly*, 12:3.

Cobbe, James H. (1992), "Lesotho and the New South Africa: Economic Trends and Possible Futures," paper presented at the annual meeting of the African Studies Association, Seattle, November.

Grundy, Kenneth W. (1986), *The Militarization of South African Politics*, (Bloomington: Indiana University Press).

—— (1973), *Confrontation and Accommodation in Southern Africa*, (Oxford: Oxford Universit Press).

Hanlon, Joseph (1986), *Beggar Your Neighbours: apartheid power in Southern Africa*, (Bloomington: Indiana University Press).

Hermele, Kenneth, and Bertil Oden (1988), *Sanctions Dilemmas: some implications of economic sanctions against South Africa*, (Uppsala: SIAS).

Jackson, Robert H. (1992), "The Security Dilemma in Africa," in Brian L. Job, ed., *The Insecurity Dilemma: National Security of Third World States*, (Boulder: Lynne Rienner): 81-94.

Johnson, Phyllis and David Martin, eds. (1986), *Destructive Engagement: Southern Africa at War*, (Harare: Zimbabwe Publishing House).

Lewis, Stephen R. (1988), "Economic Realities in Southern Africa (or One hundred million futures)," in Coralie Bryant, ed., *Poverty, Policy and Food Security in Southern Africa*, (Boulder: Lynne Rienner).

Martin, William G. (1991), "What Prospects after Majority Rule?" *Review of African Political Economy*, 50 (March): 115-134.

McCarthy, C.L. (1988), "Structural Development of South African Manufacturing Industry: a policy perspective," *South African Journal of Economics*, 56:1 (March): 1-23.

Nkiwane, Solomon (1988), "Destabilisation in Southern Africa: a historical perspective," *Dalhousie African Working Paper*, No. 12, July.

Ovendon, Keith, and Tony Cole (1990), *Apartheid and International Finance: a programme for change*, (Ringwood, Victoria: Penguin).

SADCC (1991), *SADCC: Towards Economic Integration*, (Gaborone).

Saul, John S. (1991), "The End of the Cold War in Southern Africa," *Review of African Political Economy*, 50 (March): 145-157.

—— (1976), "The Unsteady State: Uganda, Obote and General Amin," *Review of African Political Economy*, 5 (January-April): 12-38.

Shaw, Timothy M. (1993), *Reformism and Revisionism in Africa's Political Economy in the 1990s: beyond structural adjustment*, (London: Macmillan).

—— (1991), "South and Southern Africa in the New International Division of Labour: prospects for the 1990s," in Larry A. Swatuk & Timothy M. Shaw, eds., *Prospects for Peace and Development in Southern Africa in the 1990s: Canadian and Comparative Perspectives*, (Lanham: UPA): 3-25.

—— (1988), "Africa in the 1990s: from economic crisis to structural readjustment," *Dalhousie Review*, 68:1 (Spring/Summer): 37-69.

—— (1977), "Kenya and South Africa: 'sub-imperialist' states," *Orbis*, 21:2 (Summer): 375-394.

——, and Larry A. Swatuk (1993), "Third World Political Economy and Foreign Policy in the Post-Cold War Era: towards a revisionist framework with lessons from Africa," *Journal of Asian and African Affairs*, 5:1 (Fall): 1-20.

Stoneman, Colin (1991), "Future Economic Policies in South Africa and Their Effects on Employment: some lessons from Zimbabwe," paper prepared for presentation at the international conference on South Africa, Copenhagen, 21-23 February.

——, and Justin Hutchence (1991), "SADCC: Coordination of Industry and Trade — Can it Work?" draft paper for AWEPAA, April.

——, and Carol B. Thompson (1991), *Southern Africa after apartheid: economic repercussions of a free South Africa*, (Africa Recovery Briefing Paper, No. 4, December).

Stubbs, Richard (1994), "Malaysia and Thailand: models for economic development at the margins?" in Larry A. Swatuk & Timothy M. Shaw, eds., *The South at the End of the Twentieth Century*.

Swatuk, Larry A. (1988), *Security Through Development? Toward an Assessment of SADCC*, Dalhousie African Working Paper, No. 11, July.

——, and Timothy M. Shaw, eds. (1994), *The South at the End of the Twentieth Century: Rethinking the Political Economy of Foreign Policy in Africa, Asia, the Caribbean and Latin America*, (London: Macmillan).

UNCTAD (1990), *Handbook of International Trade 1990*, (New York).

Van Heerden, Auret (1991), *Issues and Trends in South Africa's Economy*, (ILO: Geneva), unpublished.

Weekly Mail (Johannesburg), various.

Weisfelder, Richard F. (1991), "Collective Foreign Policy Decision-Making within SADCC: Do Regional Objectives Alter National Policy?" *Africa Today*, 38:1, 5-17.

World Bank (1989), *Sub-Saharan Africa: From Crisis to Sustainable Growth*, (Washington).

Endnote

Reprinted from: *Journal of the Third World Spectrum*, Volume 1, Number 1, 1994, by permission of the author and the *Journal of the Third World Spectrum*, Washington, D.C.

1. Angola, Botswana, Lesotho, Malawi, Mozambique, Swaziland, Tanzania, Zambia and Zimbabwe. Namibia has since become the 10th member.

Chapter VI

Colonialism and the Integration of the Gambian Ethnic Groups

Dr. Sulayman Nyang

Historical Origins of the Ethnic Configuration

The Gambia's geographical characteristics have for several centuries made it a favorable location for human groups searching for a fertile and habitable agricultural area. The navigability of the river has always made it possible for immigrants to chart their way from one end of the river valley to the other. The sources of the Gambia river penetrated the slopes of the Futa Jalloin, near those of the Senegal, in an area associated with the Western Sudan, the terminus of trade routes, and the fulcrum of the fourteenth century empire of Mali.

Because of this favorable location of the Gambia, most of the immigrants into the country came from the north across the Senegambian plateau, from the east, and from the southeast where the northern savannah curves across the valley. And of course many of these foreign peoples flocked to the Gambia river valley immediately after long distance trade and communications were established by the expanding Ghana empire.

Many factors must have given rise to this massive influx of alien peoples into the Gambia river valley. Perhaps, like many of those fifteenth century Europeans fleeing away from turbulent Europe to America, most of these newcomers found in the Gambia a heaven where they could start a new life away from their troubled homelands. Besides this question of personal and political safety, there were also some other considerations. Many of these individuals seized upon the economic opportunities in the river valley. As a result of this foreign intrusion the Gambia soon attracted trade moving between the interior of the Sudan and the sea.

Before the Europeans reached the Gambia river, the area at the river's mouth was already flourishing as a trading center. Among the many products sold and exchanged by the traders were salt, corn and other items essential to a subsistence economy of the time. Most of the trading, however, was centered on salt which was refined from the brackish water in calabashes exposed to the sun.[1] This product was transported by canoe as far as Barrakunda Falls and from there on asses overland to the east. By the year 1620, as many as three hundred asses were reported carrying corn, hides, ivory, and ornaments of brass of British origin which had crossed the Sahara to river ports below the Falls.[2]

During the eighteenth century the trade in salt and other essentials became less and less significant. Two reasons accounted for the decline. First, there was the fact that the Songhoi empire, the last of the great West African empires, had collapsed and with it the profitable trade in Gambian salt. Second, the great growth of the slave trade was already over-shadowing the salt trade. In fact, here one can make the sad commentary that whereas formerly salt was sold to sustain the lives of the people in the interior, at this time in Gambian history, human lives were the objects of trade. Indeed, the same Bambara, Serahuli, and Mande-Dioula traders who made money on the salt trade were now the peddlers of human cargoes. They sold these slaves in exchange for manufactured goods, arms and ammunition, iron ware, tobacco, alcohol and cloth. The slaves were transshipped from saloumnniumi or Bintans Foni to James Island or Albreda, the principal European stations and from there across the ocean.[3]

The slave trade was a very lucrative business for the Mandinka kingdoms. Francis Moore tells us that many of these slaves were Bumbrongs and Petcharies peoples who spoke different tongues from the Mandinka. Besides these alien slaves, there were many others brought along the river. These were most often prisoners of war, or else men condemned for crimes, or else people stolen, which was very frequent. Since the slave trade began, all punishments were changed into slavery. Not only murder, theft and adultery are punished by selling the criminal for a slave, but every trifling crime was punished in the same manner.[4]

Francis Moore also tells us about a story of a man who was brought to him for sale in Tomany. The only crime this defenseless man committed was the theft of a tobacco-pipe. In fact, had Moore failed to intervene, the poor man was doomed to languish in the chains of slavery somewhere in the Americas. Preposterous cases like this one revealed the depravity of the slavers and their African agents.

However, the trade continued and it went on so well for the merchants that at the end of the eighteenth century as many as 3,700 human beings were exported a year at a price (to the African trader) of around F20 for healthy young men.[5] Because of the quest for easy money and other creature comforts, the political elites of the Gambian states reluctantly acknowledged the British termination of their coveted trade.

The British "abolished" the slave trade in 1807, although French and other European and American slavers continued to operate illegally in areas where British surveillance was weakest. But with the establishment of a strong task force in Bathurst in 1817, these illegal activities gradually came to a halt. The abolition of the trade, however, did not brighten the economic horizon of the Gambian states. To compensate for the loss of revenues, the British spent the next forty years searching for a respectable substitute.

In the early period of the European exploration, the Gambia was reported to be the land of gold; but as we now know such were the tales of European adventurers whose need for home support led them to such exaggeration of the Gambian realities. The Gambian peoples grew rice, millet, maize and coos. The rice was planted in fresh water swamps in the river valley, chiefly in the region midway between the Falls and the sea beyond the tidal flow.

The Gambian pasturage attracted many nomadic groups, and by the eighteenth century these peoples have established themselves in almost every part of the Gambia river. In their new locations, they sold milk and other cattle products. Many ofthese pastorialists (Fulahs) worked for the sedentary populations. Most members o the settled populations had large herds, but their cattle were generally used as a mark of wealth and status and rarely used for meat.[6] But though the Gambian peoples grew many varieties of stable food, their food provisions were always limited, particularly during the rainy season (later called the "hungry season") when little or no food was available to the rural areas. There were several reasons for this hungry season. Among these were poor cultivation techniques, climatic uncertainties and poor economics. The only cash product, after the end of the slave trade, was beeswax. In 1817, it represented nine-tenths of the total value of all the exports. In that year, besides beeswax, the only major item export was hide. There were other minor items like gold, gum and ivory, all of which were brought from areas beyond the Barrakunda Falls.[7]

However, the economic situation began to improve following the creation of marketing facilities for groundnuts. This product was brought to the Gambia from Brazil by the Portuguese.[8] The sandy soil of the dry savannah bushland on the plateau flanking the river valley was found suitable for the cultivation of this product. Though the groundnut was known to the Gambian peoples for almost a century, nothing was done to cultivate it in significant quantity. But by 1830 the product became one of the items on the export list.[9] Although the British colonial regime did not enthusiastically campaign for the widespread cultivation of the product, the Gambian farmers, in search of an alternate source of income, continued to produce large quantities. By 1850, the total number of tons exported from the Gambia exceeded 8,000 and the Gambian farmers were already receiving outside help in the cultivation of this crop.[10] The newcomers generally known as "strange farms" were mainly men from the neighboring countries who spent a year or two in the Gambia where they hired land from the various chiefs.[11] Thus the population of the river states, though long settled in many areas, was highly heterogeneous. At this juncture, one can point to the rapid transforma-tion of the human configuration in the Gambia river valley. Whereas in 1455 when European visits to this part of Africa had just begun, Alvise de Cadamiosto, the Venetian explorer commissioned by Portugal, could maintain on his first voyage that the river served as a definite dividing line in the movement of the races in Africa,[12] the observers of the eighteenth and nineteenth century Gambia could hardly say such a thing. The Tawney Moors whom Cadamosto met on the north bank seemed to have been driven northwards by the Songhai empire,[13] and their abandoned territory came under the jurisdiction of the Wolofs and Mandinka.

The Mandingo Migration

When the Mali empire was a flourishing civilization in the thirteenth century, many of her Mande-speaking inhabitants started to leave their traditional home (Manding) for the peripheral parts of the empire. The salt trade which linked the Gambia and the interior brought many merchants but the bulk of the Mandinkas who came as a result of the empire's expansion,[14] wanted to settle permanently.

These Mandinkas spread from the area of the Falleme river to the sea, over-running the peoples settled between the Casamance and the Gambia.[15] The two groups who were the indigenous inhabitants prior to the Mandinka intrusion were the Jolahs and the Sereres moved north under this pressure, across towards the Senegal.[16]

Mandinka tradition has it that when their people settled in the Gambia, the emperor appointed vassal kings or governs over these outlying areas.[17] Though we do not know exactly how long it took the Mandinkas to finish their conquest of the areas they now occupy, we do have certain historical accounts which are helpful. Between 1457 and 1460, when Diego Gomez visited the Senegambian area, he was told by Wolofs at the Gambia that the Bur Mali controlled all the interior.[18] Earlier, Cadamiosto reported that, when he sailed forty miles up the Gambia river and succeeded in establishing contact with one Battimansa, the local inhabitants told him that the Battimansa was under Forofangoli, who was the chief lord of the South Bank. This Forofangoli was a tributary to the King of Mali.[19] This same fact was reported by Jobson in 1920 when he wrote that the Mandingo "were the lords and commanders" of all Gambia.[20]

Mandinkas and their Neighbors

The relationship between the Mandinka and the other tribes is the chief variable in this case. This is due to the fact that the Mandinka is the largest group in the Gambia. The relations between Mandinkas and the other peoples of the Gambia were at best coexistential and at worst conflictive. In the early days there might have been certain villages which could claim to be wholly Mandinka; but even this is doubtful, judging from the fact that on their way to the Gambia, the Mandinkas must have enslaved some Bassaris, Patcharis and Konyajis to serve them in their new habitat. But even without these alien slaves in their midst, the Mandinkas had to coexist with these tribes, which formerly owned the land. Their relations with the Jolas had been a long story of bitterness, although it appears that by the time Moore's visit to the Gambia, the Mandinkas had overrun Foni and to a certain extent, had subjected the Jolas there.[21] The whole relationship seems to be an admixture of love and hate. There were times in the past when jolas looked up to the Mandinkas for leadership; but these instances were often followed by open rebellion.

The Mandinka-Jola relationship was based on a changing community of interests. There were times when Mandinkas and Jolas shared certain interests, particularly those relating to trade with the Europeans. For example, in 1722, when Glynne, an English employee of the African company, wanted to extend his commercial activities in Jola country, he had to consult the King of Barra who was hostile towards the Jolas. The British wanted him to "make peace with the Floops (Jolas)" or to allow them to use the port on the South bank for trade. The King of Barra who was not pleased about the whole matter simply stated the following: (1) If the British developed commercial ties with the Floops (Jolas), he would not be against it. (2) But this consent did not mean the complete cessation of hostilities against the Jolas.[22]

Actually, the Jolas and Mandinkas had a different community of sentiments, and that even their common interests against the Europeans could not be early harmonized. The Jolas, it seems to me, were very defensive about their territory and freedom and even though they were traditionally less centralized politically than their Mandinka neighbors, they did not wish to subdued totally by them. Further- more, the fact that the Europeans were not always united in their dealings with these African peoples made it difficult for the Jolas and the Mandinkas to come to terms. As a result, they soon found themselves on opposite sides--each supporting one of the competing European forces. This state of affairs in the Gambia river area resembles the present-day ideological wrangle between the big powers who are now trying to recruit clients in Africa. The only difference between the two periods is that formerly the competitors fought over markets, but today they struggle over minds and markets.

The partisanship of the Jolas and the Mandinkas was very evident in the 1780's when the British and French fought bitterly over who should control Senegambia. At this time in Gambian history, the French banked heavily on the support of the King of Barra and his people. The Mandinkas of Barra made it very difficult for the British traders to operate. For example, in 1778 they attacked and destroyed the British factories and carried off the merchandise left behind by the fleeing British.[23] The French gladly welcomed these developments, for they stood to profit from the British disaster. To crown the "good work" of the Barra people, the French sent their fleet of Corvettes to raze James Island and to take possession of any British vessels and factories in the Gambia.

While the British suffered depredations from the French and the Barra people, they received succor and friendship from the Jolas of Foni. The most striking case was in October, 1780, when Captain Daniel Haughton was chased by the French Frigate Senegal under the command of Monsieur Allery. The leader of the Jolas (described as "emperor" in the writings of the time) mobilized 400 of his people to drive back the advancing French. In the ensuing struggle which lasted for three nights, the French lost five men and the Jolas four. Eventually, the French gave up the pursuit and left.[24]

Again, in 1794, when the British found themselves in serious distress, they turned to the Jolas. And it was the protection given to the British by the Jolas that led Mungo Park to write: "during the present war they have more than once taken up arms to defend our vessels from French privateers; and English property of considerable value has frequently been left at Vintain (meaning Bintang) for a long time entirely under the care of the Feloops (Jolas)".[25]

After citing the examples of events which put the Mandinkas of Barra and the Jolas of Foni on two antipodal positions, I now continue to examine the relations between these two Gambian peoples. We have already seen that the Mandinkas to some extent had subjugated the Jolas, but that the allegiance of the conquered was for the most part nominal. Such reference as is made to the Jola-Mandinka relation-ship in the correspondence of the servants of the Royal African Company and the later Government officials of the Senegambia shows that in the late seventeenth and early eighteenth century, the Jolas were giving their conquerors a good deal of trouble. But what made it more difficult for the Jolas was the fact that they themselves were badly divided, and their nominal chiefs had to keep the peace before they could mobilize themselves against their Mandinka neighbors.

Mandinka-Jola relations stabilized for sometime; but when the Soninke-Marabout War[26] broke out, the Jolas, whose religious practices were repulsive to the Mandinka Marabouts, found themselves the objects of derision and coercion. The Mandinka Marabouts together with some Islamized Jolas stormed Foni. Many Jolas lost their lives because of their resistance to the crusaders. Today Kabba, a leading Marabout on the South Bank, tried many times to cow the Jolas into submission; but the Jolas persistently fought him out of their territory.[27]

In commenting on the Soninke-Marabout War and its implications for Mandinka-Jola relationship, it should be pointed out that the War did not take on ethnic character entirely. On the contrary: many, if not all, Soninke rulers who fought the Mandinka tribe. In fact, much of the fighting that occurred was between Serahulis, Sereres and Jolas who had little concern for the religious differences between the two parties, but were primarily interested in selling their services as mercenaries to the highest bidder.[28]

What makes the conflict a serious matter for the Jolas was the fact that they were the targets of politically ambitious men, who dared to justify their ambitions in the name of Islam. Forgetting the Quranic dictum: "Lakum dini kum waliyadin" - hold on to your religion, I will to mine - some of these Muslim crusaders disguised their political ambitions in Islamic slogans.[29] Rather than fight a jihad in defence of Islam, they sought political Kingdoms in the most depraved and venal manner. Foday Kabba could be lauded for his stand against the British and French colonization of his homeland; but one cannot commend such a man for his atrocities against the Jolas. It was reported that Foday Kabba organized some kidnapping of Jola women working in rice fields in Foni. These victims were conveyed by certain recognized "underground railroads" to the north bank of the river, where they were ferried over to Baddibu and battered for cattle, guns and ammunition.[30]

Again, after talking so much about Jola-Mandinka relations, we should say that though the Jolas fought strenuously against their Mandinka neighbors both before and during the Soninke-Marabout War, they gradually assimilated the Mandinkas; or where Mandingo gains had been consolidated, they (the Jolas) were assimilated.[31] Of course, the Mandinkas' organizational skills enabled them to wield great power among the Jolas, and the British must have sensed this when in 1894, they appointed a Mandinka agent over the Jolas. This was done to exercise more or less direct colonial control over Brefet and Baijani in Foni where the Jolas lived in small and scattered villages, had no chiefs and had not proved tractable.[32] With the help of Mandinkas agent, the British officials in Bathurst incorporated these two districts as parts of the Protectorate in the following year.

Today, the Jolas living together in the same villages. In fact, many of those who speak Mandinka in the South bank are of Jola origin who now happen to live in predominantly Mandinka areas.[33] The social, economic and political forces unleashed by the colonial era have partially created a limited community of interests between the two groups. Their new solidarity is manifested more clearly in the Gambian political arena, for since the emergence of party politics, Foni has remained a P.P.P. stronghold.[34]

Another Gambian group with which the Mandinkas had long contact is the Fulah. Fulahs-Mandinka relationship goes back long before the migration of the two groups into the Gambia. At the height of the Mali empire, the Fulahs were subjected to Mandinkas domination. This domination continued in the Gambia even after the Fulahas rebelled against their rulers in the Futa Jalloin area.

The first mention of the Fulah in Western colonial literature came from the Portuguese in Senegal. The Portuguese came in contact with this group from the Futa Jaloin south of the Gambia in the fifteenth century. Many years after this, a band of Fulahs, under an ardo (leader) named Kili Tenguela crossed the Gambia and
crossed Mandinka territories in Bondu and established the Denianke dynasty in the Futa Toro which ruled for about three centuries.[35] This migration is remembered as an exodus. It is said that the army of this Fulah general was so large that the streams which it passed were drunk dry by the men and their horses and cattle.[36]

The Fulahs conquered Bondu, but they failed to extend their sway over the Mandinkas in the Gambia river valley. And because of this, the Mandinkas continued to dominate the Fulahs who migrated into their territory. Their domination was described by Jobson in 1623, when he wrote that "the Fulahs lived in great subjection to the Mandinkas.[37] But this domination did not put a check on the flow of Fulahs into the Gambia.

By the eighteenth century the Fulahs were everywhere in the country.[38] In the 1850s, their concentration was heaviest in Wuli, Niani, Baddibu and the south districts of Kantora, Tomani and Jimara.[39] Two reasons accounted for this massive concentrations of the Fulah n these areas. First, the new waves of Fulahs that migrated into the Gambia early in the nineteenth century were of a very different metal. These were from Bondu, Futa Jallon and Futa Toro; and it should be remembered that these Fulahs had already sloughed off the yoke of Mandinka domina-tion in their place of origin.[40] Second, the Fulah states bordering the Mandinka states in the upper river area were now organized the disturb the peace. By the middle of the nineteenth century, the Fulahs had formed a powerful confederacy, and annually a force of several thousand men was sent to raid the Mandinka settle-ments.[41] The leaders of this confederation were Bakari Sardu, the ruler of Bondu, Sori or Alfa Ibrahima, the ruler of Futa Jallon, and a warrior chief Alfa Moloh.

Bakari Sardu received French education and because of his fidelity to the French, was awarded the Legion of Honor.[42] He was a man of considerable ability, but the British disliked him because he considered it necessary to give his people some outlet for their bellicosity and therefore encouraged raids into the British sphere of influence.

Alfa Molloh led a group or Rulahs from Kasonko in the Sudan and had settled in the Mandinka country, which lay between the Gambia and the Casamance. His original name had been Mozzo Egue and his original occupation that of elephant hunter. Detractors of the Molloh family made the insinuations that Alfa was once the slave of a Mandinka chief. But whatever the case may be, we now know that in 1867, Alfa led the Fulahs in revolt against the ruling Mandinkas. In that year, he defeated Lekuta Sona, the leading Mankingo chief, in a fight near the Senegalese village of Kolda. After this victory, he changed his name to Alfa Molloh.[43]

With the support of the kings of Futa and Bondu and also that of his own son, Momodou Salif, Alfa Molloh gradually made himself during the course of the next few years the supreme in the districts of Jimara, Tomni, Eropina, Pata, Kariako, Yega and Jambuntan. After the death of Alfa Molloh, his son, Musa, took over. Musa led many raids against the Mandinkas; and the areas abandoned by the fleeing Mandinkas became the settlements of the Fulahs. Today, this whole area is called Fulladu. Musa's triumph was quite unprecedented, although he failed to dominate Kantora, and his army faced tremendous resistance from the Niamina, Kiang and Foni peoples.

The Fullahs were able to defeat the Mandinkas because they had good horses and their mobility was great, and it was always difficult to forecast the direction of their operations. The Serahulis and Mandinkas occupying these areas were helpless because their troops were quite ineffective. Moreover, there were feelings of enmity among these invaded peoples, and the lack of confidence and jealousy among their leaders foolishly prevented them from joining forces and thoroughly routing these Fulah marauders.[44]

The victory of Fulahs over the Mandinkas and Serahulis enhanced the prestige among the Gambian ethnic groups. Many myths and tales about the bravery of the Fulah began to circulate throughout the country. One may even suspect that the myth of Fulah invincibility was deliberately circulated by the Fulahs to instill fear among the vanquished Mandinkas.

However, in 1855, an incident took place in Kataba. The Mandinkas decided to attack several thousand Futa Fulahs who had shut themselves up on the strongly stockaded town of Suraja. Among the Fulahs was their leader Bakary Koi, as well as Omera Katu. These two leaders gave a great deal of trouble to the British and their ally, the Mandinka king of Kataba. The king of Kataba was fighting a bitter enemy, Keluntang. He needed British support to trash this formidable foe into submission; but while he was seeking British support, Keluntang was recruiting Bambara and Fulah mercenaries.[45]

Apparently, these Fulahs supported Kenintang and for this reason, they were stormed by the Mandinkas of Suraja. The sweeping victory of the Mandinkas destroyed the vestige of the Futah Fulahs who had hitherto been considered invin-cible. This defeat was welcomed by the British colonial officials who thought that "few events could at that period have occurred so opportunely for the interest of the Gambia."[46]

In talking about the relations between the Fulahs and the Mandinkas, it would be helpful to examine closely the Fulah community itself. The Fula speak dialect of the West Atlantic group of languages. Nine dialects have been identified, reflecting different areas of origin, periods of arrival and considerable cultural diversity with-in the Fulah population as a whole.[47]

It was the Jawaranko, the Torodo and the Futangke that were the main challenges to the Mandinkas. Throughout the nineteenth century, the Jawaranko, as they were called by the Mandinkas, pushed into Tomani and Jimara districts. Today, these segments of the Fulah community constitute the largest Fula group in the Gambia, numbering some 30,000.[48]

The Torodo or Tawranka from Futu Toro came to Wuli, Niani, Baddibu and the south districts during the early part of the nineteenth century. These Fulahs under their leader Maka Cisse settled chiefly in eastern Niani, where they received lands with the permission of the Mandinka chief of Sandugu district, at Niankoui near the mouth of a large creek where they were joined by others from the Futa. The success of these Fulahs in Sandugu brought another batch of Torodo under the leadership of Ousman-Celli. The Fulahs soon asserted their freedom once it became clear to them that their Mandinka hosts were being divided. The occasion came when one Mody Fatouma, a royal slave of the deceased Mandinka chief of Sandugu, usurped power from the king's brother who was still a child.[49]

The other branches of the Fulah tribe included the Futangke, the Habobo, the Hammanabi, Jombonko, Jawando, Lorob and the Laube. The Futangke group has been discussed earlier in our accounts of the Fulah raids of Mandinka settlements in the upper river. The Laube, however, was an itinerant woodworking caste group who attached themselves to communities throughout the Gambia of all ethnic back-grounds.[50] The Lorobo were the pasteralists from Bondu. Most of these Fulahs were always reluctant to give their services to the settled populations.

During the slave trade, very few Fulahs were sold into slavery. Many of those who found themselves in the hands of slavers int he Americas were either criminals or kidnapped individuals. A good illustration of the latter case was (Ayub Ibn Sulaiman Diallo) Job Ben Solomon.[51] This young Fulah Prince, whose real name, according to J.M

Gray, was Job Jallo (should read as Ayub Ibn Sulayman Jallow). He was kidnapped by some Mandinkas on the banks of the Gambia near Joar and sold as a slave to a private trader who carried him to Maryland.[52] He was a Muslim, and during his captivity his devout observance of the rites of his religion attracted attention of a number of benevolent Marylanders. Eventually, through the good offices of General Oglethorpe he was released.[53] Job was fluent in Arabic and his mastery of this language became a useful asset. Following his release, Job went to England where he received British education before sailing for Bondu.

A Mandinka-speaking Fula named Lahamin Jay (Lamin Jaye) has been kidnapped and carried to Maryland with Job. After Job obtained his freedom he wrote to the Duke of Montagu asking him to procure the release of his friend. This was done and Lahamin (Lamin) was sent back by the African Company in 1738. Besides these two, there was another notable case--that of Abdul Rahman who was ransomed and sent to Liberia in 1838, after having been a slave in the U.S. for over forty years.[54] Rev. Wilson, an American missionary in Africa, reported that in 1856 there was yet another 85 year-old Fulah called Moro who was living in Wilmington, North Carolina. He was given the opportunity to return to his country, but was averse to returning. Moro was most likely a criminal who was sold into slavery rather than put to death; and his refusal to return indicated his previous criminal life in Africa.

The example of Job was given to show the bitterness and chaos that pervaded in the upper reaches of the Gambia river. Actually, Job's father warned him not to cross the river; but being a curious fellow, he disobeyed only to find himself a slave in the U.S. In fact the story of Job reveals a big contradiction: This young man who had sold many slaves from Futa Toro to Captain Pyke of the Arabella, was himself caught by Mankinkas in Jarra, and sold to the same captain.[55] Some colonial historians considered it a retributive justice that was not fully meted out.[56]

Today, Mandinka-Fulah relations, however, are relatively peaceful. The pastoral Fulahs still offer their services to the Mankinkas who own cattle. Fulahs are slowly but surely intermarrying with their neighbours, although not to any great extent.[57] But the evidence of integration is shown by the fact that many Gambians claiming Fulah ancestry are as dark in complexion as many other members of the society. In concluding this part of the discussion, it should be pointed out that the degree of cooperation between the Fulahs and Mandinkas has increased lately, especially after many Fulah political leaders joined in the mid-1960s what was originally-heavily Mandinkas party, is the P.P.P. We will examine this point later on in this paper.

Mandinka-Wolof Relations

This major group with which the Mandinka has some political difficulties in recent years is the Wolof. The relationship between these two groups has a long history and we shoul now try to document it. According to Sabatie the Wolofs once occupied the greater part of Futa (i.e., Futa Toro) and a vast territory on the north bank of the lower Senegal. Kayor was at that time occupied by Mandinka and Serere. The Fulah invasion, Sabatie continues, drove the Wolof westwards, while the Berber and Arab invasion drove those in Gandar (Mauretania) towards the south, presumably in the fourteenth and fifteenth centuries. These retreating Wolofs drove the Sereres and the Mandinkas (Soseh) towards the Gambia and took possession of the territory they occupy today.[58]

Whether Sabatie's contention is true or not, one thing is quite clear: that is, when the Portuguese first visited the Senegambia area, they learnt from the people that the Wolof assumed control over the whole country between the Gambia and the Senegal rivers.[59] Moore reported that all the towns of the north bank paid tribute to the ruler of Saloum, a state lying along the north frontiers of Niumi Baddibu and Bar Sally.

When J.B. Durand, a former Governor of St. Louis, reported in 1806, that eight kingdoms existed on each bank of the Gambia river and that Fogny (Foni) and Barra were the most important of all these small and petty kingdoms, he reported incorrectly; for as the Gambian Historian Dr. Florence Mahoney argues, and quite correctly, the powerful kingdoms in the river were not really Barra and Foigny, as Durand believed, but the interior kingdoms of Wuli (the most easterly state in the north), Kantora (situated opposite on the south bank), and Saloum in the middle river.[60] In fact, Jobson reported that there was a general belief in the 1600s that if the King of Saloum could find the means to transport his horses across the Gambia river, the whole south bank would have been taken over by the Wolofs from the north.

But, whatever immigration routes the Wolofs might have followed into Gambia, the point that seems to be historically significant here, at least in terms of our discussion of Wolof-Mandinka relations, is that the first Mandinkas to reach the Niumi area had to deal with the Wolof kings to the north. According to some of the traditions of the royal Mandinka families of the Niumi area, the Jamehs were the first Mandinka group to set foot in this part of the Gambia. Upon their arrival they fixed their capital at Bakendik and from there segments of the family left to establish new settlements in the surrounding areas.[61]

As soon as the Mandinkas built up their villages the Wolof rulers to the north forced them to pay tributes. The Jammehs accepted this vassal status, knowing fully well that their limited numbers put them at a terrible disadvantage. However, after sometime another batch of Mandinkas joined the Jammehs in Niumi. This group was the Mannehs who originated from Kabu. Tradition now says that the Mannehs came ostensibly to help the Jammehs throw off the yoke of Wolof domination. This act of liberation proved abortive, but the defeat did not drive the Mandinkas away. The Mannehs settled at Kanuma and latter at Bunyadu.[62]

Later still a family called Sonko, which now claims Fula origins, migrated from the east and settled near the border of Salum in a town call Bankiri. In Mandinka, this term means "by force" and the Sonkos perhaps put up this act of gallantry in the hope of impressing the Wolof rulers of Saloum. But being terribly outnumbered and being new comers in a strange land, the Sonkos had to compromise; for if their quest for liberation was too assertive, their Wolof hosts would undoubtedly have thrashed them into

,ubmission. At first they served the King of Saloum as tax collectors in the Wolof and ,erere communities around them.[63]

Eventually, they had three showdowns with their Wolof overloads, and according to ,onko tradition, all three battles resulted in their favor. Neverthe-less, they moved south o the banks of the Gambia where the Mannehs and Jammehs still sought ways of liberating hemselves from Wolof domination. This attempt at liberation from Wolof subjugation ;radually yielded fruits. The three Mandinka families which led their contingents into Niumi soon spread out to Jokadu and Baddibu. But before the dispersal, a power struggle among these Mandinka families took place. The Sonkos defeated the Jammehs and Mannehs. The reason for the struggle was that the latter went back on their word concerning he parcelling out of land following the campaign against Wolof rule. And according to radition, the Jammehs and Mannehs moved to Jokadu and Baddibu where they are still mportant. The Sonko, on the other hand, settled at Berending, then at Essau and Jiffet.

But even though these Mandinka ruling families tried to slough off the yoke of outside Jomination, they did not succeed completely until sometime in the eigh-teenth century. [n fact, one hundred and forty years ago, most if not all of the north bank states, even Wuli, paid tribute to Saloum. Every year they despatched messengers with grasses and ;rains for the Bur Salum (King of Salum at Kahore).[64] [he Mandinka states in Niumi, Jokadu and Baddibu managed to loosen the grip of their Salem overloads, and by 1850 only Barsally was really subjugated by Saloum.

The Mandinka kingdoms tried throughout the nineteenth century to curb Wolof interference in their domestic affairs. To a large extent this handsoff policy worked out well,[65] except "in 1860, when a certain Hama Bah (commonly called Mabah), who had been formerly a native trader, by degrees collected together a heterogeneous army and drove the Mandinkas from Baddibu."[66] The Sonninke-Marabout war which pitted Muslims against pagan Soninkees had devastating effects on the social and political structures of the Mandinkas.

After having discussed the historical encounter between the Wolof and Mandinka on the political level, I now attempt to examine the social and cultural links between these two branches of the Gambian people. In his excellent study of the Wolof of Senegambia, Dr. Gamble reported that Joire believed in the Serere more or less mixed with foreign elements, Mauritanian, Fulbe, Mandinka, Serahuli and Bambara.[67] This is an extreme view, and the author must have been led to such a conclusion because of the fact that there are many Wolof with many surnames belong-ing particularly to certain ethnic groups.[68]

Another point of importance in the discussion of Mandinka Wolof relations is the theory that the Gelawar, who became the rulers of Sine-Saloum, were of Mandinka origin. The theory contends that the Gelawars were Mandinkas; but being submerged in Wolof culture, they gradually became Wolofized.[69] Whether this theory is valid remains a moot point. But one thing certainly remains undisputable, that is, the mutual influence between these two cultural groups. Although there are minor differences in agricultural styles between Wolof farmers and their Mandinka counterparts, it is arguable that Wolofs borrowed groundnut and rice techniques from the Mandinkas and Serahulis. There is also a great deal of similarities between the social systems of the Wolof and the Mandinkas. In both systems, a somewhat rigid form of caste differentialtion exists, and up to the present time Wolofs and Mandinkas differentiate between the peoples of high castes and low castes.

The Mandinkas and the Wolofs have been forced by history and geography to deal with one another. And Islam, as one of the agents of history, has contributed tremendously in the development of the relations between these two subgroups of the Gambian state. Islam gives the same sets of beliefs, similar dress, etiquette and religious customs, etc. to Mandinka, Fulah, Serahuli and Wolof alike. Many Wolofs techniques, smithing, leather-work, weaving, etc., have no seriously specific character about them. Even in the customs of marriage, naming and circumcision there are extremely close parallel to Mandinka and Fulah custom.[70]

Trade between the Mandinka and the Wolof states went through three different phases, namely, the pre-colonial, colonial and late colonial. During the pre-colonial phrase, the articles of trade were mainly salt and horses. The Wolof, it seems, compensated for their aversion to long distance travel by dealing heavily in the slat and fish trade. These articles of trade found on their coast formed a lucrative part of their business with the inland states.[71] During the course of their trade with the other Mandinka states, the Wolofs developed a medium of exchange called Pagns (cloth money).

This cloth-money was used for domestic as well as external trade. The Wolofs trades their payne (cloth) for gold from the Mandinka, Serahuli and Bambara traders.[72] They had weight measures made of iron called goro, each valued at its equivalent in African country cloths. The Wolofs also traded with Serahuli and Fulah traders who brought horses, cows, donkeys, and occasionally slaves to exchange for country cloth or grain.[73]

This pre-colonial trade between the Wolofs and the Mandinkas and other minor tribes was, however, sporadic and chiefly the concern of a few wealthy persons, war-like chieftains, powerful marabouts and the like.[74] The Mandinkas was keen about salt and dried fish; and the Wolof, who was particularly enamored with horses, saw no reason why this intertribal trade should not be maximized to the fullest. During the course of this fierce trading, coastal tribes, like the Sereres and Labous, came up the river in their canoes to barter dried fish and salt for American clothe and grain.

This pre-colonial trade benefitted most of the tribes; but the Jolahs became the victims of the unscrupulous profit seekers whose morality sunk so low that they cared little about the humanity of their own fellow tribesmen. The most disturbing aspect of this pre-colonial trade between the tribes was the fact that Wolof chiefs as well as their Mandinka counterparts obtained slaves from Jola traders by raiding neighbouring districts, especially the district of Foni.[75]

As a result of this intense trading between the tribes, a real mobility became more and more accepted. But at the same time, it should be emphasized that trade was still limited because of the inaccessibility of certain parts of the country. Also, because of the dangers of travelling, and of the taxes and customs imposed by the petty rulers of villages and kingdoms, many people found it dangerous and unwise to undertake long distances trading. The Serahulis were the chief exceptions in this case. This race of determined pilots of African trading caravans in the Senegambian area were never daunted by interstate wars.[76]

But even though the Serahuli's enthusiasm for trade was never dampened, the petty rulers who controlled the trade routes were very exacting in their collection of custom duties from the Serahulis.[77] So insistent on the observance of custom laws were the petty rulers of the Kingdoms along the Gambia river that non-conformist traders often wound up in their graves. Mungo Park found himself subjected to the same pressures when he travelled across the Gambia. His most distressing experience perhaps was the one that took place at Joaq, where the men of the King of Maana accused him of evading custom duties, and told him that his properties were considered the confiscated items of the King of Maana.[78]

The pre-colonial trade between the ethnic groups was significant but not very well developed. The Mandinkas who have for centuries constituted the largest group in the Gambia river valley played a significant role in it. The Wolof, on the other hand, participated in the flourishing trade mainly to buy horses and other essential products. The other tribes partook in the trade, but either because of their numbers of their interest in other matters, they did not contribute significantly as the Mandinkas, Wolofs and Serahulis. The first two were the holders of power and the last the business genius of the area.

The Serahulis were unique in their commercial and trading activities, and this tradition has persisted up to the present. The reasons for the success of the Serahuli traders could be traced to two things: first, the Serahulis, for one thing, were indefatigably dedicated to the accumulation of wealth by the pursuit of trade;[79] second, relating to, and as a result of their commercial and trading activities, the Serahulis-particularly successful traders among them-enjoyed and capitalized on the convenience of owning domestic slaves, who farmed for them in their absence.[80]

Furthermore, some of the traders were Marabouts or related to them. These men had free recourse through all places and even interstate wars did not deter them from travelling, for they were generally privileged travellers.[81]

The second phase in the intertribal trade, particularly between Mandinkas and Wolofs, began with the establishment of the town of Bathurst in 1816. In fact, when the British decided to strengthen their position in the Gambia by setting up a military post at Bathurst, many British traders in St. Louis and Goree, (Senegal) decided to move to this new island for greater security. These merchants did not spontaneously decide to try their luck in the Gambia. On the contrary, some were already actively engaged in the gum trade with the Trarza Moors; but most of them decided to quit Goree, because of the difficulties created by their French rivals and also because of the absences of any tangible evidence of effective protection from hostile forces. The British officials charged with the task of creating a colonial outpost in the Gambia offered free lots of land on the newly acquired island of St.

Marys (Barthurst),[82] to those merchants who would undertake to build "good, airy and substantial stone or brick houses within a given time.[83]

The British merchants and their señoras (African or Mulatto women who were the wives, or mistresses, or concubines of British traders) moved from Goree, Senegal to Bathurst, Gambia. This transfer of commercial activity involved a great deal of sacrifices on the part of some of these merchants. And indeed Dr. Mahoney was correct when she wrote that the transfer from Goree to Bathurst would not have been possible, had it not been for the señoras' willingness to accompany their European lovers.[84] These merchants and señoras brought with them many Wolof artisans and slaves who helped them in their new settlement.

This new immigration was destined to change the history of the Gambia; for with the señoras and their Wolof servants a new kind of economic system began to emerge. Soon the British merchants and their señoras were actively engaged in the trade of the island states. The Mulatto women served as binding force in the hetero-geneous society of Bathurst. On the top of the hierarchy was the European mercantile class whose stay in the Gambia was largely occasioned by the will to make money as quickly as possible. Sandwiched between the common Africans, who incidentally were attendants to the mercantile community, or refugees from the surrounding independent African Kingdoms, and this mercantile group was the señora and Mulatto community. The Señoras were linked to the British traders by romance and to the Africans (particularly the Wolofs) by ethnicity. It is even said today by many of the older generation of Gambian Wolofs in Bathurst that the señoras of former days did assimilate the European life styles, but they were similarly proud of their customs and beliefs of their Wolof ancestors.

Whether this was the case or not, one thing seems to be quite definite, that is, a new situation was developing. What seemed to have been taking place was the emergence of a mercantile community whose impact on Gambia's colonial politics was to be far reaching. The Wolof artisans were also beginning to evolve as the proleta-riats of this small community of Europeans, Mulattoes and Africans. By the 1830s, these Wolof mechanics and shipwrights were already building fine cutters and ships for the European and señora merchants. And while these Wolofs from Goree and St. Louis busied themselves in shipbuilding, their racially mixed cousins (mulattoes) travelled as sailors in search of goods in the many trading centers along the Senegal, Casamance, and Gambia rivers.

This new life for the former inhabitants of Goree and St. Louis grew out of the incipient groundnut trade. Actually, by the middle of the 1830s groundnut was beginning to appear in the Blue Books of the Gambia administration. Many Wolofs became traders and undoubtedly played important roles in the commercial development of the Gambia. A statement made in 1842 before the Select Committee on West Coast of Africa (paragraphs 808, 809, 8011) reveals that Wolofs operating out of the European trading center of Bathurst travelled up and down the rivers of the Senegambia in small trading vessels and canoes, selling European goods. Many of the up-country Wolofs, in turn, acted as middlemen in trade with people living in the interior. And, in this respect, the Wolof traders may well have been the primary agents of "Financial" acculturation.[85]

David Ames, in using the term "financial" acculturation, is indicating to us that with the intensification of trading actively in the Gambian hinterland and duet to the gradual elimination of the Payne (cloth money) from the Gambian market. This transformation took place partly because the groundnut brought thousands of "strange farmers" into the Gambia; and since these farmers were more impressed by the French currency than by the traditional payne, it soon became crystal clear to the British that a revolutionary change in the economy was occurring, and the best thing to do was to follow the tide. The British responded accordingly, and soon the various Gambian ethnic groups trading with the British became acquainted with European currency.

To bolster their position, the Europeans recruited Wolof and Mandinka traders (agents) to operate their business up-river. The agents had the reputation of being clever and industrious merchants.[86] They built small crafts for the river trade; and fishermen in the river or along the seacoast traded fish for commodities produced by the inland people. The Wolofs, Mandinkas and others tribal groups from the rural areas traded their groundnuts for musket and Kola nuts during the height of the Soninke-Marabout wars in the second half of the nineteenth century.[87]

Also, in the 1830s, efforts were made to recruit discharged soldiers to serve as agents transacting business. Most, if not all, of these soldiers were men who had previously been engaged in the services of the budding colonial administrator who was responsible for British interests in the area, felt that their services would pay many dividends; for they could serve as agents transacting business "with the native merchants of Africa, the Toocolors, Sera Woolies, and Mandinkas who trade in coffles backwards and forwards from the river to Sego, Bourie, Timbuktu."[88]

This new group of intermediaries became a class of its own and its member-ship was to swell in a matter of decade or two. The increase in number was due to the inflow of creoles from Sierra Leone to the Gambia.

The Creoles

The Creoles were destined to form a part of the African mercantile class, but this was to take place only after many years of suffering, frustration and toil. These men and women were brought to the Gambia colony because the governor thought that their presence would contribute to the general welfare of the emerging colony. Governor Randall saw the planting of such government "agents" in the midst of native tribes as the building of a bridge between the government and those tribes.[89]

The second objective of the British colonial regime was never realized, and if one looks at the wider perspective of Gambian history, one may well argue that the arrival of the creoles marked the beginnings of the rift which later came to be known as the Colony-Protectorate Problem. The fact that the Liberated Africans (Creoles) had no cultural affinity with the tribes inland put them at a serious disadvantage in their new roles as "agents" of the colonial government and the mercantile community. Most of the Liberated Africans were Akus, Congolese, Ibos, Mokos, Pappaios and Hausas,[90] and they had no intention of assimilating themselves to the local cultures of the inland tribes. Actually they could not do this for two reasons: first, most of them were anxious to breathe the air of freedom once again; and in the course of their self-rehabilitation, they were more proned to Christianity and Westernization than to the cultures of these inland tribes. Second, they just could not win the favors of the tribes.

Moreover, these Creoles had a great deal of difficulties adjusting to their new habitat. Having been liberated from the burdensome yoke of slavery, they found the challenges and responsibilities of freedom too demanding. In fact, many of those who set sail for the Gambia were not the best types of settlers. Many were sick and some were just plain criminals who were hastily disposed of by the authorities at Freedom, Sierra Leone.

It is only against this background that one can understand the psychology of the Creoles and their relations with the other Gambian tribes. In keeping the record straight, one may well say that when the Creoles first came to the Gambia life was quite deplorable; for facilities were inadequate and economic means terribly limited. To minimize the crisis tormenting them and to provide favorable alternatives, a system of apprenticeship was initiated. Some of the Creoles were apprenticed was mistresses, to some of the Wolofs and the discharged soldiers.[91]

Thomas Joiner, a prosperous Mandinka trader, employed nearly a hundred apprentices within a span of five years. The majority of his apprentices were put on his vessels trading up and down the river. Others were attached to carpenters, blacksmiths, wax-cleaners and lime-burners, the rest being employed as laborers and domestic servants.[92] These Creoles were taught the principles of Christianity, and useful personal, domestic services and the English language. In short, these apprentices were to be properly acculturated to live in a colonial society.

The relations between the Creoles and the Wolofs began to sour once the former started to emerge from the depths of their misery. In the first two or three decades of their sojourn in the Gambia, the Creoles had to play second fiddle to Señors and their Wolof retinue; but once an increasing number of them secured places in society, things began to change. The Christine Wolofs (Gurrmot) were much ahead of the Creoles, and it was in recognition of this fact that Madden Report (1841) argued that though some of the Creoles were employed "as mechanics, sailors and laborers . . . (they) are far behind the Joloffs and other natives of this part of Africa."[93] At this point in Gambia history, the Creoles were just beginning to uplift themselves from the quicksand of servitude to the solid rock of hope and fulfillment. And when Dr. Madden reported that Wolof children were sent to school while Creole Children were terribly neglected, no one who was familiar with the conditions of the Creole community would disagree.

But as I mentioned above, the Creoles were gradually building up their community, and through the help and guidance of the Wesleyan missionaries, many of them found their way out of the wilderness of illiteracy and ignorance. They learnt the three Rs and gradually established a society of proud men and women. With the passage of time, they became traders rubbing shoulders with their Wolof and Mandinka associates. There was, however, one thing which restricted their range of operation, that is, their alienness. The Creoles were alien to the indigenous Gambian tribal cultures, and their presence in the Gambia added another disruptive element in a situation which was already explosive.

The Creole man had the bad luck of being a black Anglo-Saxon--an African by pigmentation, but not by culture--and since the Gambia of the nineteenth century was the theater of incessant wars, the Creole trader became a target of disgruntled petty chiefs and village alkalis. In fact, he was the victim of any embittered African who felt inclined to take revenge for past injuries suffered at the hands of St. Mary's inhabitants. The Creole middleman was faced with greater problems of adjustment than either his Wolof or Mandinkas associates.[94]

The relations between the Creoles and their African brothers was complicated by the differences in psycho-cultural makeup. The collective unconscious of the Creoles, in the language of Frantz Fanon, embodied all the prejudices and arche-types belonging to the European; and for this reason they could identify more with the European than with the African. Actually, one can say that the hostility between the Creole minority and the African majority stemmed largely from what Fanon calls the "unreflected imposition of a culture"[95] on the Creoles.

Since most, if not all, Creoles readily embraced the English colonial culture, although one must admit that certain modifications were made to this culture by the Creoles, it became only a matter of time for them to perfect their knowledge about it. What complicated things in the early nineteenth was the general practice of replacing the tribal names of the Creoles by the Europeans names of their Christian sponsors.[96] A Gambian historian noted that this de-Africanization process assumed significance among the future generations "who felt a closeness with their European employers more than with the indigenous tribes in the River states."[97]

The African members of the inland tribes, on the other hand, were psycho-culturally myopic. Their weltanchuung was that of the tribal man who does not befriend or discriminate the other on the basis of skin color or race but on the basis of tribal culture and language. This tribal man was unwilling to recognize the being of the Creole. To him, the white man was a stranger and nature has made him different; and so his deviation from the African cultural norm is naturally determined. The Creole, on the other hand, is unnatural; to the tribal man, such an existential manifestation is beyond the kin of his tribal determined consciousness. To put the whole situation into proper perspective, we may have to call on Hegal for help. Actually what divided the Creoles from the African population could be philosophically stated: that is, both groups fail to recognize themselves as mutually recognizing each other.[98]

At the foundation of Hegelian dialectic there is an absolute reciprocity which must be emphasized. It is of course in the degree to which I go beyond my own immediate being that I apprehend the existence of the other as a natural and more than natural reality. If I refuse to erect communications lines between my being and that of the other, I prevent the accomplishment of movement in two directions, and I deliberately stifle the chances for feedback. Stated another way, my non-recogni-tion of the other keeps the other within himself, and ultimately my communication blackout may well deprive the other of the being-for-itself. In the Gambia of the early and mid-nineteenth century, we may say with some justifications that this was the nature of the relationship between the Creoles and their African brothers.

Against this background, we can now understand the events which transpired between the arrival of the Creole in the early 1820s and the early 1900s. The relationship between the Creole and the inland tribes was tumultuous because the mental estates of the two peoples were stored with certain archetypes and prejudices whose manifestations in the realm of consciousness undermined relations more than anything else. These groups were suspicious of each other, and since the Creole was regarded as a "whiteman" in black skin,[99] it was not infrequent for him to be a scapegoat of the dissatisfied Africans. Dwarfed and overwhelmed by the preponderant power of the European invader, the disgruntled African vented his hostility against the invader by attacking the weakest symbol of his presence. The Creole provided an immediate object for the African's displaced aggression.

In 1860, one of the Creole traders, Mr. Thomas King, was robbed by the people in the village of Gori Bool. King begged the colonial governor to enquire into the robbery he had suffered. The trader claimed a loss of L37. 10s worth of goods.[100] To the present Gambian, this sum may look small, but in those days this was an enormous amount. This is more so, when we remember the great risk under which these urbanized African trader labored. We are not going into details here about the relations between the African middlemen and the rulers of colonial Gambia--a matter which is reserved for the succeeding sections of this paper.

In 1863, another Creole trader was the victim of the inland tribes. This time one Mr. Thomas Johnson was the scapegoat of the embittered tribesmen. The governor responded to the merchants' plea for protection. Hastily, a man-of-war was demonstrated in the Gambia river, and by this the governor hoped to impress the offending chiefs. The loud outcry of the African traders made the governor more attentive to the developments in the area. But while the governor listened carefully to the pleas of the African traders, he also suspected them of duplicity, of giving support to the wrong side, of participating in a transatlantic slave trade.[101]

The difficulties endured by the Creole traders were largely the by-products of the precarious trade between the inland tribes and the Europeans. It should be noted that before European colonization, tribes traded among themselves, with one another, and without much conflict in values. But the Euro-African trade affected this traditional framework and by the 1860s, a gradual erosion of the traditional value base was very much evident. This mutability of values led to the emergence of the colonial man--the man whose behavior could no longer be predicted on the basis of African value among tribes. The fact that a Gambian credit system steadily followed the growth of the groundnut market explains to some extent why the Creole traders could not avoid a confrontation with the inland tribes. These traders, who were described as active businessmen spared little time to make money. In 1865, one finds a description of trade in the Gambia in the following terms:

> During the four rainy months of July, August, September, October, our native trader (the liberated African) is busy. He conveys rice and corn, the property of the Europeans employer, articles at that time most in request up the river, receiving in exchange pagners or country cloths, manufactured from cotton grown in the country in the native towns by the weavers....In November he receives groundnuts, hides, and wax in exchange for those same pagnes, but his factory is now stocked by imports from home; the possession of guns, powder, Madras handkerchiefs, and rum tempts the native to industry, and the trade is very active till the rainy season comes around when the payne season again opens; the European merchant...(lives) this part of the trade to be conducted by his native agent.[102]

The early years of the groundnut trade saw the successful operation of a new credit system; the debtors returned and settled debts with little or no difficulties. However, when the winds of change, ushered in by the train of religious wars, began to sweep across the Gambian river valleys, traders particularly Creoles--had a terrible time recollecting their debts. The failure of the farming community to provide sufficient food for its members compelled the merchants to import rice for local consumption and soon foreign imports began to assume significance. In 1863, "foreign rice" made its appearance in the trade returns of the Gambia colony.

The farmer's need for imported goods along with his inability to accommodate the food crisis of the middle nineteenth century made him a difficult trade client or customer. Moreover, because of the fierce competition among both the African traders and the European merchants, trade as a lucrative business in the Gambia hinterland was ruined. As one official report puts it, "a merchant sends his trader or people to some out-of-the-way place, who return with their feet or hands cut off, or perhaps not at all, having had their heads cut off, whereupon an application is made to the government for protection."[103] The colonial administrator told one of the complaining traders that if traders sent laborers to an area which was at war with their own tribes, then they (the traders) must expect the laborers to lose their heads.

These incidents were the results of hostilities between contending forces in the Gambia area. Apart from the petty wars of the various chiefs in the region, there were many religious wars fought by the traditional rulers and those Islamic reformers bent on changing the status quo. The Soninke-Marabout war was the most significant.

Things only changed after the full weight of the Pax Britanica was thrown against the Gambian people. Actually, by 1900 most of the Gambia was under firm British control, and by the 1920s the state-building processes initiated by the colonial power were already yielding results. The Gambia was divided into a protectorate (composed of 36 chieftaincies) and a colony. This colonial machinery offered jobs at the lower and middle levels to the Africans. Most of those Africans who made it to these positions were Creoles. And it was at this time that the Creole aristocracy began to consolidate some of the gains it made in the late nineteenth century.[104]

The third phase of the intertribal trade began, and became quite developed, after the British colonial apparatus planted itself firmly on Gambian soil. But this period was a bad one for farmers because most of the Gambian cattle had been lost in the epidemic of 1892. Moreover, locusts destroyed a large quantity of rice and corn while an abnormal rainfall in December, 1893 damaged the groundnut just after they had been pulled and before they had been stored. But besides these moments of financial despair, there were also periods of prosperity. These days were well spent by the farmers and much trade between the tribes took place under the imperial roof of the British colonial power.

What facilitated the growth of intertribal trade was the colonial government's efforts to increase the groundnut yield of the Gambia as a part of its state-building effort. Knowing that a poor and hungry colonial subject is no symbol of pride to a nation of empire-builders, the British set out to promote and execute a policy of self-development within the individual colonies. In the case of Gambia, groundnut production was to be increased and efforts were to be made to tackle the recurrent food crisis in the Gambian hinterland.

It is indeed within this colonial framework that intertribal trade flourished. The safety provided by the colonial administration led to the emergence of big European companies like to United African Company, Vezia, Maurel & Prom and others. These European firms employed many Africans as agents in the rural areas. Many of these agents were still Wolofs, Creoles, and urbanized Mandinkas. These traders became more secure, and life as a trader in the Gambia Protectorate more prosperous. There are still stories about Wolof traders who lived so extravagantly that their trading days were spent sweetening their wells with bags of sugar.

Whether such stories were legends about the past history of Gambian traders or not, one thing is certain: the traders were more confident than before. The development of communications systems made it possible for these men to keep close contact with headquarters. Also, with the gradual consolidation of colonial power, many of the woes of the olden days evaporated. All of a sudden the rural man changed from being a belligerent debtor to a compromising borrower of loans to accommodate the hungry season. This change in relations between the urban trader and the farming community ushered in trains of developments which later created a crisis in the Gambian farming community.[105]

Furthermore, the peaceful co-existence of the Gambian ethnic groups, to a large extent fostered by the British colonial system, enhanced trade in another respect. The cessation of hostilities between the Muslims and the Soninkes in the Gambia made it possible for the peaceful conversion of the latter into Islam.[106]

This conversion enhanced trade; for by restructuring the value system of the converted individuals, it inclined them to buy more cotton cloth so as to make garments and dresses in the Islamic tradition. Such a peaceful islamization of the Soninke Mandinkas, Wolof tedios, Jolas and Fulahs also fostered trade. Kola nuts became more and more in demand, and the Creole women who dominated the trade since the 1850s had a lucrative business to look after.

In addition to these organized trade opportunities, there were also facilities for limited trade between the ordinary members of the individual ethnic groups. In the late nineteen forties and early nineteen fifties a fairly large number of Wolof women travelled yearly to the rice belts of the Gambia to exchange dried fish, pepper, sugar, salt, and many other products for rice, millet and coos. These women are generally known in Wolof as Norankatyi; and many of them have proved to be very good business women. Migrating to another area for trade purposes suffered a little when ethnic politics created a rift between the residents of the urban center (Bathurst and its environs) and those of the rural areas. The politicization of the notion of Norani came about in the late 1950s and the early 1960s when P.P.P. propagandists went around the rural areas telling the farmer that people from Bathurst were responsible for their destitution and wretchedness. Among those charged with milking the rural poor were the Noronkantyi. Today, very few Wolof or Creole women now venture into the rural areas. Those who still operate in the rural areas either work side by side with their husbands (who are usually traders or government employees stationed in the Provinces) or live permanently in their area of operation and commute from time to time,[107] or conduct their business in areas where their ethnic group is predominant.

Interethnic relations has also been enhanced in other ways throughout the country. David Ames reported in the early fifties that the Wolofs had a kind of symbiotic relationship with the Fulani-cattle-herding people, as exemplified by the regular exchange of grain for curdled milk.[108] The Wolofs also turn to the Fulah medicine men in the case of distress, and this usually take the form of a request for magical charms and amulets. During the dry season, Fulah shepherds bring their cattle down from Senegal to the Gambia river to water and pasture them. Wolofs often house the Fulani in their compounds, and in return receive milk, and manure for their fields. The Fulahs also benefit from the limited Wolof economy, for during their stay in the Wolof community they could receive loans front their Wolof hosts.

The colonial era also witnessed a gradual change in the attitudes of the Wolof and Creole toward one another. Whereas in the early and middle nineteenth century Wolofs and Creoles constituted one and the same class of people under the same colonial roof, by the 1920s many Creoles had uplifted themselves front he quicksand of poverty to the solid rock of financial success. And moreover, by the 1930s most of the political agitation in the Gambia was from the Creole community.[109] Since the African middle class was heavily Creole, the African leadership had to be Creole.

It should, however, be pointed out that besides the Creole elites there were a few Muslim leaders (mostly Wolof). In addition to the names of M.S. Richards, J.A. Mahoney, S.J. Forster, B.J. George, H.M. Jones, P.A. Jones, E.F. Small, J.C. Rendall, E.A.T. Nicol, etc., there were men like Ousmen Njie, Amar Gaye, Omar Jallow, Jatta Joof, Sheih Omar

Fye and Alhadji Ousman Jeng. Actually, what divided the Wolof Muslims from the Creole Christians were both their religious and their ethnic identity. On the one hand, the Wolof Muslim feared the power of the Creoles; on the other hand, the Wolof suspected the intentions and ambitions of Creole leaders. Langley in his study of the activities of the Gambia section of the National Congress of British West Africa, found the Muslim (Wolof) community terribly divided over the Congress issue. The struggle in the 1920s was mainly centered around two personalities--Alhadji Ousman Jeng and the Hon. Sheikh Fye. The former championed the cause of the Muslim majority and the latter led the "influential minority" which supported the Congress.[110]

Wolof-Creole relations remained lukewarm up to the 1962 elections, when these two Gambian minorities found themselves, for the first time, under the leadership of the Mandinkas. In the early forties when local government politics came to Bathurst many influential Creoles participated. At this time the Creole leadership was firmly entrenched and many Wolofs looked up to some of them for leadership. An outstanding case was Pa Edward F. Small, the most active of Gambia's political leaders in the 1930s and 1940s.

The Wolofs seriously threatened Creole power in the 1950s. But before the Wolofs completely took over Bathurst, they had to sweep Reverend J.C. Fye, a Wolof-Serere Protestant Minister, out of their way. Fye was a very powerful bridge linking the Wolofs and the Creoles.

The main group that seriously challenged Creole power in the city of Bathurst was the young Muslim Society--a social and cultural organization which later became the political mouthpiece of one segment of the Bathurst Muslims. In the 1950s, this group was called the "Ndongo group" because most of its leaders were young Wolof Muslims. Actually, in retrospect, one can argue that the young Muslim Society was a socio-religious group whose main agenda was to get jobs and political recognition for the interwar generation of young Muslims in the capital of colonial Gambia. Their limited success in wringing out concessions from the colonial government later led to the political career of Mr. I.M. Garba Jahumpa. This Muslim youth leader of the interwar period would later become a political activist on behalf of the Muslims in the late forties and early fifties. His political career took off with the formation of the Gambia Muslim Congress. Although this political party failed to capture the hearts of the majority of the Banjul people in the late fifties and beyond, the efforts of Mr. Jahumpa and his cohorts certainly changed the nature of the power relationship between the Creole and the rest of the population. In response to the increasing demands for political participation among the Non-Creole members of Gambian society, the British colonial government started a series of constitutional changes which eventually extended the franchise throughout the country. This constitutional advance eventually led to one person-one vote. With this new arrangement Creole power in Banjul declined sharply, and the Wolofs became the successors to the Creoles as the dominant custodians of social and political power. This new dispensation would be further complicated by the rise of national political parties after the 1960s. Because of the emergence of the PPP and the UP as the two dominant political parties in the country, Banjul became for a brief period the battleground between the predominantly Mandinka-led PPP and the predominantly Wolof-led UP. As a result of the electoral victory of the PPP, the Creole-Wolof rivalry became irrelevant. It was soon replaced in the minds of certain ethnically chauvinistic Gambians by the old Colony-Protectorate rivalry. By the mid-sixties, the new post independent leadership of the Gambia was face with the task of nation-building and Banjul was seen as a testing ground of national unity. Prime Minister D.K. Jawara tried his best to create a government of national unity. In these early days of independence his administration was certainly representative of the ethnic composition of both the nation's capital and the country at large.

CONCLUSION

In concluding, three points need to be noted here. First of all, it should be stated that the history of the Gambia shows a country whose peoples came from different parts of the West African region. Except for the Jola and the Serere, all the other main groups of Gambian ethnic groups are immigrants from ancient Mali, ancient Tekrur or ancient Jollof. The Mandinkas of the Gambians are the descendants of people from Mali who came by way of Kabu in present day Guinea, Bissau; the Fulas are the descendants of many subgroups of the Pular-speaking groups from northern Senegal and Southern Mauritania; and the Wolofs are also immigrants who came to the Gambia by way of the Senegalese regions of Cayor Sin and Saloum. Equally true is the story of the Serahuli, whose history goes back to ancient Ghana. Like Americans, Gambians must now be too self-conscious about their ethnic origins because they have been too mixed to make any credible claim of ethnic purity. Secondly, it should be concluded that inter-ethnic struggles for resources and living space and foreign encroachments in the area have together shaped the nature of the relationship between the different groups. The different histories of the relationships between the various groups in the country have definitely define the attitudes, the images and the stereotypes about each other. What has kept the peace among these groups are the following: the cementing power of religion, inter-ethnic marriages and responsible social and political leadership. The third conclusion is that the history of ethnic relations in the Gambia reveals a pattern in the struggle for power in Banjul. The city or town has always served as a social elevator for the different groups converging on its limited territorial space. The first African group to enjoy some social significance were the Señoras, a mulatto group of Africans who benefitted from their cultural and biological links to the European colonizers. They were followed by the Creoles from Freetowne, Sierra Leone by the colonial government. The Wolofs came after the Creoles in the fifties, when the colonial government extended the electoral franchise to the people of the Old Colony. By virtue of their numbers they have continued to exercise influence in the social, political and cultural life of the city. This pattern will eventually be replaced by a more nationally representative order of social integration. The emergence of Serrekunda and Bakau as urban centers have led to a new ethnic mosaic which is increasingly representative of the wider ethnic mix in the country. It has also created new conditions which deserve to be studied separately.

Bibliography

1. H. Reeve, *The Gambia, Its History, Ancient, Medieval, and Modern* (London: John Murray, 1912), p. 59. For an interesting account of the salt trade in the Sudan area, see E.W. Bovill, *The Golden Trade of the Moors* (London: Oxford University Press, 1958), pp. 236 ff.
2. See Especially Phillip D. Curtin.
3. Francis Moore, *Travels into the Inland Posts of Africa.* (London: 1738), p. 20; Mungo Park, *Travels of Mungo Park,* Ronald Miller, ed. (London: Dent, 1954), p. 18; H.F. Reeve, *op cit.,* p. 25
4. Francis Moore, *op cit,*; Fenwick Reeve, *op cit.,* p. 74; C. Quinn, *op cit.,* p. 35
5. J.M. Gray, A History of the Gambia, (N.Y.: Noble Inc., 1966), p. 303; Mungo Park, *op cit.*
6. Francis Moore, *op cit.,* p. 30.
7. J.M. Gray, *op cit.,* p. 379.
8. Lady Balla Smithorn, *The Gambia: The Story of the Groundnut Colony,* (London: George Allen Unwin, 1952), pp. 187-188.
9. Gray, *op cit.,* pp. 379-380
10. *Ibid.,* p. 383.
11. D.P. Gamble, *Contributions to a Socio-Economic Survey of the Gambia.* (London: 1949), p. 73; "Notes on the Strange Farmers" (Dept. of Agriculture, 1946) *The Golden Trade of the Moors,* No. 15 of 1946, pp. 1-9.
12. Hakluyt Society, *The Voyages of Cadamiosto and Other Documents on Western Africa in the Second Half of the Fifteenth Century,* (London: 1937), pp. 29
13. H. Gailey, *op cit.,* pp. 9-10.
14. Mungo Park, *op cit.,* p. 13.
15. Charlotte Quinn, *op cit.,* p. 23.
16. L. Berenger-Feraud, *Les Peuplades de la Senegambia,* (Paris, 1979).
17. Florence Mahoney, Stories of the Gambia with Supplement (1976 Editon), (Bathurst, Gambia: Government Printer, 1967), p. 49.
18. *Ibid*
19. Fenwick Reeve, *op cit.,* p. 36. J. M. Gray tells us that the Battimansa must have been the king of Baddibu. See J.M. Gray, *op cit.,* pp. 7-8, particularly footnote 1.
20. Jobson, *op cit.,* p. 51.
21. Gailey, *op cit.,* p. 14; F. Reeve, op cit., p. 180; Gray, *op cit.,* p. 326.
22. John Milner Gray, *op cit.,* p. 179.
23. Roberts, "An Account of the Situation of Senegal and Gambia, " P.R.O., C.O. 267/   19 and Egarton M.S. 1162 A, f. 242.
24. J.M. Gray, *op cit.,* p. 270.
25. Mungo Park, *op cit.,* p. 16.
26. The Soninke-Marabout wars could be divided into three phases: (1) 1850-1859; (2) 1859-1866; (3) 1866-1887. The word Soninke was a socio-political cflassificatory term used to differentiate those Africans who held on the traditional religious beliefs from those who were devout Muslims (Marabouts).

27. *Annual Report for 1888.*

28. J.M. Gray, *op cit.*, p. 288; Harry Gailey, *op cit.*, p. 41

29. See *Quran,* Ch. 109, V. 7 (translated by Maulawi Yusuf Ali), p. 632

30. J.M. Gray, *op cit.*, p. 469.

31. It should be mentioned here that the Jolas defeated another Mandinka Marabout Chief Foday sillah in 1873. See Florence Mahoney, *Stories of the Gambia with Supplement, p. 30.*

32. J.M. Gray, *op cit.*, p. 484.

33. Peter Weil "Language distribution in the Gambia 1966-1967," *African Language Review,* Vol. 7, 1968.

34. P.P.P. is the leading Gambian political party. Originally, it was designed to serve as the mouthpiece of the Protectorate Peoples, who claimed that the urbanites of the Gambia mistreated them in the past.

35. Henry F. Reeve, *op cit.*, p. 39.

36. Reeve, *op cit.*, 178.

37. R. Jobson, *The Golden Trade,* (N.Y.: Da Cappo Press, 1968), p. 35.

38. Moore, *op cit.*, p. 30

39. H. Hecquard, *Voyage sur la Cote et Dans l'interior de l'Afrique Occidentale,* (Paris, France: Bernard, 1855). Quinn, *op cit.*, p. 40.

40. J.M. Gray, *op cit.*, p. 326.

41. *Ibid.*, p. 446.

42. *Ibid.*, p. 447.

43. *Ibid.*, p. 448.

44. Francis Bisset-Archer, *The Gambian Colony and Protectorate,* (London: Frank Cass, 1967), P. 54.

45. J.R. Gray, *op cit.*, p. 370.

46. Francis Bisset-Archer, *op cit.*, p. 56.

47. J. Greensberg, *Studies in African Linguistic Classification* (New Haven 1955), p. 10.. In the Gambia these dialects fall into thre linguistic groupings: (1) Jawarangko, Jombonko, Habobo, Lorobo, Hammanabi; (2) Torodo, Jawado, Laube; (3) Futangkesea, Bayley, Notes on the Ethnological Division of (Gambia Archives, 27 September, 1939):_____.

48. Charlotte Quinn, *op cit.*, p. 41.

49. *Ibid.*, p. 43.

50. Forde, *op cit.*, p. 12ff.

51. This author believes that this is an Anglicized version of the Arbic or Fulah name - Ayub Ibn Sulaiman.

52. J.M. Gray, op cit.,, p. 109. See also my "Islam in the United States of America: A Review of the Sources," *Islamic Culture*, July, 1981.

53. For a detailed account on Job, see J.M. Gray, *op cit.*, p. 21.

54. Rev. John Leighton Wilson, *Western Africa: Its History, Condition and Prospects* (N. Y.: Harper Brothers Publishers, 1856), pp. 80-8.

55. Reeve, *op cit.*, pp. 78-79.

56. *Ibid.*

57. Lady Bella Southern, *op cit.*, p. 43.

58. Sabatie, 1926, p. 297.

59. W. Hamlyn, *A Short History of the Gambia,* (Bathurst, 1931), p. 31.

60. Florence Komolara Mahoney, *Government and Public Opinion 1816-1901,* (Ph.D. Dissertation, University of London, 1963), pp. 3-4.

61. Charlotte Quinn, *op cit.*, p. 81.

62. *Ibid.*

63. *Ibid.*

64. 10/87/57, O'Connor to Newcastle, 10 May, 1854; Charlotte Quinn, *op cit,* p. 51.

65. Major W. Gray and Surgeon Durhard, *Travels in West Africa,* (London: Murray, 1825), p. 75.

66. 1885 Annual report cited in D.P. Gamble, *Economic Conditions in Two Gambian Mandinka Villages - Kerewan and Keneba,* (London: Colonial Office, 1955), p. 40.

67. D.P. Gamble, *The Wolof of Senegambia,* (London: Int. African Inst., 1957), p. 14. See also Vincent Monteil's article in Daryll Ford and P.M. Kaberry (eds.), *West African Kingdoms in the Nineteenth Century,* (London: Int. African Institue, 1967, p. 261).

68. Actually, there is a Wolof saying: Santa Amut Ker (Literally, a surname has no home--i.e., one cannot determine a person's ethnic background solely from his surname).

69. For this and other related theories, see D.P. Gamble, *The Wolof of Senegambia,* (London: Int. African Inst., 1957), P. 14.

70. Gamble, *op cit.,* p. 20-21.

71. Mahoney, *op cit.,* p. 15.

72. David Ames "The Use of a Transitional Cloth-Money Token Among the Wolofs", *American Anthropologist,* (Vol. 57, No. 5), October, 1955, p. 1019.

73. David Ames, "The Rural Wolof of the Gambia" in *Markets in Africa,* (Eds. by Paul J. Bohannan and George Dalton), Northwestern University Press, n.d., p. 36.

74. *Ibid.,* p. 30.

75. *Ibid.*76. Mahoney, *op cit.,* p. 16.

77. Gaspard Mollien, *Travels in the Interior of Africa to the Sources of the Senegal and Gambia,* (London 1820, Edited by T.E. Bowdich, p. 308; Mungo Park in *West African Explorers.*

78. Mungo Park, *The Life and Travels of Mungo Park,* (N. Y., Harper & Brothers, 1841), pp. 48-49.

79. Mungo Park reports that a successful Serahuli merchant received congratulations from friends and neighbours; but an usuccessful merchant is derided for his failure to "bring back nothing but the hair upon his head." Mungo park, *op cit.,* p. 47.

80. Mahoney, *op cit.,* p. 13.

81. R. Jobson, *The Golden Trade,* 2nd ed. (N.Y.: Da Capo Press, 1968), p. 78.

82. The island of St. Mary's was purchased from the King of Kombo for a poetry sum.

83. P.R.O. Co. 267/42 12th June, 1816. Brereton to Bathurst.

84. Florence J. Mahoney, "Notes on Mulatto".

85. D. Ames, The Use of a Transitional Cloth-Money Taken among the Wolof" *American Anthropolgist,* Vo. 57, No. 5 (October, 1955), p. 1022.

86. MacBriar, p. 6; Hungting p. 142.

87. A.B. Ellis, *The Land of Fettish,* (London: 1883), p. 4.

88. C.O. 87/5, 1831, 17th May , Rendall to R. W. Hay.

89. C.O. 267/65, 1825, Vol. 1. 1st December, 1824, Randall to Hamilton.

90. C.O. 87/16, 1835-1836, Gambia Returns of Liberated Africans, 22 July, 1835, Rendall to Glenely.

91. Florence Mahoney, *Government and Opinion in The Gambia,* (Ph.D. Dissertation, London University, 1963), p. 75.

92. Mahoney, p. 78.

93. Madden Report, 1841, Lt. Governor Huntly to Dr. Madden.

94. Mahoney, *op cit.,* p. 128.

95. Frantz Fanon, *Black Skin, White Mask,* (N.Y.: Grove Press, 1968), p. 191.

96. A correspondent for *West Africa,* in talking about the first Gambian Accountant Genral, wrote in 1951 that he hoped future historians would not mistake the Gambian man for one of the

European members of the Gambia Colonial Civil Service. 97. Mahone, *op cit.*, p. 82.

98. G.W.F. Hegel, *The Phenomenology of Mind*, trans., by J.B. Baillie, 2nd rev. ed., (London, Allen & Unwin, 1949), pp. 230-231.

99. Here, whiteness is a symbol representing all that was characteristic of European culture in the Creole's life.

100. C.O. 87/69--9th March, Thomas King to D'Arcy.

101. C.O. 87/80, 1864, Vo. 2, 25th September, D'Arcy to Newcastle.

102. *Annual Report of the Gambia*, 1865. Cited in D.P. Gamble, *Contributions to a Socioeconomic Survey of the Gambia*, (London: Colonial Office, 1949), p. 60.

103. *Annual Report of the Gambia*, 1869.

104. For a good discussion on the role of Creoles in early Gambian colonial politics, see Florence Mahoney, "African Leadership in Bathurst in the Nineteenth Century." *Tarikh*, Vol. 2, No. 2, 1968, pp. 25-38.

105. See my "The Administrative Problems of Gambian Cooperative and their Impact on National Development." (Unpublished M. A. Thesis, University of Virginia, 1971), Chapter 1.

106. For some discussion on the evolution of Islam in the Gambia, see my Islam in the Gambia" *Journal of the Pakistan Historical Society,* 1977.

107. This kind of woman is not counted as a Norankat.

108. David Ames, *op cit.*, p. 46.

109. For a good discussion of political agitation in the Gambia of the 1920s and 1930s, see J. Ayodele Langley, "The Gambia Section of the National Congress of British West Africa, "*Africa* Vol. XXXIV, No. 4 (October 1969), pp. 382-395.

110. Langley, *op cit.*, p. 387.

Chapter VII

Africa and the Demise of the Soviet Bloc

Dr. F. UGBOAJA OHAEGBULAM

This paper examines the proposition that the demise of the Soviet bloc of powers has produced repercussions in, and new challenges, to Africa. It is evident that the excruciating humanitarian crisis in Somalia, which at long last in December 1992 prompted President George Bush of the United States to initiate a humanitarian military intervention, under United Nations' auspices, in the devastated country on Africa's Eastern Horn, is in part a legacy of the cold war and the result of the collapse of the Soviet bloc. The U.S.-led intervention under UN auspices probably would not have occurred had the climate of the cold war continued to prevail.

The Somali crisis, like similar African crises, stemmed largely from stockpiles of armaments built by the cold war and used after the demise of the Soviet bloc by rival groups against each other. It represents a historic expression of forces repressed for a long time by an artificial stability built into the respective camps of the cold war. Thus, like the antagonism between the Soviet bloc and the Western bloc of powers, the collapse of the Soviet bloc itself is being felt in the African continent. Consequently, Africa is reaping the bitter harvest of the cold war. The continent had existed on the periphery of world politics during the cold war. It may become even more peripheral after the end of the cold war and the collapse of the Soviet bloc than before.[1]

AFRICA AND THE COLD WAR

Africa was under Western European imperial domination during the emergence of the Soviet bloc of powers. During the entire period of the imperial domination the continent and its inhabitants were insulated from the Soviet Union and the Soviet bloc so as to prevent the penetration of the region by the bloc. As colonial subjects Africans were not to travel to Soviet bloc countries. They were not to study there, nor to read literature produced in the bloc, and were not to trade directly with the countries of the bloc. Similar imperial restrictions kept Soviet citizens out of Africa too. Yuri Popov, formerly head of Chair of World Economy at the Soviet Academy of Labor and Social Relations, and Deputy Chairman of Soviet Association of Friendship with Peoples of Africa, wrote that even in December 1960--labelled then as Africa year--when he was in Rome, he was taken off the plane of a British airline the only one operating direct flights from Europe to Nigeria at the time. A British Overseas Airways official, he affirmed, bluntly told him: "There have been no Russians in Africa, and there won't be any."[2]

Post-World War II anticolonial nationalism in Africa became a critical vehicle through which the Soviet bloc sought to expand ideologically and politically to the continent. Initially, however, Soviet leaders regarded the African nationalist movements as illusory and the movements' leaders as bourgeois nationalists within a firm grip of the Western European capitalist camp.[3] Meanwhile, the independence of more than thirty-one African countries, during the period of the intensification of the cold war, offered the Soviet bloc opportunities to gain an entry into Africa through diplomatic relations, trade, and cultural exchanges. Accordingly, during the 1950s and the 1960s, the Soviet Union, leader of the bloc, resolved to establish a presence and influence in Africa appropriate to its global power status and to ensure that Africa would no longer be absolutely controlled by the West.[4]

This ambition of Soviet leaders collided head-on with the interests of the United States and its Western allies, already antagonized by Soviet territorial and ideological expansion in Eastern Europe. Africa thus became part of the arena of the ideological struggle between the Soviet and the Western bloc of powers. The respective leaders of the blocs, the Soviet Union and the United States, frequently based their actions on Africa more with reference to each other than to the needs of the continent and its peoples.[5] In the midst of their actions and struggle, therefore, Africa's weakness was to make the continent a pawn in the conflict. Africa's weakness, above everything else, subjected the emergent African nations to external pressures and facilitated great power meddling in the continent.

For their part, African rulers and political elite used the international politics of the cold war to promote their own interests. They played the Soviet Union against the United States in their efforts to deal with their parochial problems of political insecurity and material resources. To do so was easy because the ideological conflict, as a function of the competition between the Western and Eastern power blocs for advantage and influence, conferred on Africa a false importance in world affairs which African political leaders exploited to their own advantage. The competition drew the great powers into deep involvement in Africa's political and economic developmental processes. Viewed in zero-sum terms, in which an adversary's gain represented a loss for the other side, the competition rendered the great powers vulnerable to pressures from their African allies. It was such vulnerability of the great powers that gave African leaders a false sense of their importance.

African Marxist-oriented regimes exploited that false sense of importance as they sought Soviet help additionally on the basis of their ideological compatibility with the bloc. For their part, the white minority regimes in southern Africa and other authoritarian regimes elsewhere in Africa used appeals to anticommunism to seek to obtain the support of the Western powers, especially that of the United States, for their own interests.

The measures employed in the international politics of the cold war by African Marxist-oriented governments, rebel groups, and authoritarian regimes, and by the governments of the ideological rivals themselves, often escalated and prolonged conflicts in Africa with devastating consequences for such African countries as Angola, Mozambique, Ethiopia, and Somalia. Frequently the measures betrayed an insufficient knowledge on the part of the superpowers of a specific African region's internal dynamics and so prevented African issues from being seen in their local and regional contexts. One immediate consequence was that the cold war helped to prolong authoritarian rule in Africa as the continent passed from European imperial dictatorship to the authoritarianism of local regimes--one man, single party, Marxist ideologues, military officers, propped up by one or the other rival great power.

Political miscalculations of the leaders of the rival blocs and the strategies employed by both power blocs in their ideological competition for global hegemony contributed to undermine respect for human rights, the nurturing of democratic governance, and the process of national consolidation and economic development in post-colonial Africa. Much of the responsibility for this is clearly attributable to the Western practice of deifying and demonizing political leaders, movements, and ideologies, and championing individuals rather than the formation of democratic institutions in the continent.

Measures most frequently used by the rival blocs were very similar. They included military transfers,[6] foreign aid, covert, and sometimes overt, political and military intervention in support of groups or authorities the rival groups believed could best promote their interests. Sometimes the rival powers shared intelligence with client governments and denied economic, including sometimes food, assistance to governments sympathetic with the goals of their ideological rivals.

Perhaps, the most devastating impact of the cold war on Africa is that it deprived the African states forty-five critical years during which they themseleves should have dealt very realistically with their own urgent and complex problems of political consolidation and economic development with every measure of creativity and original thinking. Instead of doing this, African leaders paid lip service to the concepts of self-reliance and nonalignment as they uncritically adopted the capitalist and socialist approaches of the ideological power blocs and the former colonial powers to development. In the process critical thinking and original strategies for Africa's political and economic development were sacrificed to ideologies and policies that served to perpetuate Africa's dependence, marginalization, and peripheral economic and political status in world affairs.

THE END OF THE COLD WAR

Developments occurring over the years culminated in the dramatic collapse of the forces that comprised the Soviet bloc--communist regimes in Eastern Europe, the War Saw Pact, the Berlin Wall in 1989.[7] The forces also brought about the reunification of Germany in 1990. These occurrences were followed dramatically also by the disintegration of the Soviet Union itself in December 1991. The high cost of the arms race between the Soviet Union and the United States, the overextension overseas of itself by the Soviet Union, internal economic and agricultural difficulties in the Soviet bloc countries and the widespread dissatisfaction of nationals of the bloc generally, acclerated the internal contradictions within the communist system to undermine the bloc.[8] But perhaps, the most important of the developments that brought about the collapse of the Soviet bloc and the Soviet Union was the emergence of Mikhail Gorbachev in 1985 as the General Secretary of the Communist Party of the Soviet Union. This occurred amidst worsening perennial economic problems, the failure of Soviet agriculture to provide enough food to feed the Soviet population, and the frustrations of costly military involvements in Afghanistan, Angola, and Ethiopia. Steadily, Gorbachev initiated a new thinking and a reappraisal of both Soviet domestic policies and role in the world.[9]

Gorbachev's reappraisal of Soviet domestic policies and role in the world led him to specific strategic conclusions. The first was that the Soviet economy had to be restructured. The second was that Soviet exercise of military power abroad, including armed intervention in Eastern Europe, had led directly to the political and economic disasters that afflicted the Soviet Union; that new interventions abroad would defeat the goal of restructuring and resuscitating the Soviet state and economy; that a calm on the international scene was equally essential to the implementation of his perestroika which required massive infusion of financial and technological inputs from the West. Gorbachev recognized that for this calm and the opportunity to develop a new economic and political relationship with Western Europe to occur, it was critical that the Soviet Union develop a good working relationship with the United States.

Gorbachev's conclusions from his reappraisal of the Soviet situation at home and abroad culminated in concrete steps to transform the Soviet Union, to retrench the Republic gradually from overcommitment abroad, and to accelerate a process of rapprochement with the West, especially the United States. This will at modernization in the Soviet Union begun by Gorbachev to replace the earlier will to imperial expansion and the use of force contributed to bring about the end of the cold war and the emergence of a new world order.

TRENDS PRECEDING THE END OF THE COLD WAR: THEIR IMPACT ON AFRICA

Although the new world order is as yet largely uncharted, its impact is beginning to be felt in Africa in a variety of ways. That impact was presaged by trends that already had been emerging prior to the end of the cold war and the collapse of the Soviet bloc. The trends were a consequence, among others, of US-Soviet detente, important changes in global economic relations (especially the emergence of West Germany and Japan as economic superpowers, and the steady erosion of US economic hegemony),[10] and domestic socio-economic problems within both the United States and the Soviet bloc countries. These developments facilitated corresponding adjustments in the way the superpowers defined their security interests in Africa. The eventual consequence for the superpowers was that the United States and the Soviet Union began to reduce their security commitments in Africa and to cooperate diplomatically in finding solutions to such African regional problems as Angola, Namibia, and the suffering in Ethiopia due to civil wars, drought, and famine.[11]

For African states the developments foreshadowed a reduction in the preparedness of the Western and Soviet blocs to respond, or commit resources, to their needs.[12] Access to such resources as were available from the West, including the International Monetary Fund and the World Bank, were made highly competitive and conditional on democratic reforms, belt tightening, and structural adjustment of the economies along captitalist lines consistent with Western experiences and preferences.

Three other trends, with specific impacts on Africa, also preceded the end of the cold war and the dissolution of the Soviet bloc. First, Soviet views of political and economic developments in the Third World generally had begun to change a few years before the accession of Gorbachev to power in the Soviet Union in 1985. Policy alterations that resulted from such changes were accelerated by Gorbachev's accession to power, revisionist interpretations of the cold war and strategic changes in Soviet diplomatic style.[13] However, they were eclipsed by improvements in East-West relations and the sudden demise of the Soviet bloc.[14]

Indeed, before the dramatic events of 1989 and 1990 in Eastern Europe and in the Soviet Union itself in 1991, Soviet leaders, disappointed at the apparent failure of Soviet policy in the Third World, had begun to look inwards and to believe that retrenchment from the Third World was urgent so as to accord with their critical domestic reforms. This meant that whatever priority of attention that had been given to African states was downgraded and replaced with a firm intention to disengage from African conflicts.[15] In response to outcries from a broad section of the Soviet populace, including parliamentarians and striking miners, agencies and organizations responsible for aid to African and other Third World countries were directed by presidential decree to cut such assistance.[16] Thus, to Soviet leaders Africa was no longer to be an arena for zero-sum competition and confrontation with the West. Consequently, African governments whose military and economic support derived from the competition between their super-power patrons were immediately affected by a new international understanding brought about by the new thinking in the Soviet Union.[17] In such countries as Angola, Namibia and Ethiopia, the two super-powers began to support directly and indirectly negotiations towards political settlement of ongoing conflicts and national reconciliation.[18]

In the economic field, the expansion of the nominal trade relations between the Soviet Union and African states continued to be hampered by a variety of constraints. Economic difficulties and political uncertainties in both the Soviet Union and in Africa militated against efforts at expansion. In addition to its problem of heavy budget deficit, the Soviet Union itself was reeling under a huge foreign debt of about $56 billion owed mainly to the West.[19] This situation was compounded by the lack of complementarity between the Soviet economy and those of African states and by the problems of scarcity of currency resources and modern technology in both areas. Like many developing nations, the Soviet Union remained predominantly an exporter of fuels and raw materials and an importer of manufactured goods and food stuffs. Relatively few of these imports came from Africa whose countries the Soviets complained had yet to start supplying them with goods they needed.[20] The structural and institutional foundation for a dynamic and expanding commercial relationship with Africa was therefore lacking. Private African business could not establish any economic ties with the Soviet states. Soviet enterprises could not trade on the external markets since all economic cooperation was conducted through the central government agencies.[21]

Another significant trend that preceded the demise of the Soviet bloc was in the area of Africa's export trade with the non-communist world. By 1988 the value of Africa's percentage of total world exports had decreased from 6 percent in 1980 to 2.5 percent.[22] Also, before 1989, Africa's most important trading partners, Britain, France, and the other members of the European Economic Community, while maintaining their share of total exports to African countries, had begun to import less from them.[23] Their share in African exports declined from an average of 63 percent in 1958-1963 to 45 percent in 1974-1986.[24] This situation increased the inability of African countries to generate foreign exchange by exports to provide their fledgling industries with critically needed imports. In addition, the situation contributed to the balance of payments difficulties, the debt crisis, and the economic marginalization, of African states. Closely related to this problem is that the European Community heavily subsidizes European farmers for food they would not otherwise grow competitively. Because of the estimated $55 billion a year subsidy to European farmers African countries are unable to export advantageously to Europe such products as sugar. Also, the prices of African exports globally are depressed because the

European Community dumps excess commodities, such as cereals, on the world market in order to avoid incurring storage costs.[25]

The additional major trend which preceded the end of the cold war occurred in the investment field where foreign investors, mainly Western, wary of the the risks entailed in Africa's political conflicts and instability, held back their investments in the continent. As a consequence direct foreign investment in Africa "fell from $2.4 billion in 1982 to $0.86 billion in 1987."[26] This apparent economic disengagement of the Western nations from Africa deepened the continent's economic crisis even before the collapse of the Soviet bloc.

NEGATIVE REPERCUSSIONS OF THE DEMISE OF THE SOVIET BLOC ON AFRICA

According to a Bambara, West Africa, proverb "whether elephants fight or make love, the result is the same: after them the grass no longer grows."[27] Indeed, what we are witnessing is that the end of the cold war, brought about by the demise of the Soviet bloc, has increased the peripheralization of Africa. Having won the ideological war, the West lost interest in Africa. The components of the former Soviet bloc, for their part, abandoned the continent.[28] This is not just a function of the end of the cold war, it is also a result of a general disillusionment with the economic and political performance of post-colonial African states, and the preoccupation of the former ideological rivals with their own complex domestic problems.[29] In addition to these, conflicts in the Persian Gulf, the Balkans, especially in the former Yugoslavia, and in the economically troubled states of the former Soviet Union, virtually forced Africa off the screen in the major powers of the Western world. The United States appeared not to care about what was going on within the borders of its client states Liberia, Sudan, and Somalia, for example.

It is clear from these that the demise of the Soviet bloc produced negative repercussions in Africa. Politically, the collapse of the bloc brought about a new international environment in which the Western powers have again become the dominant influence especially in Africa. It is true that the Soviet bloc was unable to address the issue of neocolonialism of the West in Africa successfully, yet the role which the bloc had played as a relatively countervailing force in the Western bloc's political domination and economic exploitation of Africa has been removed by the dissolution of the bloc. There is a question now as to whether the nonaligned movement, born of the cold war, by which African and other member states had played a balancing role for international peace and stability retains any steam and usefulness.

The economic repercussions are much clearer. To the direct loss of aid from the former Soviet bloc, attributable to the demise of the bloc, is now added the apparent diversion of scarce foreign investment capital away from Africa to the countries of Eastern Europe and the Commonwealth of Independent States (CIS). These countries have the advantages of proximity, cultural affinity with Europe, a better infrastructural base for investment.

These advantages add to make the massive mobilization of resources by the Western powers for them to stand in stark contrast to the modest response of those powers to the development needs of African states during the years of the cold war and thereafter. The Western powers' preoccupation with the economic restructuring of Eastern Europe and the CIS is demonstrated by their announcement in April 1992 of $24 billion official aid package for Russia alone and their earlier pledges in January 1992 of an estimated $80 billion to the CIS. Added to these were the estimated pledges of $45 billion to Eastern Europe by twenty-four members of the Organization for Economic Cooperation and Development (OECD) in November 1991.[30]

Also in 1991, because of severe budgetary pressures and a decision to support economic reforms in Eastern Europe and the former Soviet Union, the Nordic countries--traditionally among the most generous and flexible of Africa's aid donors--cut and began to reorient their aid to the continent.[31] In April 1993, President Clinton of the United States pledged to provide upwards of $1.6 billion to Russia and to mobilize America's Western friends to pledge more to promote Russia's rebirth which he said is in the economic interest of the American people.

The Secretary-General of the African, Caribbean and Pacific (ACP) grouping of signatories to the Lome Convention with the European Community, Gehbray Berhane, argues that Western Europe is looking for closer relations overall with the East, at the expense of African relations. In the pursuit of the closer relations Western Europe, he adds, "is devoting more resources to promote not only industry and agriculture in East Europe and the CIS, but also technical assistance and institution building" while it places less emphasis on these things for Africa.[32]

Between 1990 and April 1992, Germany, which led in providing aid and investment capital to Eastern Europe and the CIS, channelled more than $120 billion to the former German Democratic Republic and about $36 billion to the CIS. Its aid of about $2 billion a year to Africa could in no way match those figures.[33]

In addition to receiving more resources from Western Europe, Eastern European nations and the CIS have become competitors with African and other less industrialized countries for official multilateral credits from such institutions as the International Monetary Fund (IMF) and the World Bank. In 1991 the IMF committed $4.7 billion to five Eastern European countries compared to $1.8 billion which it committed to thirteen African states.[34]

The current state of commercial relations between African states and the former countries of the Soviet bloc provides additional evidence of the negative repercussions of the demise of the bloc in Africa. The commercial relations, which historically have been concentrated in a few countries, are now mostly in chaos.[35] The economic situation in the former Soviet bloc and in the economically troubled countries of the former Soviet Union in particular, has reduced exports to those countries from Africa[36] and jeopardized a number of multi-year trade deals signed with the Soviet Union prior to its disintegration in 1991. A case in point is the five-year deal Cote d'Ivoire had signed with the Soviet Union in 1990 for the export of 100,000 tonnes of cocoa a year to the republic. Egypt suffered a similar fate when a five-year trade accord it had negotiated with the Soviet Union in 1991 for the export of 10,000 tonnes of cotton per year collapsed after the break up of the Soviet Union. Consequently, Egypt was compelled to search elsewhere for more than half the 500,000 tonnes of coal the former Soviet Union had been expected to supply.[37] The Soviet Union's decision to demand hard currency for all exports from January 1991 terminated its barter and counter trade deals with a number of African countries. Perhaps, the most adversely affected by the decision was Mozambique which had received manufactured goods from East European countries and the former Soviet Union at favorable terms. The southern African country's hope to strengthen its development through a joint development of natural gas with the Soviet Union is now out of the picture.

In general Soviet enterprises have neglected the establishment of links with Africa owing to their concentration on establishing contacts with Western and Japanese firms.[38] It is also noteworthy that beginning in 1989 the Soviet Union began a drastic reduction of aid allocations to Third World countries. Sub-Saharan African states received a smaller share of the drastically reduced aid allocations.[39] In October 1991 the reform program outlined by Boris Yeltsin, who became president of Russia after the resignation of Gorbachev in December of that year as the President of the Soviet Union, included a ban on foreign aid.[40]

The timing of these developments when expectations of new demands for African exports to Western Europe are receding compounds the economic difficulties of African states. Moreover, there are fears that the former Soviet bloc countries which are already competing with African countries for aid from Western Europe and and America, will also become competitors of African states in the vital markets of the European Community. Some of them, like Czech republic, Slovakia, Hungary and Poland, are considered likely prospective members of the European Community by the year 2000.[41]

The demise of the Soviet bloc marked the dramatic beginning of the end of a thirty-year period of educational and specialized training assistance to Africans states by the former bloc. It created immediate problems for more than 8,000 African students in the countries of the former bloc. Over 600 Ugandan students and hundreds more from other African countries in the former Soviet Union were stranded after their scholarships were withdrawn by the new independent states and after Aeroflot's airfare soared to an extent that they and their governments could not afford. Many of the students left East Germany, Czechoslovakia and Bulgaria in 1990-91. Some left Russia in 1991/92. Prior to 1991 African students throughout the Soviet Union had been victims of black bashing and anti-black sentiments let loose by Gorbachev's glasnost.[42]

THE SILVER LINING OF THE DEMISE OF THE SOVIET BLOC

Shakespeare wrote that there is some soul of goodness in things evil would men observingly distill it out. The demise of the Soviet bloc may, indeed, have its silver lining for African states. Its immediate salutary political effects are not inconsiderable. With vision they could be magnified in the long run for Africa's overall advantage. Thanks to the demise of the Soviet bloc, Africa is no longer a pawn in the cold war. It is henceforth spared the privations which the erstwhile implacable ideological struggle had brought its peoples. Africa now receives significantly less arms deliveries from the former ideological rivals than it did during the years of the cold war. For example, in 1990 African nations spent $1.316 billion in arms purchases from the Soviet Union compared to $5.595 billion they had spent eight years before in 1982.[43] Consequently, Africans can now truly attempt to rely first and foremost on themselves and on nonviolent means to resolve their local conflicts. African scarce resources would now be devoted to meeting the basic needs of African peoples rather than being squandered on arms purchases in the pursuit of military solutions to local conflicts.

Furthermore, resurgent interest in Africa in multiparty democracy was fuelled by the popular upheavals of 1989-1990 in Eastern Europe which brought about the collapse of the communist dictatorships in that region of Europe. The disintegration of those regimes caused nervousness among Africa's authoritarian regimes. In such one party states as Mauritania, Kenya, and Zaire, students and masses of the citizenry seized the opportunity to call for democratic governments on the basis of plural politics. Between 1989 and 1991 ruling parties in Angola, Mozambique, and Congo--Brazzaville, formally abandoned their Marxist-Leninist ideology and declared their intention to hold multi-party elections. In 1991 legislative and presidential elections removed Marxist leaderships from power in Benin, Cape Verde, and Sao Tome and Principe. "There is no doubt" wrote *West Africa*,"that it is the amazing collapse of one party authoritarian regimes in Eastern Europe which has sown the seeds of a real desire for change in African one party authoritarian regimes. . . . The wind from the East is shaking the coconut trees. . . ."[44] Olusegun Obasanjo, formerly Nigeria's head of state (1976-1979), added that the winds of change in Eastern Europe provided "considerable opportunities for the African people . . . to intensify their struggle for democracy. . . . The people in almost every country on the continent," he went on, were demanding "radical political changes which alone would usher in a new era of economic and social transformation."[45] General Obasanjo affirmed that, strenghtened by the developments in Eastern Europe, a new era in Africa was in the offing when leaders would no longer choose to ignore the voices and votes of their people and their people's fundamental human rights; that the "Ceauscescu factor" was the most important single event that caused many African leaders to embark upon political and economic reform programs that, in varying degrees, aimed at introducing accountablity of the political leaders and institutions, multiparty system, rule of law, and observance of human rights. The critical need now is to sustain these trends and reform programs.

The demise of the Soviet bloc has had additional salutary impact on Africa. It has reduced the opportunity for the politicising of Western aid to Africa as a cold war weapon--a prophylactic against the spread of communism to Africa. During the era of the cold war, Western aid donors, including the IMF and the World Bank, had tolerated the corrupt practice of Third World elite to use grants, loans, and credits to transfer capital to Europe or to purchase luxury homes in the area rather than using the resources to meet critical needs of their societies. Now that the cold war is over, they sharply criticize the practice. Also, unlike their practice during the years of the cold war, they factor into their aid to African states the human rights record of applicants and potential recipients of such assistance. As a consequence, fear has struck at the corrupt state bureaucracies and the hearts of those senior civil servants who had engaged in the practice.[46]

Finally, the demise of the Soviet bloc definitively discredited the Soviet system of economic development in the eyes of Africans as a social model on a global or regional level. It provides a challenge to Africans to develop their own model of economic development. Between 1989 and 1991, in some cases earlier, most of the nations of Africa had moved rapidly towards adopting free market economies. The road remains rough as they chart new paths.

CONCLUSION

It is clear that the demise of the Soviet bloc, indeed, produced repercussions in, and new challenges for, Africa. But the magnitude of the those repercussions and challenges is not greater than that posed by the erstwhile ideological struggle between Soviet and Western power blocs. With the end of that struggle, Africans now have an unfettered opportunity, such as they never had under the cold war, to redouble their efforts at attempts to adjust economic and political institutions to African realities. Given this opportunity, the governments of African states and their officials must now pay more attention to the concrete needs and aspirations of the masses of their people. They must demonstrate more willingness to be accountable. They must demonstrate by their life styles and leadership genuine sacrifice in the overall interest of their nation and public good. Above all, they must recognize, and act on such recognition, that post-cold war Africa desperately needs an infusion of indigenous economic and political thinking and structures to deal with the particular and pervading problems of the peoples of Africa--a low rate of economic development, political cleavages, and the brutal impoverishment of large peasant communities. Continued attempts to graft Western economic and political structures to African conditions are likely to fail as they did during the years of the cold war.

The demise of the Soviet bloc might thus be auspicious for Africa. It might set the stage for an African cultural and structural renaissance that brings with it more viable approaches to political consolidation and sustainable economic development for Africa. Such a process might well establish the "foundation for a genuine [African] autonomy, facilitating the transformation of the continent's peripheral status [in world affairs] in times to come."[47] Finally, a transformed Africa may have better political and economic relations with a politically and economically restructured Russia and other members of the Commonwealth of Independent States as well as the established Western Democracies.

ĿDNOTES

1. John W. Harbeson and Donald Rothchild (eds.), *Africa in World Politics* (Boulder, Colo.: Westview Press, 1991), p. 1.

2. Yuri Popov, "Africa and the Soviet Peretroika," *International Affairs* (Moscow) No. 3 1991), p. 41.

3. F. U. Ohaegbulam, "Africa and Superpower Rivalry: Prospects for the Future and Possible Remedies," *Journal of African Studies*, Vol. 8, No. 4 (1981/82), p. 164; David Morrison, *The U.S.S.R. And Africa* (London: OUP, 1964), pp. 1-58; David E. Albright," The USSR and Africa: Soviet Policy, "Problems of Communism (Jan/Feb. 1978), P. 21; Robert Legvold, *Soviet Policy in West Africa* (Cambridge: Harvard University Press, 1970), pp. 1-39.

4. "Soviet Union in Africa," *Africa Recovery*, Vol. 6, No. 1 (April 1992), p. 15. Mark Webber, Soviet Policy in Sub-Saharan African: The Fihnal Phase," *The Journal of Modern African Studies*, 30, 1 (March 1992), pp. 1-30; Arthur Jay Klinghoffer, "The soviet Union and Superpower rivalry in Africa, "in Bruce E. Arlinghaus (ed.), *African Security Issues: Sovereignty, Stability, and Solidarity* Boulder, Colorado: Westview Press, 1984), pp. 64-74.

5. Andrei Kozyrev & Andrei Shumikhin, "East and West in the third World," *International Affairs* (Moscow), No. 3 (1989), pp. 64-74.

6. Stephanie G. Neuman, "Arms, Aid and the Superpowers," *Foreign Affairs*, 66, 5 (Summer 1988), 1044-1066; Leonid L. Futurie, "Russia's Arms Sales to Africa: Past, Present, and Future," *CSIS Africa Notes*, No. 140 (September 1992), p.1; David E. Albright, "Moscow's African Policy in the 1970s," in D.E. Albright (ed.), *Africa and International Communism* (London, 1980); Bruce D. Porter, *The USSR in the Third World Conflict: Soviet Aims and Diplomacy in Local Wars, 1945-1980* (Cambridge, 1984), chap. 3; Roy Pateman, "Soviet Arms Transfers to Ethiopia," *TransAfrica Forum*, 8, 1 (Spring 1991), pp. 43-57.

7. Richard Ullman, "Ending the Cold War," *Foreign Policy*, No. 72 (fall 1988), pp. 130-157; Robert G. Kaiser, "The USSR In Decline," *Foreign Affairs*, 67, 2 (1988), pp. 97-113; Robert Tucker, '1989 And All That," *Foreign Affairs*, 69, 4 (1990), pp. 93-114; William McNeil, "Winds of Change," *Foreign Affairs* 69, 4 (1990), pp. 152-175; Michael Howard, "The Springtime of Nations," *Foreign Affairs*, 69, 1 (1990), 17-32; Milan Svec, "The Prague Spring: Twenty Years Later," *Foreign Affairs*, 66, 5 (1988), 981-1001.

8. Kozyrev & Shumikhin, in *International Affairs* (Moscow), No. 3 (1989), pp. 68-69.

9. Archie Brown, "Change in the Soviet Union," *Foreign Affairs*, 64, 5 (1986), 1048-106; Seweryn Bialer & Joan Afferica, "The Genesis of Gorbachev's World," *Foreign Affairs*, 64, 3 (1986), 605-644; Dimitri K. Simes, "Gorbachev: A New Foreign Policy," *Foreign Affairs*, 65, 3(1987) 477-500; David Holloway, "Gorbachev's New Thinking," *Foreign Affairs*, 68, 1 (1989), 66-81, Robert Legvold, "The Revolution in Soviet Foreign Policy," *Foreign Affairs*, 68, 1 (1989), 97-113; Jerry Hough, "Gorbachev's Politics," *Foreign Affairs*, 68, 5 (1989), 26-41; Robert G. Kaiser, "Gorbachev: Triumph and Failure," *Foreign Affairs*, 70, 2 (1991), 160-174.

10. Jeffrey E. Garten, "Japan and Germany: American Concerns," *Foreign Affairs*, 68, ! (Winter 1989/90), pp. 84-101; Felix Rohatyn, "America's Economic Dependence," *Foreign Affairs* 68, 1 (1989), pp. 53-65; Samuel P. Huntington, "The United States--?Decline Or Renewal?" *Foreign Affairs*, 67, 2 (Winter 1988/89), pp. 76-96.

11. Webber, in The Journal of Modern African Studies, 30, 1 (March 1992), pp. 5-15.

12. Vladimir Iordansky, "Russia: No Bear Hugs for Africa," *Africa Recovery,* Vol. 6, No. 1 (April 1992), p. 17.

13. Iordansky, in *Africa Recovery*, 6, 1 (1992), pp. 15-17; Kozyrev & Shumikhin, in *International Affairs* (Moscow), No. 3 (1989), pp. 64-74.

14. Margot Light, "Soviet Policy in the Third World," *International Affairs*, Vol. 67, No. ? (April 1991), pp. 263-280.

15. Jiri Valenta, "Moscow's New Thinking and Third World Regional Conflicts: Some Conclusions," in Valenta and Frank Cibulka (eds.), *Gorbachev's New Thinking and Third World Conflicts* (London: 1990), pp. 291-293; Webber, in *The Journal of Modern African Studies*, 30, 1 (March 1992), pp. 1-5.

16. Charles Quist Adade, "Soviets Abandon Africa," *West Africa*, (Oct. 8-14, 1990), pp. 2606-2607; Yuri Popv, "Africa and the Soviet Perestroika," *International Affairs* (Moscow), No. 3 (1991) pp. 43,50; Konstantin Ovchinnikov, "Third World Markets, Mirages and Prospects,: *International Affairs* (Moscow), No. 5 (1991), P. 54.

17. Light, in *International Affairs*, 67, 2 (April 1991), p. 269.

18. Webber, in *The Journal of Modern African Studies*, 30, 1 (March 1992), pp. 7-15.

19. Charles Quist Adade, "Soviets Abandon Africa," *West Africa*, (Oct. 8-14, 1990), p. 2606.

20. Grigori Polyanov, "What Shall We Buy in Africa," *International Affairs* (Moscow), October 1989), p. 69.

21. Popov, in *International Affairs* (Moscow), No. 3 (1991), p. 48; Ovchinnikov, in *International Affairs* (Moscow), No. 5 (1991), pp. 54-58.

22. General Agreement on Tariffs and Trade, International Trade 1988-1989, Vol. 2 (Geneva GATT., 1989), p. 28, Cited in Harbeson & Rothchild (eds.), *Africa in World Politics*, p. 170.

23. Harbeson & Rothchild (eds.), *Africa in World Politics*, p. 9.

24. Joanna Moss & John Ravanhill, "Trade Diversification in Black Africa," *The Journal of Modern African Studies*, 27, 3 (Sept. 1989), pp. 521-545; Harbeson & Rothchild (eds.), *Africa in World Politics*, pp. 179-201.

25. Harbeson & Rothchild (eds.), *Africa in World Politcs*, p. 171.

26. Harbeson & Rothchild, *Africa in World Politics*, p. 9; Olusegun Obasanjo, "Eastern Promises," West Africa, (7-13 May 1990), p. 762; Editorial, "France, Africa, Africa And Democracy, *West Africa,* (9-15 April 1990), p. 567; Shada Islam, "Lome IV: Frayed Tempers," *West Africa* (16-22 April 1990), p. 636.

27. Cited in Yuri Popov, "Africa and the Soviet Perestroika," *International Affairs* (Moscow) No. 3 (1991), p. 44.

28. Michael Clough, "The United Sates and Africa: The Policy of Cynical Disengagment, *Current History*, 91, 565 (May 1992), 193-198; David D. Newsom, "After the Cold War US Interest in Sub-Saharan Africa, " *Washington Quarterly*, 13, 1 (Winter 1990), 99-114; Carol Lancaster "U.S. Aid to Sub-Saharan Africa: Challenges, Constraints and Choices," *CSIS Significant Issue Series*, 10, 16 (1988); "USA/Africa: Policy? What Policy? *Africa Confidential*, Vol. 32, No. 1 (1 January 1991), pp. 1-6 ;Shada islam, "Lome IV: Frayed Tempers," *West Africa* (April 16-22 1990), p. 567.

29. Salim Lone, "UN Confronts Tough New Africa Challenges," *Africa Recovery,* Vol 6, No. 3 (Nov. 1992), p. 1; Roy Laishley, "Africa Faces Aid Cuts: Recession Preoccupies Major Western Donors, "*Africa Recovery,* Vol. 6, No. 3 (Nov. 1992), pp. 3, 24-25; Michael Clough, *Free At Last?: U.S. Policy Toward Africa And The End Of The War* (N.Y.: Council of Foreign Relations Press, 1992); Pauline H. Baker, "Africa in the New World Order," *Sais Review,* Vol 10, No. 2 (Summer/Fall 1990), pp. 139-152.

30. Tim Wall, "Soviet Demise Brings Africa New Challenges," *Africa Recovery,* Vol 6, No. 1 (April 1992), p. 14.

31. "Nordic Aid Cuts," in *Africa Recovery,* Vo. 6, No. 1 (April 1992), p. 36.

32. Wall, in *Africa Recovery,* 6, 1 (April 1992), p. 14; Olusegun Obasanjo, "Eastern Promises," West Africa (May 7-13-1990),

33. Wall, in *Africa Recovery,* 6, 1 (April 1992), p. 15.

34. Wall, in *Africa Recovery,* 6, 1 (April 1992), p. 15.

35. "Soviet Union and Africa," *Africa Recovery*, Vol. 6, No. (April 1992), pp. 15; Tim Wall, "Soviet Demise Brings Africa New Challenges," *Africa Recovery*, Vol. No. 1 (April 1992), p. 17.

36. Roy Laishely, "Commodity Prices Deal Blow to Africa," *Africa Recovery*, 6, 1 (April 1992), pp. 1, 8-10.

37. Laishley, in *Africa recovery,* 6, 1 (April 1992), p. 17.

38. Popov, in *International Affairs* (Moscow), Number 3 (1991), p. 48.

39. Webber, in *The Journal of Modern African Studies*, 30, 1 (March 1992), p. 26.

40. Webber, in *The Journal of Modern African Studies*, 30, 1 (March 1992), p. 29.

41. Webber, in *The Journal of Modern African Studies*, 30, 1 (March 1992), p. 19.

42. "Black Bashing: Perestroika Breeds Anti-Black Sentiment," *West Africa* (Oct. 8-14, 1990), pp. 2606-2607; Popov, in *International Affairs* (Moscow), No. 3 (1991), p. 43.

43. Leonid L. Fiturie, "Russia's Arms Sales to Africa: Past, Present and Future," *CSIS Africa Notes*, No. 140 (Sept. 1992), p. 1.

44. Editorial, "France, Africa and Democracy," *West Africa*, (April 9-15, 1990), P. 567; Popov, in *International Affairs* (Moscow), No. 3 (1991), pp. 40-50.

45. Olusegun Obasanjo, "Eastern Promises, "*West Africa* (May 7-13, 1990), p. 762.

46. Popov, in *International Affairs* (Moscow), No. 3 (1991), pp. 44-45.

47. Harbeson & Rothchild, *Africa in World Politics*, p. 14.

Chapter VIII

Prospects for the Development of Higher Education in Kenya*

Dr. John C. Weidman

I t is important that any consideration of prospects for the development of higher education in Kenya be understood within the more general context of the East African region. Consequently, in the first part of this discussion I describe the economic and social development context of East Africa. Then, I draw on the more general context of the African continent, summarizing several major issues that have been identified by various experts as being of contemporary significance for the continued growth and development of African higher education. This leads to a discussion of five major themes that I believe are particularly important for Kenya, followed by some concluding suggestions for the future development of its university system.

The Regional Development Context: East Africa

Kenya and its neighboring East African countries are in a very poor economic condition, as is shown in Table 1. Kenya is just above the mean in per capita GNP for low- and middle-income countries in Sub-Saharan
Africa, but all of the bordering countries except Sudan are considerably below the regional mean. Kenya is the 23rd poorest nation in the world, but all of its East African neighbors

Table 1.   Development Status of Countries in East Africa

Country/Region	Rank	1989 per Capita GNP	1989 Life Expectancy at Birth	1985 Adult Illiteracy Women All	Rate of Population Growth
Ethiopia	2	$ 120	48 yrs	--- 38%	3.4%
Kenya	23	$ 360	59 yrs	51% 41%	3.4%
Somalia	4	$ 170	48 yrs	94% 88%	3.1%
Sudan	40	$ 550	50 yrs	--- ---	2.8%
Tanzania	3	$ 130	49 yrs	--- ---	3.3%
Uganda	14	$ 250	49 yrs	55% 43%	3.5%
Low- and Middle-Income SubSaharan Africa		$ 340	51 yrs	65% 52%	3.2%

Source: World Bank. 1991. *World Development Report 1991*. New York: Oxford University Press.

are even poorer. The region is also characterized by high rates of adult illiteracy. Hence, it is important that there be serious consideration of investment that will enhance the capacity of universities in the region to further national development. It is anticipated that the Treaty for East African Cooperation, signed 30 November 1993, will facilitate cooperative work among universities in Kenya, Uganda, and Tanzania. This treaty specifically identifies education, research, and communications as important areas for cooperation.

Background: Issues in African Higher Education

African leaders and higher education experts who participated in seminars held in Accra, Ghana, in 1991 (UNESCO, 1992), and in Dakar, Senegal, in 1992 (UNESCO, 1993), identified ten major areas of concern about the current status and future prospects of African higher education. The following summarizes the observations and recommendations made as a result of these seminars (Consultation of Experts on Future Trends and Challenges of Higher Education in Africa, 1992): (1). Mission of Higher Education in African Society: There is a need to build institutions that are truly oriented toward the development of African societies and the promotion of African cultures. This will require greater efforts at producing the kinds of graduates who will not only be adaptable to the rapidly changing needs of African society but also contribute to innovation and development. (2). Access to Higher Education: Rapid increases in enrolments have occurred without consideration of the distribution of students by discipline and the extent to which current patterns will satisfy African manpower needs. Guidance and counseling of students should take African development needs into account along with more careful attention to the ability and aptitude of entering students. (3). Women's Access to Higher Education: The participation of women in African higher education is very low compared to many countries. This is in large part due to traditional cultural values that emphasize women's roles as wife and mother. Specific actions should be taken to encourage the continuation of girls and women through primary and secondary school. Both material and academic incentives should be offered that will facilitate their entrance into and successful completion of higher education. (4). Quality and Content of Education: There are serious problems in Africa with the quality of instruction, the size of classes, availability of up-to-date materials and equipment, the relevance of the curriculum to current conditions, and the integration of higher education with the world of work. Higher education institutions should begin to provide pedagogical training to their teachers as well as to their graduate students seeking to become teachers at the tertiary level. Students should have opportunities to experience the world of work through such experiences as internships, cooperative placements with employers in their field of study, and off-term jobs. Specific plans should also be developed for the acquisition of needed materials and equipment. (5). Harmonization of Curricula and Academic Mobility: Mobility among countries in Africa is hindered by the "critical mismatch between curricula and societal needs," and the "lack of mutual recognition" of academic degrees and qualifications. Institutions need to "intensify information exchange." Member states should "ratify and effectively enforce the Arusha Convention on the Recognition of Studies, Diplomas and other Qualifications." (6). Inter-University Cooperation and Pooling of Resources: Institutions of higher education in Africa are more inclined toward developing joint activities with countries in the North rather than with their African neighbors. They should join forces to develop "centres of excellence" in Africa and seek external resources that would facilitate this process such as the UNESCO UNITWIN and UNESCO Chairs programmes. (7). Higher Education as a Factor of Social Change: There is a need to recognize the unique contributions that African higher education institutions have made to the adoption of innovation in a variety of fields. Greater efforts should be made to strengthen the contribution of higher education to "innovation, especially in the promotion of endogenous technologies and cultural heritage." (8). Teachers' Status: Teachers in African universities continue to be underpaid in comparison to those with similar qualifications working in other economic sectors. This has contributed to "brain drain" as highly respected academics have been sought by other universities and left Africa for different parts of the world. Efforts must be made to upgrade academic salaries so that teachers will not be motivated to leave higher education in search of higher pay and status. (9). Research: Research "should keep abreast with teaching and should help to raise the quality of higher education, in particular, and of social life, in general." The contributions of research in Africa, however, are hindered by the lack of adequate resources and limited applicability to societal needs. Attention must be paid to (a) improving both basic and applied research, (b) furthering work on advanced technologies of critical social and economic need in Africa, (c) improving the preparation of researchers, (d) setting up "adequate structures for the coordination, dissemination and publication of research results," (e) working to make research activities an integral part of institutions' public service functions, and (f) reducing duplication through inter-institutional cooperation involving both researchers and facilities. (10). Financing: Government budgets in Africa ave been inadequate to fund the actual needs of institutions. Higher education should be given a major priority because of its significance for social and economic development. In addition, institutions should seek to diversify their funding base through a variety of *cost-recovery* measures such as rental of facilities, charging fees for services to non-university constituencies, and contracting for professional consulting services.

Higher Education in Kenya: Significant Themes

The foregoing list of issues suggests five themes which are particularly significant when considering the future of higher education in Kenya. Not surprisingly, these five themes also appear throughout recently published materials on higher education in Africa: (1) access and gender equity (Alele-Williams, 1992; Lamptey, 1992); (2) increasing the use of technology to improve management, instruction, and research (Fall, 1992); (3) providing continuing professional development for academic staff (both teaching and research) and administrators (Mohammedhai, 1992; M. Thiam, 1992); (4) establishing the capacity for reform and innovation through systematic planning and policy analysis (Taiwo, 1992); and (5) diversifying finance (Koso-Thomas, 1992). (1). Access and Gender Equity: With respect to access to education, virtually all (94%) children in Kenya enter primary school. However, only half of the original entering students are still enrolled at the end of primary school. Since just half of the primary school graduates gain admission to secondary school, there is an effective secondary school enrolment ratio of 24% of the nation's young people of secondary school age (Opondo & Noormohamed, 1989, p. 88). In 1990, there were enough available university places for just 7.5% of the secondary school graduates (Mwiria & Nyukuri, 1992, pp. 17-18), therefore the effective university enrolment ratio was less than 2% of university age Kenyans. Despite the rapid expansion of enrolments in higher education in Kenya over the thirty years since independence that is shown in Table 2, the system still can accommodate only a very small fraction of the nation's young people.

According to Table 2, virtually equal numbers of boys and girls begin primary school in Kenya. However, by secondary school, there are 1.33 boys for every girl. The public university sex ratio is double that of secondary schools at 2.68 males for every female! Only for the Teachers' College sector of higher education is there reasonable gender equity (1.15 males per female). There are many cultural reasons for the low participation of women in African higher education, especially traditional family patterns which emphasize that the proper role of women is to stay in the home and care for their families (Alele-Williams, 1992). Parents often discourage their daughters from obtaining advanced education (beginning as early as the transition from primary into secondary school) because they believe potential husbands will not be interested in marrying highly educated women (Lamptey, 1992).

Many strategies for increasing the participation of women in higher education have been advocated, e.g., counseling and the creation of awareness of educational opportunities among girls, reorienting attitudes of male counterparts, changing attitudes of parents, reforming organizational management practices that exclude women from senior administrative posts in African higher education, development of an indigenous women's movement, and government promulgation and enforcement of affirmative action policies (Lamptey, 1992). There continues to be much room for improvement with respect to gender equity in Kenyan higher education.

Table 3 shows the distribution of academic courses of study for first-time undergraduates who enrolled in 1992/93. For both genders, the most popular courses were B.Ed.(Arts) and Arts. The combination of Science and B.Ed.(Science) was the next most popular, also for both genders. Only for B.Ed.(Home Economics/Home Science Technology) did women outnumber men, and there were almost equal numbers choosing Cultural Studies. While an arts (social science or humanities) emphasis was being pursued by almost half of all undergraduates entering Kenyan public universities in 1992/93, there were also substantial numbers studying science, engineering, and business management/commerce. This distribution of academic courses suggests that the universities are contributing to the goal of educating students according to their expressed academic interests as well as filling the high-level manpower needs of a developing nation. (2). Increased Use of Technology: Most African universities have very limited access to modern computing and communications technology, so it is increasingly difficult for teachers and students to keep abreast of current developments in their academic areas. As financial constraints and the complexity of managing financial resources increase, having access to relevant computer soft- and hardware could greatly improve financial management in African higher education. Universities should also be in the forefront of helping to plan and develop national and international communication systems in order to facilitate rapid dissemination of information as well as to keep up-to-date with current literature in the academic disciplines (Fall, 1992). Given the budget constraints of most African universities, it is important to investigate technological needs from both an intra- and an inter-institutional perspective so that strategies for equipment acquisition and seeking donor funding can maximize their impact across the entire range of instructional (including library), research, and public service activities. Of course, advanced communications technology requires access to a reliable, efficient, and affordably priced telephone system. Improving Kenya's outmoded telecommunications system should be a major government priority. (3). Continuing Professional Development of Academic Staff (Teaching and Research) and Administrators: It has been suggested that the quality of research produced in African universities is rather poor, not only due to the lack of adequate facilities, but also because teachers are not well-prepared to do research (M. Thiam, 1992). Consideration must be given to the strategies that might be used to improve research training, including the advantages and disadvantages of sending people abroad for study as opposed to organizing local training

Table 2 -- **Kenya Education Trends by Type of Institution, 1963-1992 (Selected Years)**

	1963	1973	1983	1986	1987	1992
Primary Schools						
No. of Schools	6,058	6,932	11,966	13,347	13,849	15,465
Total Enrollment						
(in thousands)	892	1,816	4,324	4,843	5,031	5,530
Sex Ratio *	192	130	108	108	107	103
Secondary Schools						
No. of Schools	151	964	2,230	2,417	2,592	2,632
Total Enrolment	30,120	174,767	493,710	458,712	522,261	621,443
Sex Ratio *	215	204	148	141	144	133
Teachers' Colleges **						
No. of Institutions	37	21	21	22	22	29
Total Enrolment	4,119	8,905	13,657	15,644	17,817	19,154
Sex Ratio *						133
National Polytechnics						
No. of Institutions	1	2	2	2	3	3
Total Enrolment	864	3,721	5,398	5,313	5,186	9,029
Institutes of Technology						
No. of Institutions		1	4	16	16	17
Total Enrolment		110	456	4,694	4,248	5,633
Government Universities ***						
No. of Institutions	1	1	1	4	4	4
Total Enrolment	571	5,149	9,223	10,143	17,538	40,748
Sex Ratio*						270

Notes:
* Males per 100 females.
** The drop in number was due to conversion of some into secondary schools. By 1992, these colleges prepared only primary school teachers.
*** "Double intakes" (two different groups of secondary school graduates admitted to university simultaneously) occurred in 1987/88 and 1990/91.

Sources:
Republic of Kenya. 1989. *Development Plan, 1989-1993.* Nairobi: Government Printer.
Republic of Kenya. 1994. *Development Plan, 1994-1996.* Nairobi: Government Printer.

programs and the consequences of each for "brain drain" (the failure of highly trained personnel to return to Kenya following completion of their programs). Academic staff must also remain up-to-date in their knowledge of the fields in which they are teaching (M. Thiam, 1992). Because of limited student access to textbooks and other instructional materials, academic staff in many fields must deliver the primary content of courses through classroom instruction. Consequently, it is very important that teachers be skilled in the pedagogy of higher education, especially those aspects unique to higher education in the African context. (4). Establishing Capacity for Reform and Innovation: Because the post-colonial history of African higher education is relatively brief, it is important to build the capacity for continual reform and innovation so that vitality and productivity can be enhanced (Taiwo, 1992). This might encompass developing alternative modes of instructional delivery (including distance education); evaluation and use of results to modify programs (including paying attention to content and facility duplication); and developing strategies for the acquisition and maintenance of necessary instructional materials and equipment. It would also include forging more democratic governance structures in which teachers, other staff, and even students participate in significant decision-making processes such as the recommendation of candidates for administrative appointments.

Reform and innovation need to be based on a firm foundation of planning and policy analysis. A wide variety of statistical data are collected routinely by the government, but they tend not to be used for systematic analysis. There needs to be better use of the many knowledgeable and highly skilled academics in Kenyan universities for providing expert advice on policy options. There has been a tendency to bring in external consultants to do projects that could be done by people already working in Kenya. Examples are the three research projects recently let for bid by the Kenya Commission for Higher Education, using World Bank *loan* funds: (a) graduate labor market survey (focus on employment,

Table 3 -- First Year Undergraduate Enrolment in Public Universities, 1992/93 *

Selected Courses **	Males	%	Females	%	Total	%
Agriculture Education	73	1.0%	42	1.5%	115	1.1%
Agriculture ***	248	3.3%	110	4.0%	358	3.5%
Horticulture	91	1.2%	33	1.2%	124	1.2%
Arts	1440	19.4%	584	21.1%	2024	19.9%
Anthropology	151	2.0%	67	2.4%	218	2.1%
B.Ed.(Arts)	1913	25.8%	851	30.7%	2764	27.1%
B.Ed.(Science)	447	6.0%	116	4.2%	563	5.5%
B.Ed.(Home Economics/ Home Science Tech.)	7	.1%	134	4.8%	141	1.4%
Business Management/ Commerce	440	5.9%	109	4.2%	549	5.4%
Science	969	13.1%	273	9.9%	1242	12.2%
Engineering ****	380	5.1%	33	1.2%	413	4.1%
Veterinary Medicine	86	1.2%	14	.5%	100	1.0%
Medicine	129	1.7%	19	.7%	148	1.5%
Natural Resources	87	1.2%	15	.5%	102	1.0%
Animal Production	62	.8%	33	1.2%	95	.9%
Agriculture and Home Economics	54	.7%	33	1.2%	87	.9%
Cultural Studies	131	1.7%	120	4.3%	251	2.5%
(Total Enrolment for All Courses)	(7418)		(2771)		(10,189)	

Notes:
* All data for 1992/93 are "provisional," i.e., government estimates (in recent years, very close to final figures).
** Only those courses enrolling more than 85 students are listed, but the total in the bottom row is for all entering undergraduates.
*** Includes B.Sci.Agri., Food Science Tech., and Agri. Economics.
**** Includes civil, mechanical, electrical, agricultural, and building construction.

Source: Republic of Kenya. 1993. *Economic Survey 1993*. Nairobi: Government Printer.

unemployment, and underemployment); (b) alternative funding models for higher education, including private institutions; and (c) women in higher education, access and equity. Given the type of public bidding procedure involved, it is quite likely that the projects will be awarded to foreign consultants. It would be unfortunate if these projects are not awarded to academic and research staff in the universities of Kenya where considerable relevant expertise exists and where the studies could also provide training opportunities and contribute to the development of institutional research capacity. (5). Diversifying Finance: Over the past five years, there has been a sharp decrease in the proportion of the Kenya national budget for *recurrent* (e.g., salaries, pensions, benefits, utilities, facilities maintenance, etc.) expenditures that is being allocated for education. In 1988/89, education received 38% of the total *recurrent* budget funds (Maina, 1989, p. 110). In 1992/93, estimated *recurrent* government expenditures for education were only 18% of the total national *recurrent* budget (Republic of Kenya, 1993, p. 88). While a natural tendency is to blame the government for neglecting education, this is not entirely fair because other international agencies (most notably, the World Bank and the International Monetary Fund) are staunch advocates of "structural adjustment" policies. These policies require that national budgets be structured in such a way that the broad spectrum of national development needs are addressed. What this has meant, in practice, is pressure on developing countries to reduce expenditures in historically high-cost areas such as education and human services so that more funds can be allocated to other development needs, e.g., making infrastructure (especially transportation, communication, and resource management) improvements that are necessary to facilitate national development.

It cannot be said that the government in Kenya is failing to spend a significant amount on higher education. To the contrary, in 1992/93 higher education was allocated 19% of the total national *recurrent* budget and just over half (56%) of the government's *development* (e.g., funds for buildings, equipment, and other capital investment) budget (Republic of Kenya, 1993, p. 184). Clearly, the government of Kenya is conforming to external expectations that its budgetary policies reflect efforts at structural adjustment. Even so, higher education is being funded much more generously than any other level of education. Table 4 shows Kenya government expenditures per student in 1992/93, calculated by dividing the Ministry of Education *recurrent* budget figures (Republic of Kenya, 1993, p. 184) by the enrolment figures shown in Table 2. According to Table 4, national *recurrent* expenditures per student in public universities for 1992/93 were *46 times higher than those for each primary school student*.

However, in the context of African Higher education, Kenya's expenditures are not unusual. Sanyal and Martin (1991) describe "the relatively high cost of African higher education" as follows:

> ...cost of a graduate of Sub-Saharan Africa, according to one estimate is eight times GNP per capita whereas it is only 3.7 times the GNP per capita for all the developing countries combined (Mingat and Psacharopoulos, 1985). The ratio between unit costs in higher and in primary education varies between 30:1 and 50:1 in African countries as against 10:1 in Asia or Latin America (Hinchcliffe, 1987).

It must be noted that projected 1992/93 government "development" expenditures for universities were quite high and, hence, may not be repeated in the near future. Taking both the *recurrent* and *development* parts of the Ministry of Education budget together, per capita expenditures per student in public universities were an astonishing *68 times greater than those for each primary school student*.

Despite the overall decrease between 1987/88 and 1992/93 in the proportion of total government funding for education, the per capita student expenditure ratio between university and primary education, when based on *recurrent* expenditures only, did not change between 1987/88 when it was 47 (Opondo & Noormohamed, 1989, p. 92) and 1992/93 when it was 46. Given this pattern, it is unlikely that the proportion of government expenditures allocated to higher education will increase significantly. Consequently, it is necessary for universities to begin exploring alternative sources of funds and developing strategies of "cost-sharing." Ten options for "widening and diversifying sources of finance" (Woodhall, 1993, pp. 8-10; 1991) are (a) charging students for tuition and/or other types of fees (e.g., registration, examination, etc.); (b) charging students a larger share of actual board and lodging costs (including reducing governmental stipends for student housing and other personal expenses); (c) encouraging the establishment and growth of private institutions within a context of effective government regulation (James, 1991); (d) deferred cost recovery (e.g., payroll tax paid by employers of graduates); (e) work-study aid or national service programs; (f) business sponsorship of students; (g) contracting for consulting and applied research with industry, commerce, and government; (h) sales of goods and services; (i) private contributions and endowments, including gifts from alumni and staff as well as from business and industry; and (j) student loans or other forms of deferred payment.

In Kenya, only 20-25 percent of students ever pay back their loans (Woodhall, 1991, p. 55). This is unfortunate, since repayment replenishes the loan fund, and as such, can be thought of as an investment in future generations of students who will be contributing to national development. The failure to recover loan funds from Kenyan students is due to lack of both strong legal sanctions and an effective collection agency. If cost-sharing and cost-effectiveness are underlying goals, a higher education student loan program should have the following characteristics:

First, a deferred payment program requires the participation of a *credible collection institution with incentives to collect*, which in most instances required the direct participation of commercial banks, a taxation department or a social security agency...Second, with loans, there must be a willingness to charge interest rates equal to or above *inflation* in order to minimize subsidies...Third, the relationship between necessary repayments and the likely income of students must be examined to ensure that repayment burdens never pose an *excessive burden* on graduates...Fourth, developing a means of *targeting* support to needier and more academically deserving students will be crucial to a program's efficiency...Fifth, loan losses can be justified if there are *potential social gains* that would not be reflected in a graduate's income (Albrecht & Ziderman, 1992, p. 100).

Institutions *must be financially autonomous*, as well as able to control and monitor their own expenditures (preferably with a computerized financial accounting system). They must also be able to keep revenue generated and not return it to the government or have subsequent budget allocations reduced by the amount of the revenue (Woodhall, 1993, p.

12). Institutions must also receive their funds (government allocation, other revenue) in a *timely and regular way* (Passi, 1992). It is important to emphasize that cost recovery is not meant to substitute for effective government funding policy which provides funds for investment in tandem with funds for systematic maintenance of facilities and equipment, for acquisition of library materials and teaching resources, and for institutional development:

> ...in practice, cost recovery operates in tandem with, and complements, state subsidy of higher education. Characterizing a system as one of cost recovery in practice relates to the breadth of student coverage of fees and their size in relation to costs (Albrecht and Ziderman, 1992, p. 11).

Discussion

With respect to each of the foregoing significant themes, Kenya is making progress but much remains to be done. Access and gender equity in the public universities are still not at the levels that one would wish to see in a developing country. Because there are places for less than 2% of the eligible age cohort to attend university, it is important that serious consideration be given to increasing the enrolment capacity of the university system. Rather than founding new universities, this could be done by expanding already existing institutions which are now relatively small when compared with those in other countries (Nairobi University, the largest, has 13,000 students; Moi University, the smallest, has fewer than 7000) so that "economies of scale" could be realized. Young men enrolling in universities outnumber young women by a ratio of 2.7 to 1, even though both groups start primary school in equal numbers. Ways will have to be found to improve gender equity not only in universities but also throughout the educational system if the human resources of Kenya are to be utilized fully. Such efforts will have to be grounded in the very strong cultural traditions present among the various tribal groups of Kenya.

Increasing the use of technology requires both technical knowledge and the funds necessary to purchase, effectively use, and maintain sophisticated equipment. Donor agencies such as the World Bank have been helpful, but more broadly-based approaches that do not depend on external donors are needed if the country as a whole is to benefit along with the universities. Significant improvement of Kenya's telecommunications system is also essential.

Professional development of academic staff and administrators continues to occur, but approaches need to be varied and oriented toward pressing problems of teaching, research and administration in higher education. There also must be a purposive mix of in-country and foreign training programs. Kenya has received a loan from the World Bank (Universities Investment Project) which is being used for training higher education staff as well as to acquire books and scientific equipment. Further, institutions need to look beyond themselves to build regional coalitions that enlist the expertise of academic and administrative

Table 4 -- Kenya Recurrent Expenditures Per Student by Level of Education, 1992/93 *

Level	Enrolment	Education Ministry Recurrent Budget (Kenya Pounds)	Per Student Expenditure (Kenya Pounds)**
Primary Education	5,530,000	346,330,000	62.63
Secondary Education	621,443	97,240,000	156.47
Teachers' Colleges	18,992	12,870,000	677.65
Public Universities	41,062	118,620,000	2888.80

Notes: * All data are "provisional," i.e., government estimates (in
        recent years, very close to final figures).
       ** 1 Kenya Pound - 20 Kenya Shillings.

Source: Republic of Kenya. 1993. *Economic Survey 1993.* Nairobi: Government
        Printer.

staff from the universities within Kenya as well as from neighboring countries in Africa (King, 1990).

Building the capacity for reform and innovation depends, in part, on the development of planning and policy analytical skills at both the institutional and national levels. It also requires that universities have sufficient autonomy to be able to pursue initiatives without government intervention as well as to control their own affairs. More participatory governance structures are necessary. Saint (1992, p. 71) identifies the following three areas of particular importance for African higher education, more generally, that are also relevant for Kenya:

> Existing governance structures need to be strengthened, and new ones created if necessary, to make them more sensitive to the needs of all the university's stakeholders. Greater dialogue among the university's various constituent groups, at both formal and informal levels, is desirable. Improved information flows between university administration and its staff and students is needed

Institutional staff and students should have a significant voice in the appointment of administrators. Even though all administrative appointments are ultimately made by the Chancellor of the public universities (under current law, the President of Kenya), academic and non-academic staff as well as students should play more than a token role in the selection process. Because of this strong influence, it is often difficult for stakeholders in higher education to communicate concerns without having them construed as being criticisms of the government. Consequently, it is sometimes difficult to engage in the dialogue necessary for addressing the problems. The unwillingness of the President to meet with representatives of academic staff seeking formal government recognition for their union led to an unauthorized strike felt primarily at the universities located in the Nairobi metropolitan area. Under such conditions, academic freedom can also be threatened

Finally, it is incumbent upon universities to develop a broader funding base so that they are not entirely dependent upon the government. It is certainly reasonable to expect the government to pay a substantial portion of faculty salaries and benefits (especially health care and pension contributions), but costs of most things must be shared, with student fees being a more significant source of funds. Better ties must be forged with the private sector which also benefits greatly from highly educated manpower. The government of Kenya needs to find better ways to collect loan payments in order to make certain that future generations can benefit from the fund created through loan repayment.

Kenya has a stable government, good relationships with neighboring East African countries cemented by a recently signed treaty for cooperation, and renewed support from the international donor community. All of these bode well for a promising future in which higher education can play a significant role. There is, however, a need top improve governance structures so that there can be significant dialogue both among stakeholders and with the government. It is up to members of the university community to make certain that the human resources and expertise represented therein are utilized as fully as possible in the service not only of personal goals, but also to facilitate local, regional, and national development.

References

Reprinted from: *Journal of the Third World Spectrum*, Volume 2, Number 1, 1995, by permission of the author and the *Journal of the Third World Spectrum,* Washington, D.C.

* Revised text of a public lecture presented 1 December 1993 at Maseno University College, Maseno, Kenya.

Albrecht, Douglas and Adrian Ziderman. 1992 (August). *Financing Universities in Developing Countries.* Washington, D.C.: Education and Employment Division, Population and Human Resources Department, The World Bank (Document No. PHREE/92/61).

Alele-Williams, Grace. 1992. "Major Constraints to Women's Access to Higher Education in Africa." Pp. 71-76 in UNESCO/BREDA. *Higher Education in Africa: Trends and Challenges for the 21st Century.* Dakar, Senegal, UNESCO Regional Office.

Consultation of Experts on Future Trends and Challenges of Higher Education in Africa. 1992. "Appendix: Plan of Action, 1992-2002." Pp. 325-334 in UNESCO/BREDA. *Higher Education in Africa: Trends and Challenges for the 21st Century.* Dakar, Senegal, UNESCO Regional Office.

Hinchcliffe, Keith. 1987. *Higher Education in Sub-Saharan Africa.* London: Croom Helm.

Fall, Brahim A. 1992. "Use of New Information and Communication Technologies and their Impact on the Management of Higher Education." Pp. 215-245 in UNESCO/BREDA. *Higher Education in Africa: Trends and Challenges for the 21st Century.* Dakar, Senegal, UNESCO Regional Office.

James, Estelle. 1991. *Private Finance and Management of Education in Developing Countries: Major Policy and Research Issues.* Issues and Methodologies in Education Development: An IIEP Series for Orientation and Training, 5. Paris: International Institute for Educational Planning (UNESCO).

King, Kenneth. 1990. "The New Politics of International Collaboration in Educational Development: Northern and Southern Research in Education." *International Journal of Educational Development,* 10 (No. 1): 47-57.

Koso-Thomas, K. 1992. "Innovative Ways of Financing Higher Education in Africa." Pp. 121-

133 in UNESCO/BREDA. *Higher Education in Africa: Trends and Challenges for the 21st Century*. Dakar, Senegal, UNESCO Regional Office.

Lamptey, Alice Sena. 1992. "Promoting Women's Participation in Teaching, Research, and Management in African Universities." Pp. 77-94 in UNESCO/BREDA. *Higher Education in Africa: Trends and Challenges for the 21st Century*. Dakar, Senegal, UNESCO Regional Office.

Maina, S.N. 1989. "Provision of Education through Cost-sharing." Annex 5 (pp. 109-113) in J.E.O. Odada and L.O. Odhiambo (Eds.), *Report of the Proceeding of the Workshop on Cost-sharing in Kenya: Naivasha 29 March -2 April 1989*. Nairobi: UNICEF, Kenya Country Office, Ministry of Planning and National Development, and Kenyan Economic Association.

Mingat, Alain and George Psacharopoulos. 1985. "Financing Education in Sub-Saharan Africa: Issues of Equity and Efficiency of Investment - Some Policy Alternatives." *Finance and Development*, Vol. 22 (March), pp. 35-38.

Mohammedbhai, G.T.G. 1992. "A Review of Training Activities in African Universities." Pp. 137-156 in UNESCO/BREDA. *Higher Education in Africa: Trends and Challenges for the 21st Century*. Dakar, Senegal, UNESCO Regional Office.

Mwiria, Kilemi, and Mulati S. Nyukuri. 1992. "The Management of Double Intakes: A Case Study of Kenyatta University." Paris: International Institute of Educational Planning (UNESCO), Document IIEP/RP/49.13.

Opondo, Fred and Sodik Osman Noormohamed. 1989. "Cost-sharing in Education." Annex 4 (pp. 87-107) in J.E.O. Odada and L.O. Odhiambo (Eds.), *Report of the Proceeding of the Workshop on Cost-sharing in Kenya: Naivasha 29 March - 2 April 1989*. Nairobi: UNICEF, Kenya Country Office, Ministry of Planning and National Development, and Kenyan Economic Association.

Passi, F.O. 1992. "Implementing Change to Improve the Financial Management of Makerere University, Uganda." Paris: International Institute of Educational Planning (UNESCO), Document IIEP/RP/49.5.

Republic of Kenya. 1994. *Development Plan, 1994-1996*. Nairobi: Government Printer.

Republic of Kenya. 1993. *Economic Survey 1993*. Central Bureau of   Statistics, Office of the Vice President, and Ministry of Planning and National Development. Nairobi: Government Printer.

Republic of Kenya. 1989. *Development Plan, 1989-1993*. Nairobi: Government Printer.

Saint, William S. 1992. Universities in Africa: Strategies for Stabilization and Revitalization. World Bank Technical Paper Number 194, Africa Technical Department Series. Washington, DC: World Bank.

Sanyal, Bikas C. in association with Michaela Martin. 1991. "Staff Management in African Universities." Document prepared within the framework of the IIEP research programme on "Improving the Effectiveness of Higher Education Institutions: Studies of the Management of Change." Paris: International Institute for Educational Planning (UNESCO). Document IIEP/Prg.BS/91.160.

Taiwo, Adediran A. 1992. "Innovations and Reforms in Higher Education in Africa: An Overview." Pp. 157-171 in UNESCO/BREDA. *Higher Education in Africa: Trends and Challenges for the 21st Century*. Dakar, Senegal, UNESCO Regional Office.

Thiam, Magatte. 1992. "An Overview of Trends and Challenges of Higher Education in Africa." Pp. 19-41 in UNESCO/BREDA. *Higher Education in Africa: Trends and Challenges for the 21st Century*. Dakar, Senegal, UNESCO Regional Office.

UNESCO. 1993. "Development of Higher Education in Africa: DAKAR Seminar (19-24 November 1992)." Priority: Africa Programme of Action proposed by the Director-General (1990-1995). In cooperation with the Association of African Universities (AAU) (Publication CAB-93/

WS).

UNESCO. 1992. "Development of Higher Education in Africa: Accra Seminar (25-29 November 1991)." Priority: Africa Programme of Action proposed by the Director-General (1990-1995). In cooperation with the United Nations Development Program (UNDP) and the Association of African Universities (AAU) (Publication CAB-92/WS-1).

Woodhall, Maureen. 1993 (September). "Financial Diversification in Higher Education: A Review of International Experience." Unpublished paper.

Woodhall, Maureen. 1991. *Student Loans in Higher Education: 3. English-speaking Africa.* Educational Forum Series No. 3. Paris: International Institute for Educational Planning (UNESCO).

World Bank. 1991. *World Development Report 1991.* New York: Oxford University Press.

(Dependency Theorist)

Chapter IX

The Dynamics of the State Boundaries in Post-Colonial Africa: The Prospects for the Future.

Dr. F. Ugboaja Ohaegbulam

Prior to its conquest and accupation by European nations during tha last quarter of the nineteenth century, Africa had a mosaic of lineage and clan groups, city states, kingdoms, empires, and acephalous states whose boundaries were not clearly defined or fixed. European scramble for, and consequent partition of Africa led ultimately to the creation of about fifty new political territories with relatively clearly defined boundaries. The post-colonial experience of African states, especially the current genuine crisis of the nation state in Sub-Saharan Africa, has demonstrated that the European-carved boundaries have proven to be more of a liability than an asset to the emergent African states. The explanation for this outcome lies in the arbitrary manner in which the boundaries of the colonial states were drawn and in the dynamics that have maintained them since independence.

The boundaries were not laid down in accordance with any well-defined, rational criteria, or in full recognition of the ethno-cultural, geographical realities of Africa. Rather, they were artificially drawn by the imperial European powers to suit their own economic, political, and strategic interests. While such imperial interests were successfully promoted during the years of colonial occupation especially, the artificiality of the boundaries created for Africans serious domestic problems that persist. The artificiality of the boundaruies has been a source of ethnic rivalries and conflicts over the control of both political authority and the allocation of scarce resources. Waves of refugees and people displaced by such rivalries and conflicts have created their own problems and complications.

Furthermore, the arbitrary and illogical boundaries created the problem of uneven sizes and unequal natural resources and economic potentials of African states. This situation has been a source of inter-state boundary disputes in Africa since the formal demise of European colonialism in the continent. Such disputes themselves have undermined national cohesion, economic and social development as they caused the diversion of limited resourses away from such development to purchases of arms and military hardware for warfare.

However, inspite of this reality, the artificial and arbitrarily created boundaries, ironically, have remained relatively stable since independence. Since then only a few boundaries have either changed or disappeared. In each case the change which occurred did not do so against the wishes of an existing government nor was it brought about by violent means or the threat of violence. In 1961 the formerly British-administered Southern Cameroon reunited with the formerly French-administered Cameroon after a United Nations supervised plebiscite. Earlier in 1958, Senegal and the former French Sudan united as the Mali Federation but the entity died shortly thereafter, a victim of ideological and economic differences between the two former French colonies. Sudan retained the name Mali for itself. For similar reasons, especially economic ones, the two French federations of West and Equatorial Africa had disintegrated into eight and four political territories respectively after the Loi Cadre [Outline Law] of 1956. Leopold Sedar Senghor of Senegal and Sekou Toure of Guinea had supported the continuation of the two federations. But Felix Houphouet Boigny, whose territory, Cote d'Ivoire, after World War II, had become the richest of the twelve French West and Equatorial African colonies, opposed the notion of a federation. He was afraid that Cote d'Ivoire would always subsidize the poorer members of the federation. He preferred instead membership by each of the territories in the French Community which he believed would offer better conditions for the economic and social development of his people.

Later in 1960, former British and Italian Somalilands united as Somalia. In 1964 Tanganyika and Zanzibar merged to form the United Republic of Tanzania. Recently in 1993 Eritrea, which had been an Italian colony and subsequently became part of Ethiopia from the late 1950s, achieved independence as a separate state from Ethiopia after about thirty years' liberation struggle. Other attempts at separatism, such as those of Shaba from Zaire, Biafra from Nigeria, and Southern Sudan from Sudan, failed to succeed even though the fundamental causes of the attempts at separatism persisted. Thus, the stability of the boundaries of Africa's weak states for a period of about forty years is seen as "an extraordinary occurrence in the history of international relations.[1]

What are the dynamics that have sustained state boundary stability in post-colonial Africa despite the evidence that the boundaries, as constituted, are more of a liability than an asset to African states? In what ways have the boundaries proven to be a liability? What are the prospects for their continued stability or revision in view of their perceived liability and the apparent erosion of the concept of state sovereignty, part of the dynamics that have sustained them?

This study attempts to answer these questions. It identifies the dynamic forces responsible for the stability of state boundaries in Africa as well as the liabilities of the continent's colonially-inherited boundaries. The study notes that some of the forces that sustained those boundaries are eroding. It concludes that the prospects for the stability of the boundaries in the future are problematic. It suggests that the alternative and ultimate choice for Africa is a United States of Africa that ensures one organic nation for all Africans.

The Dynamics of State Boundary Stability in Africa

A number of dynamics combined to sustain state boundaries in independent Africa. International acceptance and adherence to the concept of state sovereignty is a significant part of the dynamics. The notion of state sovereignty is the idea that "there is a final and absolute political authority in the political community."[2] This concept arrogates to every political community, the state, regardless of its size, the strength, or the weakness of its political and economic institutions, internal and external authority subject to no control except that which it imposes upon itself. In international law the concept assures the state recognition of its independence and respect for its territorial integrity. The concept also implies that all states or political communities are juridically equal since each is sovereign, politically independent, and under no higher authority. International law, therefore, explicit requires sovereign states to respect and, in cases of treaty or mutual defense pacts, to defend the territorial integrity of each other and to refrain from interferring in matters which are purely within each other's domestic jurisdiction.

For years a pillar of international law and the state system, adherence to this concept through international practice has fostered the membership of states in the international community as sovereign equals regardless of their credibility or lack of it as authoritative and capable political organizations. Under this concept, therefore, upon attaining independence, African states became members of the United Nations. The right to belong to the family of nations, as represented by the United Nations, legitimized the existence of independent African states, including the inviolability of their boundaries. This international legitimacy protected African states and their governments from external interference in their domestic affairs and from any tampering with their boundaries. Support for the territorial status quo was based on the belief that if such support were discarded, all borders would be suspect, and the potential for chaos considerable. The stability of state boundaries in Africa is thus attributable in large measure to the international community's adherence to the concept of state sovereignty and support for the principle of the sanctity of existing borders.

African states and their boundaries might have been considered legitimate and their sanctity supported by the international community, but the reality is that they were not considered legitimate and supported by all the nationality groups that resided within them. Some of those groups identified themselves as nations or clan members and flatly rejected the arbitrarily drawn boundaries, established without the consent of the governed, as unjust. The tendency, therefore, has been for such groups to seek their own states as an expression of their right to national self-determination. The right to national self-determination is a norm of international law which recognizes the right of every nationality group to form its own state and to determine the form of government under which it will live.

In the African political sphere, the legal norms of the international community, reinforcing the concept of state sovereignty, seldom supported the concept of national self-determination upon which, hitherto, Africans had waged their struggle against Western European colonialism. Biafra's claim during the period 1967 to 1970 to independence from Nigeria was rejected by the international community despite the people's suffering and legitimate claim to being a viable sovereign nation state. The rebels in southern Sudan whose struggle for independence from Sudan began in the 1950s have been recognized by no state against the wishes of the Arabic and Islamic government in Khartoum. Katanga, now Shaba province of Zaire, was forced by the international community from 1960 to 1964 to remain an integral part of the former Belgian Congo. Northern Somalia, which declared itself independent as the Republic of Somaliland in 1991, has not secured recognition from any state within or outside Africa. Eritrea's struggle for independence from Ethiopia fared a little better. It was supported by Arab states. Even so the struggle had to last over thirty years until the Ethiopian government of Mengistu Haile Mariam in Addis Ababa collapsed in 1991 and the successor government expressed its willingness to recognize an independent Eritrea.

Thus, although rebels may establish de facto control over a piece of territory, current international law, rooted in the concept of state sovereignty, denies them sovereignty and international recognition. Neither the United Nations, the major world powers, nor African states and the Organization of African Unity [OAU] will grant them recognition, unless the sovereign government they challenge accepts their demand for self-determination. The case of Biafra which was recognized by four African states--Tanzania, Zambia, Gabon and Cote d'Ivoire--and one Caribbean state--Haiti--was an exception to this practice, albeit Biafra never survived as a sovereign state against the wishes of sovereign Nigeria. The practice of the international community which recognized, legitimized, and upheld the political independence and territorial integrity of post-colonial African states since independence, in essence, has virtually frozen the political map of Africa in its colonial shape.

One of the objectives of emergent African states that has been maintained since independence is the respect for and preservation of the boundaries they inherited at independence regardless of how illogical and artificial those boundaries might be. Believing that those boundaries were a tangible reality, and apprehensive that boundary changes by force might cause widespread chaos and suffering, African leaders who met at Addis Ababa in May 1963 to create the Organization of African Unity agreed to leave those boundaries alone. This became and has remained a cardinal principle of the OAU. Accordingly, the organization has consistently refused to countenance attempts at boundary chages by force.

The initial measures of the OAU for preserving the territorial integrity of Africa's post-colonial states were taken at the time the organization was established in May 1963. At that time the organization recognized Mauritania as a sovereign member state against the wishes of Morocco. King Hassan II had sought to incorporate the West African country into Morocco on alleged historical grounds.

Support for the territorial status quo by the OAU was a function of the recognition of the perceived vulnerability of its member states as well as the insecurity of their statesmen. It was the same perception of common vulnerability and insecurity that fostered the establishment of the OAU itself. By creating the pan-African organization, Africa's new statesmen agreed to associate themselves "in a common continental body whose rules would legitimize existing jurisdictions and specify any international actions that would be considered illegitimate."[3] By the principles of the organization, they agreed to affirm: the sovereign independence and equality of all members, large or small; non-interference in each other's internal affairs; peaceful resolution of all disputes; and the illegitimacy of subversion.[4] By recognizing their common vulnerability to external incitement to rebellion and secession, members of the organization sought to ensure the general advantage that would accrue to them all by a reciprocal respect for their boundaries and abstention from attempts at the boundaries' immediate revision.[5]

In at least three cases of secession and civil war in Zaire 1964-65, 1977-1978; Nigeria 1967-1970; and in the Sudan 1964-1971, the OAU supported the existing government against its challenger. Its mediation or attempts at conciliation in a number of territorial disputes, for example, Algeria-Morocco 1963-65; Somalia-Ethiopia, Kenya 1964, 1967, 1973; Ghana-Burkina Faso 1964-65; Equatorial Guinea-Gabon 1972; Burkina Faso-Mali 1977; and the Sudan-Ethiopia 1977, helped to preserve the territorial status quo in the disputed areas. The OAU also has consistently sought to preserve the colonially established territorial status quo in Western Sahara. The territory which Polisario nationalists declared independent as Saharan Arab Democratic Republic [SADR] in February 1976 has been occupied militarily by Morocco since 1976 when Spain withdrew from the territory. But the OAU has flatly refused to recognize the legitimacy of Morocco's presence in, or incorporation of the territory. Rather, in keeping with its declared policy of opposition to involuntary revision of colonially-established boundaries in Africa, the organisation granted recognition to Polisario and admitted SADR into the pan-African organisation. Morocco's response to this move was to withdraw from the organisation.

The great powers and the international community generally have supported the OAU principle of the sacrosanctity of boundaries African states inherited at independence. The former colonial powers, especially Britain, France, and Belgium, demonstrated their vested interests in the political, and territorial status quo in their former colonial wards by rushing to their rescue whenever they confronted internal rebellion. The opposition of African states and of the international community has therefore reinforced the legitimacy of the boundaries African states inherited at independence.[6]

Furthermore, during the cold war, the leaders of the ideological rivalry believed it was in their best interest to support and uphold the OAU's norm of maintaining the inviolability of boundaries African states had inherited from European colonial powers. They expressed their preference for international stability over territorial chaos that could result from irredentist wars or self-determination conflicts that threatened boundary stability by supporting norms that made forcible boundary changes illegitimate. They employed not only a legal frame work, in the form of international sovereignty, to justify the territorial status quo, but also provided African rulers military weapons to suppress and crush internal challenges and rebellions. They also frowned upon inter-state wars that had the potential of upsetting regional or global *status quo*.

The Liability of the Boundaries

The liability of state boundaries in post-colonial Africa is essentially a product of the nature of those states. In Africa the state is an arbitrary creation of European impperial powers which has remained "far from a credible reality."[7] Cohesive social groups such as the Somali, the Bakongo, the Ewe, were separated by European colonial map makers. Other groups, such as the Hausa-Fulani, the Igbo, and the Yoruba, that were overtly hostile or that had little to do with each other, were combined into an artificial state. Surely they were combined but they have failed to mix, to cohere, and to become blended and diffused into each other. Hence such a state has been unable to become an organic whole, nurturing and fostering political and social development, growth, healing, and political stability.

Frequently, throughout Africa, the government and its officials who wield the powers of the state promote their personal, parochial, or factional interests rather than those of inidividual citizens. Their overwhelming political ambition poisons their amorphous political communities, corroding the moral legitimacy of the government and the bond of trust between the leaders and the led, a bond which is essential in a democracy, and to political and economic development. Thus, membership in the nationality group, clan, ethnic community, or religious sect, wielding state power confers more substantial rights on the individual than the individual's citizenship in the state. This practice has negatively affected state building, especially national cohesion and the loyalty of all segments of the citizenry to the state. Also, the practice has been a major source of divisiveness and political instability within African states. The divisiveness and series of conflicts it has generated have spawned great population movements and waves of displaced persons and refuges. By these means it has affected the conomic development of Africa by discouraging foreign investment in, and promoting the flight of local capital and skilled manpower from Africa.

African leaders who indulge in this negative practice have managed to sustain themselves and to preserve the colonial jurisdictions they inherited mainly through arbitrary and autocratic rule supported by established international practice and neocolonialism. Established international practice traditionally recognizes governments regardless of their domestic policies so long as they fulfill their external obligations and comply with the rules and regulations of the United Nations. Neocolonialism maintains them in political power so long as, client governments, they faithfully serve the needs of their external patrons. The state, therefore, becomes not a tool for economic and social development of the territory and its people but a major apparatus to enrich the rulers and to enhance the interests of their defenders, supporters, and patrons.

This situation sustained and still sustains gross abuses of fundamental human rights and, as already indicated above, has been a definite source of political instability and ethnic conflict in post-colonial Africa. It has also given rise to secessionist movements as those of Biafra in Nigeria and Southern Sudan in the Sudan. It has emphasized and perpetuated local or group particularisms at the expense of national cohesion and consensus. Thus, in general elections individuals tend to vote for candidates who are members of their nationality group rather than on the basis of the ideology or the qualification of the candidate.

The problem of uneven sizes, unequal natural resources and economic potentials, lack of access to the sea, and the balkanization of ethnic communities inherent in the arbitrariness of the state boundaries has been a source of inter-state territorial disputes. Ethiopia fought over Eritrea for thirty years in order to secure and maintain access to the sea. Nigeria and Cameroon have engaged in periodic clashes over natural resources in a disputed coastal territory.[8] Libya seized uranium-rich Aouzou strip from Chad whose entire territory Khaddafi sought to annex in the 1980s but for international pressure. Morocco laid claims to parts of the Algerian Sahara rich in mineral resources and has fought since 1976 to incorporate into Morocco phosphate-rich Western Sahara which it also claims on historical grounds. Algeria and Tunisia clashed over a portion of Sahara where there was found oil and natural gas. The two countries agreed to a joint exploitation of the minerals but failed to resolve the territorial dispute. Somalia fought with Kenya and Ethiopia in order to reunite all Somali clans into a "Greater Somalia." The late Obafemi Awolowo of Nigeria at one time had cherished an ambition to reintegrate the ethnic Yoruba in Benin into Nigeria, where the bulk of the Yoruba people live. The late Joseph Kasavubu of Zaire led a Bakongo state movement to incorporate the Bakongo in Zaire, Congo, and Angola into an independent Bakongo state.

These ambitions and disputes adversely affected inter-African state relations. They led to hostile propaganda, subversion, inimical alliances, breaks in diplomatic relations, warfare, and foreign intervention. The warfare meant a diversion of critical meager resources away from economic and social development to arms purchases and efforts to prosecute the war. The disputes undermined or prevented cooperative efforts in essential aspects of political, economic, and social development. Somalia's irredentism in the

Horn of Africa made the region an area of ideological rivalry and tension between the superpowers who, during the cold war especially, saw their interests in global terms.[9]

The general tendency in Africa for political authorities to hold on to power indefinitely and to preserve the inherited colonial jurisdiction ensured the ruling authorities, civilian or military regimes, the perquisites of office--international recognition and status, control over financial and wealth generating resources, access to foreign aid donors--for life while denying them to their rivals. But it does more than that to the detriment of the state and its people. It militates against voluntary creation of more rational geographical jurisdictions with greater developmental potentials. It undermines ideas to pool scarce resources and to rationalize governing structures and practices that are duplicated all over an underdeveloped continent. Furthermore, the practice: (i): "recognizes and respects any and all governments even if they exploit their jurisdictions mainly for their own benefit; (ii): provides aid to such regimes without requiring that such governments secure a mandate from their populations; (iii): promotes strict adherence to the practice of nonintervention, thereby tolerating all kinds rulers and rule in existing jurisdictions."[10] The practice is the major explanation for the collapse of both the Mali Federation in West Africa and the East African Community of Kenya, Uganda, and Tanzania. The practice defrauds the peoples of Africa in general.

Prospects for Boundary Stability

Although state boundaries in contemporary Africa will likely continue to be protected by the general norm that existing international boundaries are legitimate, various developments in the contemporary world environment make the prospects for their stability in the future problematic. One of those developments is the end of the cold war. The cold war had imposed upon disparate groups artificial loyalty to authoritarian regimes in Africa. It had provided those regimes, in the face of challenges by their dissident citizens, resources, counter-insurgency equipment, guns, and money, for the suppression of what they saw as centrifugal political dissidents. Now those restraints have been removed by the end of the cold war. Primary group loyalties in several states have come to the fore.

Furthermore, the former ideological rivals have now other priorities, especially their internal economic and social problems. They no longer perceive the African region as strategic. They now have no incentive to assist troubled African political leaders. Instead, they are retrenching from the continent.[11] This retrenching process occurring after the end of the cold war has undermined their exaggerated sense of Africa's importance and the opportunity the cold war had provided African regimes to manipulate the West against the East. The support the superpowers had provided their African clients against challenges to their authority by rebel or self-determination forces is no longer as forthcoming as it had been during the cold war. The abandonment of troubled African regimes such as those of Samuel Doe of Liberia and Mohammed Siad Barre of Somalia by the United States, and of Mengistu Haile Mariam of Ethiopia by the Soviet Union, and the accords the two powers helped to mediate over the conflicts in Angola and Namibia illustrated the emergence of the new reality.

The new reality is further illustrated by the fact that no great power has used the excuse of humanitarian concern to intervene in Rwanda to stop the apparent genocide Hutu and Tutsi political rivals are perpetrating upon their people. In these post-cold war days citizens of the great powers have no inclination whatsoever to pay the price of humanitarian intervention not to mention that of sustaining dictators in power.

In addition, the Western powers are attaching more stringent conditions on their financial and technical assistance to African states. Critical are their demands for democratization and higher standards of respect for fundamental human rights. Thus, after the cold war, it is becoming more difficult for African regimes to crush nationalist rebels and opponents than it had been hitherto with the support of the ideological rivals and the international community.

Economic decline, in addition to pressures for political and economic liberalization which preceded the end of the cold war and were later reinforced by that development comprise another force putting enormous pressure on the stability of the boundaries of African states. In Liberia the pressures contributed to the bloody overthrow of President Samuel Doe. In Somalia they led to the overthrow of President Mohammed Siad Barre and the proclamation of Northern Somalia as the Republic of Somaliland in 1991.

Furthermore, continuing economic decline will exacerbate unhealthy rivalry and ethnic conflict as the populations contest the control and authoritative allocation of limited resources. The incompetent and corrupt ruling authorities, who have not demonstrated a political will to foster national unity, will aggravate the situation further still and provide rebels justification for secessionist movements. Developments in Nigeria, especially since June 1993 when President Ibrahim Babangida suspended the results of democratic elections, appointed a civilian administration controlled by his military regime, and was himself subsequently removed from office, have not augured well for the stability of the Nigerian state. General Abacha who ousted Babangida from power and has called for a constitutional conference has learned that the people do not believe that Nigeria's problem is a new constitution. The problem, as they have expressed it, is whether Nigeria can survive as a single political entity, a confederation, or should be broken up into more cohesive political jurisdictions.

In addition to the impact of economic decline and the pressures for economic and political liberalization, international support for the norm of state sovereignty is steadily declining, especially as the concept applies to incompetent and corrupt regimes experiencing self-inflicted wounds. The international community which legitimized the emergence of African countries as sovereign nation states now hesitates to interfere in the internal affairs of such regimes simply to preserve state sovereignty. The leading members of the community, the great powers, aid donors, and international economic institutions, such as the International Monetary Fund and the World Bank, are imposing economic and political liberalization requirements for providing African states assistance.

Hitherto such conditionalities and structural adjustment programs that they impose would have been considered as an infringement on state sovereignty.

In recent years also, the international community which had not protected the welfare of individuals and private groups within a political community has begun to pay increasing attention to the protection and promotion of fundamental human rights of individuals, women, children, religious and ethnic minorities within the jurisdiction of member states. Very significantly also, public attitudes have shifted towards the "belief that the defense of the oppressed in the name of morality should prevail over frontiers and legal documents."[12] The focus by the international community on the plight of the Kurds in Iraq illustrates the trend. Also such international non-governmental human rights organizations as Amnesty International are adding their voice and pressure to ensure that the international community and its member states enforce human rights instruments that they have so far adopted and ratified.

CONCLUSION

The international community, together with its institutions and organizations, has served to legitimize and preserve African states and their territorial jurisdictions. So far, with the exception of Eritrea, they have effectively prevented the emergence of new states in Africa by violent means. Thus, given the weaknesses and the vulnerabilities of African states, the survival of contemporary African territorial jurisdictions is essentially an international achievement. This state of dependence on the international community, its norms and institutions for survival is not wholesome for African states. The situation underlines the need for African states to acquire those critical aspects of empirical attributes of statehood that will enable them to maintain, independently, compulsory jurisdiction and to exercise continuous organization, and a monopoly of force over the entirety of their territory and its population.

To do so will require: (i): a voluntary creation of more rational territorial or regional jurisdictions with greater developmental potentials from the existing colonially-inherited fifty or so political communities. Such jurisdictions will be so demarcated that each will have access to the sea and strong institutions that can shelter them from the kinds of difficulties existing African states have experienced. (ii): a voluntary development of a new basis for the creation of a common identity for the citizens of a number of a loose federal or confederal arrangements among existing states such as Nigeria. Such a loose arrangement may require the partitioning of some existing states and making the split units parts of other states. For example, the Sudan may be divided along two justified orders North and South. The North becomes merged with Egypt and the South with Uganda. Nigeria, likewise, may be partitioned into three regions. The Northern region federates with Niger, and Chad; the West with Benin, and the East with Western Cameroon. The remaining part of Cameroon federates with Equatorial Guinea, Gabon, Central African Republic and Congo.

New arrangements, such as the two suggested above, will facilitate pooling of resources and rationalizing governing and economic structures and practices that are duplicated throughout the African continent. This is also necessary, among others, for three reasons.. First, there are definite limits to the kinds of role the international community can play to contribute to the resolution of problems and difficulties of African states and to further development of their capabilities. Secondly, the international community is becoming weary of sustaining and perpetuating incompetent and corrupt governments and suppressing legitimate demands for respect for human rights and self-determination. Thirdly, the continued existence of a large number of weak, incompetent, and corrupt governments to be indefinitely protected, preserved, and nurtured at the expense of their citizenry constitutes an immediate and present danger to the international community itself. Indeed, the international community will do itself and the peoples of Africa a disservice by perpetuating Africa's underdevelopment through its provision of support and resources to Africa's incompetent and corrupt regimes. Existing African states themselve, therefore, must voluntarily reorganize themselves along more rational territorial jurisdictions in order to survive. Ultimately, the path to survival and greatness for Africa and its peoples lies in the realization of a United States of Africa.

Ednotes

[1] Jeffrey Herbst, "Challenges to Africa's Boundaries in the New World Order," *Journal of International Affairs*, Vol. 46, No. 1 (Oct. 1992), p.21.

[2] F.H. Hinsley, *Sovereignty*, 2nd edition (London: Cambridge University Press, 1986), p. 26.

[3] Robert H. Jackson & Carl G. Rosberg, "Why Africa's Weak States Persist: The Empirical and the Juridical in Statehood," *World Politics*, Vol. 35, No. 1 (October 1982), p. 18.

[4] Zdenek Cervenka, *The Organization of African Unity and Its Charter* (NY: Praeger, 1969), pp. 232-233.

[5] Jackson & Rosberg, in *World Politics*, Vol. 35, No. 1 (Oct. 1982), p. 18.

[6] Robert H. Jackson & Carl G. Rosberg, "Why Africa's Weak States Persist: The Empirical and the Juridical in Statehood," *World Politics*, Vol. 35, No. 1 (Oct. 1982), p. 15.

[7] Robert H. Jackson, "Juridical Statehood in Sub-Saharan Africa," *Journal of Internal Affairs*, 46, 1 (Summer 1992), p. 1.

[8] See: Thomas E. Stauffer, "Border Dispute Between Nigeria and Cameroon Affects Offshore Oil Patch and Threatens France's Interests," *The Christian Science Monitor* (22 March 1994), p. 9.

[9] Peter Schwab, "Cold War on the Horn of Africa," *African Affairs*, Vol. 77, No. 306 (January 1978), pp. 6-21.

[10] Jackson, in *Journal of International Affairs*, 46, 1 (Summer 1992), p. 9.

[11] Marguerite Michaels, "Retreat From Africa," *Foreign Affairs*, Vol. 72, No. 1 (1993), pp. 93-108; David Newsom, "After the Cold War US Interests in Sub-Saharan Africa," *Washington Quarterly*, Vol. 13, No. 1 (Winter 1990), pp. 99-114; Michael Clough, "The United States and Africa: The Policy of Cynical Disengagement," *Current History*, Vol. 91, No. 565 (May 1993), pp. 193-198. See also: Thomas E. Stauffer, "Border Dispute Between Nigeria and Cameroon Affects Offshore Oil Patch and Threathens France's Interests," *The Christian Science Monitor* (22 March 1994), p.

9.

[12] Michael Mandelbaum, "The Reluctance to Intervene," *Foreign Policy,* No. 95 (Summer 1994), p. 13.

INDEX